T0215166

Communications
in Computer and Information Science   491

Weixia Xu   Liquan Xiao   Jinwen Li
Chengyi Zhang   Zhenzhen Zhu (Eds.)

Computer Engineering and Technology

18th CCF Conference, NCCET 2014
Guiyang, China, July 29 – August 1, 2014
Revised Selected Papers

 Springer

Volume Editors

Weixia Xu
Liquan Xiao
Jinwen Li
Chengyi Zhang
Zhenzhen Zhu

National University of Defense Technology
School of Computer Science
Changsha, Hunan, P.R. China

E-mail:
weixia_xu@263.net
marshell.xiao@gmail.com
lijinwen@sina.com
chengyizhang@nudt.edu.cn
493403049@qq.com

ISSN 1865-0929   e-ISSN 1865-0937
ISBN 978-3-662-45814-3   e-ISBN 978-3-662-45815-0
DOI 10.1007/978-3-662-45815-0
Springer Heidelberg New York Dordrecht London

Library of Congress Control Number: 2015932495

Typesetting: Camera-ready by author, data conversion by Scientific Publishing Services, Chennai, India

Printed on acid-free paper

Springer is part of Springer Science+Business Media (www.springer.com)

Preface

We are pleased to present the proceedings of the 18th Annual Conference on Computer Engineering and Technology (NCCET 2014). Over its short 18-year history, NCCET has established itself as one of the major national conferences dedicated to the important and emerging challenges in the field of computer engineering and technology. Following the previous successful events, NCCET 2014 provided a forum to bring together researchers and practitioners from academia and industry to discuss cutting-edge research on computer engineering and technology.

We are delighted that the conference continues to attract high-quality submissions from a diverse and national group of researchers. This year, we received 85 paper submissions, among which 18 papers were accepted. Each paper received three or four peer reviews from our Technical Program Committee (TPC) comprising a total of 61 TPC members from academia and industry.

The pages of this volume represent only the end result of an enormous endeavor involving hundreds of people. Almost all this work is voluntary, with some individuals contributing hundreds of hours of their time to the effort. Together, the 61 members of the TPC, the 16 members of the External Review Committee (ERC), and the 13 other individual reviewers consulted for their expertise wrote about 300 reviews.

Every paper received at least two reviews and many had three or more. With the exception of submissions by the TPC, each paper had at least two reviews from the TPC and at least one review from an outside expert. For the second year running most of the outside reviews were done by the ERC, which was selected in advance, and additional outside reviews beyond the ERC were requested whenever appropriate or necessary. Reviewing was "first read double-blind," meaning that author identities were withheld from reviewers until they submitted a review. Revealing author names after initial reviews were written allowed reviewers to find related and previous material by the same authors, which helped greatly in many cases in understanding the context of the work, and also ensured that the author feedback and discussions at the PC meeting could be frank and direct. For the first time in many years, we allowed PC members to submit papers to the conference. Submissions co-authored by a TPC member were reviewed exclusively by the ERC and other outside reviewers, and these same reviewers decided whether to accept the PC papers; no PC member reviewed a TPC paper, and no TPC papers were discussed at the TPC meeting.

After the reviewing was complete, the PC met at the National University of Defense Technology, Changsha, during June 6–7 to select the program. Separately, the ERC decided on the PC papers in email and phone discussions. In the end, 18 of the 85 submissions (21%) were accepted for the conference.

First of all, we would like to thank all researchers who submitted manuscripts. Without these submissions, it would be impossible to provide such an interesting technical program. We thank all PC members for helping to organize the conference program. We thank all TPC members for their tremendous time and efforts during the paper review and selection process. The efforts of these individuals were crucial in constructing our successful technical program. Last but not least, we would like to thank the organizations and sponsors that supported NCCET 2014. Finally, we thank all the participants of the conference and hope they had a truly memorable NCCET 2014 in Guiyang, China.

November 2014

Xu Weixia
Xu Daoyun
Zhang Minxuan
Xiao Liquan

Organization

General Co-chairs

Xu Weixia — National University of Defense Technology, China
Xu Daoyun — GuiZhou University, China
Zhang Minxuan — National University of Defense Technology, China

Program Chair

Xiao Liquan — National University of Defense Technology, China

Publicity Co-chairs

Zhang Chengyi — National University of Defense Technology, China
Li Jinwen — National University of Defense Technology, China
Yu Liyan — National University of Defense Technology, China

Local Arrangements Co-chairs

Zhao Haixing — Qinghai Normal University, China
Li Jinwen — National University of Defense Technology, China
Wang Qinghai — Qinghai Normal University, China

Registration and Finance Co-chairs

Geng Shengling — Qinghai Normal University, China
Wang Yongwen — National University of Defense Technology, China
Li Yuanshan — National University of Defense Technology, China
Zhang Junying — National University of Defense Technology, China

Program Committee

Han Wei — 631 Institute of AVIC, China
Jin Lifeng — Jiangnan Institute of Computing Technology, China

Xiong Tinggang   709 Institute of China Shipbuilding Industry,
                                      China
Zhao Xiaofang   Institute of Computing Technology Chinese
                                      Academy of Sciences, China
Yang Yintang   Xi Dian University, China
Dou Qiang   National University of Defense Technology,
                                      China
Li Jinwen   National University of Defense Technology,
                                      China
Zhang Chengyi   National University of Defense Technology,
                                      China

Technical Program Committee

Chen Shuming   National University of Defense Technology,
                                      China
Chen Yueyue   Hunan Changsha DIGIT Company, China
Dou Qiang   National University of Defense Technology,
                                      China
Du Huimin   Xi'an University of Posts &
                                      Telecommunications, China
Fan Dongrui   Institute of Computing Technology Chinese
                                      Academy of Sciences, China
Fan Xiaoya   Northwestern Polytechnical University, China
Fang Xing   Jiangnan Institute of Computing Technology,
                                      China
Gu Tianlong   Guilin University of Electronic Technology,
                                      China
Guo Donghui   Xiamen University, China
Guo Wei   Tianjin University, China
Hou Jianru   Institute of Computing Technology Chinese
                                      Academy of Sciences, China
Huang Jin   Xi Dian University, China
Ji Liqiang   Cesller Company, China
Jin Jie   Hunan Changsha Fusion Company, China
Li Ping   University of Electronic Science and
                                      Technology of China, China
Li Qiong   Inspur Information Technology Co. Ltd, China
Li Yuanshan   Inspur Information Technology Co. Ltd, China
Li Yun   Yangzhou University, China
Lin Kaizhi   Inspur Information Technology Co. Ltd, China
Li Zhenghao   Tongji University, China
Sun Haibo   Inspur Information Technology Co. Ltd, China
Sun Yongjie   Hunan Changsha DIGIT Company, China
Tian Ze   631 Institute of AVIC, China

Wang Dong   National University of Defense Technology,
                             China
Wang Yaonan   Hunan University, China
Wang Yiwen   University of Electronic Science and
                             Technology of China, China
Xing Zuocheng   Hunan Changsha DIGIT Company, China
Xue Chengqi   Southeast University, China
Yang Peihe   Jiangnan Institute of Computing Technology,
                             China
Yang Xiaojun   Institute of Computing Technology Chinese
                             Academy of Sciences, China
Yin Luosheng   Synopsys Company, China
Yu Mingyan   Harbin Institute of Technology, China
Yu Zongguang   China Electronics Technology Group
                             Corporation No. 58 Research,
                             Institute, China
Zeng Tian   709 Institute of China Shipbuilding Industry,
                             China
Zeng Xifang   Hunan Great Wall Information Technology
                             Co. Ltd, China
Zeng Yu   Sugon Company, China
Zeng Yun   Hunan University, China
Zhang Jianyun   PLA Electronic Engineering Institute, China
Zhang Lixin   Institute of Computing Technology Chinese
                             Academy of Sciences, China
Zhang Shengbing   Northwestern Polytechnical University, China
Zhang Xu   Jiangnan Institute of Computing Technology,
                             China
Zhang Yiwei   709 Institute of China Shipbuilding Industry,
                             China
Zhao Yuelong   South China University of Technology, China
Zhou Ya   Guilin University of Electronic Technology,
                             China

Table of Contents

Processor Architecture

Application Specific Processors

Computer Application and Software Optimization

Technology on the Horizon

An Efficient Vector Memory Unit for SIMD DSP

Haiyan Chen, Zhong Liu, Sheng Liu, and Sheng Ma

School of Computer, National University of Defense Technology,
Changsha, Hunan 410073, P.R.China

Abstract. The SIMD DSP is highly efficient for embedded applications whose parallel data are aligned. However, there are many unaligned and irregular data accesses in typical embedded algorithms such as FFT, FIR. The vectorization of these kinds of algorithms will need many additional shuffle instruction operations in the SIMD architecture with alignment restriction, which greatly decreases the computation efficiency with the increasing SIMD width. This paper proposes an efficient vector memory unit (VMU) with 16 memory blocks on a 16-way SIMD DSP, M-DSP. Each memory block contains four groups of multi-bank memory structure with most-lowest-bit interleaved addressing and affords double bandwidth as needed to reduce the parallel vector access conflicts. A high-bandwidth data shuffle unit capable of dual vector accesses alignment is carried out in the vector access pipelining, which not only efficiently supports the unaligned access but also the special vector access patterns for FFT. The experimental results have shown that the VMU could afford conflict-free parallel accesses between DMA and vector Load/Stores operations with no more than 10% area overhead, and M-DSP achieves an ideal accelerate rate for FFT and FIR algorithms.

Keywords: SIMD, access conflict, vectorization, unaligned access, data shuffle.

1   Introduction

With the development of the integrated circuit technology, many processors have employed the Single Instruction Multiple Data (SIMD) architecture [1] to achieve high computation performance for multimedia applications. To further improve the peak performance and reduce the hardware costs, the SIMD architectures are integrating more and more processing elements (PEs) to manipulate wider and wider data streams with a single instruction. For example, the imagine stream microprocessor [2] developed by W. J. Dally integrates 8 SIMD processing units/elements (PEs). The AnySP microprocessor [3] proposed by Michigan University SDR group, which aims to software defined radio applications, contains 1 RISC microprocessor and 8 groups of 8-way SIMD vector processing units. The Tensilica BBE-128 [4] microprocessor contains a 32-way SIMD processing unit. The SIMD architecture can efficiently accelerate the data intensive applications with regular memory access modes, such as contiguous address accesses and aligned

W. Xu et al. (Eds.): NCCET 2014, CCIS 491, pp. 1–11, 2015.

address accesses. For more complicated access modes, memory access conflicts will appear, and additional shuffle instructions will be needed. They reduce the automatic vectorization efficiency [5] and also the performance gain. Thus, providing an efficient vector memory to meet with the massive computation power of the SIMD processor is a great challenge [6].

In a SIMD processor, the number of PEs controlled by a single instruction is defined as the SIMD width L [7]. In order to simplify the hardware implementation, L is generally chosen to be 2^n, where n is a positive integer. In order to provide enough memory access bandwidth for PEs, the vector memory usually consists of multiple memory modules with the same number as L. Assuming W is the bandwidth of one memory module, the bandwidth of the vector memory is $L*W$. Conventionally, it can always support the vector access whose address is contiguous (unit strides) and the beginning address is aligned with the SIMD width. But there are many unaligned vector access and non-unit strides access modes in the multimedia algorithms, such as Finite Impulse Response Filter (FIR), Fast Fourier Transform (FFT), image matching and Sum of Absolute Difference (SAD). If the vector memory only supports aligned vector accesses, the vectorization of these algorithms will need a great deal additional instruction overheads to implement data shuffles and alignments, which will increase code density and execution cycles. In Imagine processor [8], each PE can only access a fixed memory module in the stream register file. The data exchange between PEs needs to use the communication functional unit in the computation kernel (PEs). The AnySP processor provides a flexible configurable swizzle network[3] between PEs to support any shuffle patterns. Some SIMD microprocessors afford "gather and scatter" instructions, which have many different address generation units to rebuild one SIMD vector data, such as Larrabee [9]. All the above design methodologies need additional cycles and the full crossbar hardware costs for data shuffle operations increase rapidly with the SIMD width, which will bring on larger silicon area, power costs and longger layout latency.

This paper presents an efficient design of Vector Memory Unit (VMU) in a SIMD DSP, M-DSP. M-DSP is mainly deployed for wireless communication applications. A high-bandwidth data shuffle unit is carried out in its vector access pipelining to support unaligned and several special access modes, which makes VMU very efficient to carry out FFT and unaligned unit-stride vector access with quite low hardware costs. The rest of the paper is organized as follows. First, we analyze the vector access patterns of FFT and FIR algorithms in the SIMD DSP. Then, we introduce the architecture of M-DSP and illustrate the structure of the proposed VMU in detail. Finally, we show the synthesis and performance evaluation results.

2   The Vector Access Patterns of FIR and FFT Algorithms

FFT and FIR are the core algorithms in media applications that have massive data parallelism and are well suited for the SIMD architecture [10].

2.1   Vectorization of FIR

A FIR algorithm formula with coefficient length N is as follows.

$$y(n) = \sum_{i=0}^{N-1} h(i)x(n+i) \tag{1}$$

where $i=0,1,2,...,N-1$, $h(i)$ is the filter coefficient, $x(i)$ is a set of input sampling points.

Let Y, X, H represent the output vector, input vector and coefficient vector respectively, then for Sconsecutive input signal x, the Sconsecutive output of FIR filter with N coefficient should be $Y=XH$, or:

$$\begin{bmatrix} y_n \\ y_{n+1} \\ \vdots \\ y_{n+S-1} \end{bmatrix} = \begin{bmatrix} x_n & x_{n+1} & \cdots & x_{n+N-1} \\ x_{n+1} & x_{n+2} & \cdots & x_{n+N} \\ \vdots & \vdots & \vdots & \vdots \\ x_{n+S-1} & x_{n+S} & \cdots & x_{n+S+N-2} \end{bmatrix} \begin{bmatrix} h_0 \\ h_1 \\ \vdots \\ h_{N-1} \end{bmatrix} \tag{2}$$

To avoid the data exchange and addition reduction between different PEs, the vectorization of FIR makes all the multiplication and addition for the computation of a single component $Y(y_i)$ being calculated by a single PE [11]. The computation of FIR contains two levels of loop: the index of the outside loop is the input signal length S, and the index of the inside loop is the coefficient length N. There will be N vector multiplications and $N-1$ additions calculated within each PE in order to generate a single output value y_i. Every PE needs to load consecutive inputs of length N and the same H.So besides the conventional address aligned vector access mode, it should support some extra features like: (a) vector loading with data duplication, which can load the same set of coefficient of FIR to every PE, (b) unaligned vector access, i.e., continuous access from arbitrary beginning address of memory bank.Provided these two features, along with software pipelining, multiple PEs can generate output in parallel mode, and the FIR algorithm will be vectorized more efficiently.

2.2   Vectorization of Radix-2 FFT

The DFT formula of N points is as follows.

$$X(k) = \sum_{n=0}^{N-1} x(n)W_N^{nk} \tag{3}$$

where $0 \leq k < N$, $j = \sqrt{-1}$, $W_N = e^{-j2\pi/N}$.

Since twiddle factor W_N^{nk} is symetric, periodic and reducible, we also have the following equation.

$$X(k) = \sum_{n=0}^{N/2-1} [x(n) + (-1)^k x(n+N/2)]W_N^{kn} \tag{4}$$

The decimation-in-frequency radix-2 FFT algorithm divides N points $X(k)$ into 2 DFT both of $N/2$ points according to the parity of frequency domain signals:$X(2r)$ and $X(2r+1)$, where$r$=0,1,2,...,$N/2$-1. Let $N = 2^M$, and divide$x(n)$ (n=0,1,...,N-1) to 2 equal parts by order of n, let :

$$x_1(n) = x(n) + x(n + N/2),$$
$$x_2(n) = [x(n) - x(n + N/2)]W_N^n \tag{5}$$

then we have:

$$X(2r) = \sum_{n=0}^{N/2-1} x_1(n)W_{N/2}^{rn}$$

$$X(2r+1) = \sum_{n=0}^{N/2-1} x_2(n)W_{N/2}^{rn} \tag{6}$$

Equation (6) indicates that the radix-2 FFT with $N=2^M$ points needs butterfly operations of M levels. In every level of butterfly operations, if the input data are accessed continuously, its butterfly operations outputs will be in the bit-reversal fashion and performed in place [12].Figure 1 represents the final 4 levels of the data flow in the butterfly computations of a radix-2 FFT.

As shown in Fig.1, the vectorization of a radix-2 FFT based on a 16-way SIMD architecture needs 4 groups 16×1 butterfly operations in its final 4 levels SIMD operation respectively. Therefore, four kinds of specific data shuffling patterns are needed.

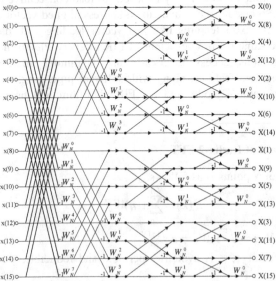

Fig. 1. The data flow in the butterfly operations of a radix-2 FFTbased on M-DSP

According to the overall structure of M-DSP and the feature of vector access patterns in FIR and FFT, M-DSP facilitates VMU that supports unaligned and four specific FFT data shuffling vector access patterns.

3   The Overall Architecture of M-DSP

M-DSP is a 32bit 16-way SIMD DSP developed for the applications of Software Defined Radio (SDR) wireless base station. Fig.2 illustrates its overall structure. M-DSP adopts a parallel architecture with a Scalar Processing Unit (SPU) and a Vector Processing Unit (VPU). Its scalar and vector instructions are both dispatched by a specific function unit. M-DSP leverages a Very Long Instruction Word (VLIW) paradigm with 10 instruction slots in each VLIW packet. Every VLIW packet contains 5 scalar instructions and 5 vector instructions. The SPU is responsible for the scalar instruction execution and the scalar data processing. The VPU applies a 16-way SIMD structure that is composed of 16 isomorphic PEs. Each PE has a 32-bit Multiply Accumulate Unit (MAC). It can execute vectorlogic and arithmetic instructions with the way of SIMD. The on-chip memory is divided into the Scalar Memory Unit (SMU) and the Vector Memory Unit (VMU). They execute scalar load/store and vector load/store instructions respectively. In order to meet with the operational requirement ofevery PE, VMU supports two parallel vector load/store instructions (VLS0/VLS1). VMU can also response to memory access request of SMU, and exchange data between peripherals or other memory by the direct memory access(DMA) controller. VMU is a large capacity local memory on chip, which adopts the 16-way SIMD memory blocks (BK0~BK15) to afford enough parallel memory bandwidth for vector computation.

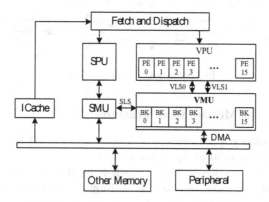

Fig. 2. The overall architecture ofM-DSP

4   The Implementation of VMU

4.1   The Overall Structure of the VMU

In order to meet with the real-time processing demands for multimedia applications, VMU adopts the scratchpad memory [6] structure with determined access latency. The total capacity of VMU is 1MB. It supports four parallel accesses that come from dual vector load/store instructions (VLS0/VLS1), one scalar load/store (SLS) and the DMA. Its function structure diagram is shown in Fig. 3. VMU is composed of the Vector Address Generator (VAG), the Vector Access Alignment Unit (VAAU), the Vector Access Controller (VMC), the Vector Write-back Reorder Unit (VWRU) and memory banks. VAG is responsible for the vector memory address calculating, and VAAU implements the address extension and alignment of the vector memory access data. VMC controls and synchronizes the VMU pipelining after of address calculation stage. The VWRU is responsible for the special vector data shuffle and aligning of vector load access (VLoad) instructions and writing back to PEs.

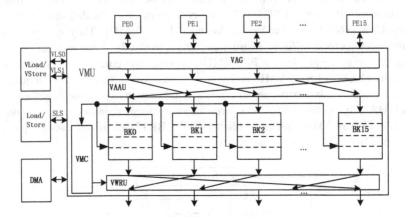

Fig. 3. the structure of the VMU

4.2   Organization of Memory Bank Structure

The 1MB VMU memory space consists of 16 memory banks (BK0~BK15), which is addressed by the lowest 4 bits of the vector address.

The memory access conflicts will lead to whole pipeline stall and bring additional latencies which strongly reduce the system performance of SIMD DSPs. In order to decrease the conflicts, Gou C put forward an un-matching memory bandwidth scheme [13], it can offer no conflicts access for different stride SIMD accesses in certain scope. To satisfy the request of 4 parallel memory accesses and reduce the access conflicts, the access bandwidth of each BK is designed as twice as needed. Each BK consists of 8 single port 8KB SRAM banks, and these banks are interleaving addressed by the two MSBs and one LSB of BK address. So each BK is divided into four consecutive memory spaces with the same capacity of 16KB. Each space is composed of two SRAM banks. Under such an organization of memory banks, the memory access conflict only occurs when the 3 bits bank address are identical. But for the access of the vector data with consecutive memory addresses, there are adequate available bandwidths and no conflict will occur. Because four continuous 16KB addresses are implemented by different memories, it can be programmed to let DMA and SLS access different 16KB memory spaces. This design totally eliminates the conflicts among the dual vectorload/stores, DMA and SLS.

This complex memory bank organization may slightly increases the area overhead, but for FIR and FFT, it will directly bring many advantages, such as supporting non-conflicting parallel memory accesses from the DMA and the core, hiding the latency of DMA data operation, and completely eliminating the stall caused by memory access conflicts. Table 1 shows the area results for 1MB VMUs that are composed of 8KB and 16KB single port memory banks manufactured with 65nm technology. Compared with the two diferent implements of VMU with the same memory capacity, the area overhead of our VUM only increases by 7%.

Table 1. The area comparison between two implementations

The access bandwidth of one BK	One SRAM bank	Area of one bank (um^2)	The number SRAM banks of VMU	The total area of memory banks (um^2)
Twice	8KB	320.09*154.69	8*16=128	6337884
Equal	16KB	588.89*157.035	4*16=64	5918486

4.3   The Hardware Support for Unaligned Vector Memory Access

VMU supports the linear addressing mode, implements the operations of vector load/store instructions with consecutive byte, half-word or word data granularity. The implementation architecture is shown in Fig.3. Firstly, the VAG performs decoding and address calculation functions. The calculated vector access address VADDR can be divided into two parts, a vector row address and an offset address of row address (ShiftAddr). The Vector Access Alignment Unit (VAAU) will realize access alignment according to ShiftAddr: if the ShiftAddr is 0, it means the vector memory access operation is aligned with the SIMD width, the row address will be extented to 16 copies, and the 16 sets of memory access data are directly sent to the corresponding BKs. If the ShiftAddr is not 0, it means the memory accessing is unaligned. The VAAU will realize the row address plus 1 operation, and align memory access data. So a cyclic aligning shifter and a row address adder function unit controlled by ShiftAddr are deployed in VAAU. Then the aligned access signals are sent to the corresponding BKs to finish following pipeline operations.

As for each Vload operation, the ShiftAdd is also needed to transform to the pipeline stage of write-back. The VMU write-back pipeline stage will also implement a Vector Write-back Unit (VWRU) that is another cyclic shifter. In accordance with the ShiftAddr, VWRU implements the cyclic shifting operation with the reading data from BK0 to BK15 with reverse direction. Then it writes back the aligned data to the corresponding PE0-PE15 registers. Each of the two cyclic shifters is carried by a 16:16 multiplexer.

4.4   The Hardware of Vector Load/Store with Special Data Shuffle Patterns

According to the situation where the multiple PEs need to share a coefficient in some algorithms such as FIR, VMU also supports a special vector load/store instruction (CVload/CVstore) with copy function. It means the CVload instruction can read one datum and broadcast it to all the PEs. The CVstore instruction can store one datum from a PE to one of BKs. VAG only generates a valid store access request to one of BKs according to the decode result. The memory access address and other access informations will be sent to the corresponding BK to complete the access memory operation after the cyclic shift alignment. But in the stage of write-back, 16:1 multiplexer is realized in VWRU to select the valid output datum and broadcast it to all the 16 PEs. The special vector load/store operation can eliminate the data copying operation between PEs and improve the efficiency of vector memory access.

According to the vector memory access requirement of Radix-2 FFT, the vector implementation of FFT with M-DSP will need four kinds special data shuffle operations between the dual vector accesses within the last 4 stages SIMD operations.

The VMU realized four kinds of vector load/store instructions for four data shuffle modes between dual vector load/store: VLS0 and VLS1, as shown in Fig.4. It needs groups of 2:1、3:1、4:1 multiplexers logic within VAAU and VWRU of VMU. The longest latency of the logic is 4:1 multiplexer.

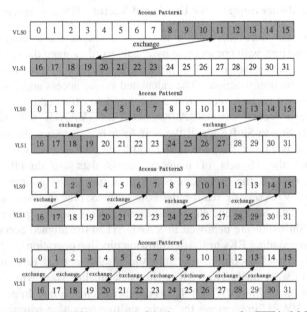

Fig. 4. Four Data shuffling pattern of dual vector access for FFT in M-DSP

4.5   Vector Memory Controller

M-DSP adopts the VLIW techology. Its instructions are executed and submitted in order. The SIMD vector memory controller (VMC) is responsible for controlling VMU access pipelining and implementing the parallel memory access arbitration and synchronization among other vector and scalar instructions, which are dispatched at the same cycle.

The VMU access pipelining is divided into six stations: address calculation, arbitration, decoding, memory access (read/write), data selection and write back. If a global stall caused by other function components appears, VMC will pause the VMU access pipeline. If the parallel memory access conflicts appear, the instruction dispatch unit will stop dispatch the next instruction until the conflicts are released. VMC will control the conflict memory access to execute serially and submit delayed 1-3 clocks. So VMC designs a two depth input buffer in arbitration pipeline station and a four depth output buffer in data selection pipelining station, The writings of the buffers are controlled by the global stall and the memory access conflicts.

5   Performance Evaluations

5.1   Synthesis Results

The design synthesis uses Design Compiler of the Synopsys® company with a 65nm technology. The synthesis constraints are set under the condition of TT, with a 0.95ns clock cycle and a 0.1ns path uncertain latency. The frequency of the VMU can reach 1GHz. The results are shown in Table 2. The control logic units with unaligned access and dual access data shuffling are only of 10% of the VMU's total area.

Table 2. VMU Synthesis results

iterms	area
Memory banks	6337884 um^2
Total cell area of VMU	7046613 um^2
Percent of area of controlling units of VMU	10%

5.2   Performance Evaluation of FFT and FIR

M-DSP is a SIMD DSP with 16 PEs. Its fixed-point arithmetic performance is about 16X of TI TMS320C64x, so the ideal speedup should be 16. This paper evaluated the performance of 2048 points 32-bit fixed plural FIR of different taps and 32-bit decimation-in-frequency radix-2 FFT of 256, 512, 1024, 2048 points on system-level experiment platform of M-DSP with assembly instructions. The speedups compared with the performance of TMS320C6416 [14] is shown as Fig. 5.

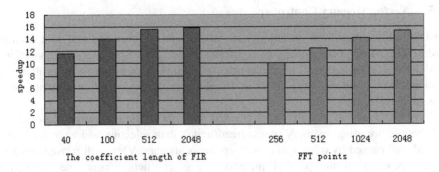

Fig. 5. The speedup of M-DSP in contrast withTMS320C64x

As shown in this figure, the speedup of FFT is not very high for a small set of input points because the overhead of outside loop initialization and communication in software pipelining is quite higher. With the increase of input data size, the speedup increases significantly and it reaches 15.3 when the points are added up to 2048. For FIR, the additional shuffle instructions are completely eliminated. With the increase of taps, the speedup finally reaches 15.88[11].

The Fig.6 has shown that the percentage of stalls cycles brought by memory access conflicts have decreased more than 50% for FFT compared twice bandwidth with equal bandwidth of VMU.

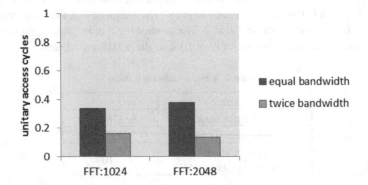

Fig. 6. The stall cycles caused by memory access conflicts before and after optimized

6   Conclusion

This paper delves into the design of a vector memory structure with 16-way SIMD. Compared with the traditional multiple bank memory, the proposed novel multiple bank memory structure induces a ~7% area overhead. But this structure decreases distinctly the stalls caused by parallel access conflicts in the FFT algorithm. The SIMD unaligned vector access mode in VMU supports the 16 PEs to access any consecutive data with SIMD width and eliminates the shuffle operations in the FIR algorithm. The special vector load/store instructions with copy and data shuffle modes needed by FFT vectorization can eliminate the additional shuffle instructions. So the VMU improves the vectorization efficiency for certain access patterns, and brings a significant acceleration for the FIR and FFT algorithms.

References

1. Keller, R.M.: Look-ahead microprocessors. ACM Computing surveys 7(4), 177–195 (1975)
2. Khailany, B., Dally, W.J., Chang, A., Kapasi, U.J., Namkoong, J., Towles, B.: VLSI design and verification of the Imagine microprocessor. In: Proceedings of the IEEE International Conference on Computer Design, pp. 289–296 (September 2002)
3. Woh, M., Seo, S., Mahlke, S., et al.: AnySP:Anytime Anywhere Anyway Signal Processing. In: Proceedings of the 36th Annual International Symposium on Computer Architecture, Austin, Texas, USA, pp. 128–139 (June 2009)
4. Rowen, C., Nicolaescu, D., Ravindran, R., et al.: The World's Fastest DSP core: Breaking the 100 GMAC/s Barrier. In: Proceedings of the 23rd Hot Chips Conference. Memorial Auditorium, Standford University (August 2011)
5. Chang, H., Sung, W.: Efficent vectorization of SIMD programs with non-aligned and irregular data access hardware. In: CASES 2008, pp. 167–175 (2008)
6. Sheng, L.: Researches on On-chip Parallel Data Access Techniques for SIMDDSPswith Very Wide Data Path. PhD Thesis, NUDT, Hunan, China (April 4, 2012)
7. Berkel, K., Heinle, F., et al.: Vector processing as an enabler for software-defined radio in handheld devices. EURASIP Journal on Applied Signal Processing 16, 2613–2625 (2005)
8. Khailany, B., Dally, W.J., et al.: Imagine: media processing with streams. IEEE Micro 3 (2001)
9. Seiler, L., et al.: Larrabee: A many-core x86 architecture for visual computing. In: SIGGRAPH 2008, New York, NY, USA, pp. 1–15 (2008)
10. Pajuelo, A., Gonzalez, A., Valero, M.: Speculative dynamic vectorization. In: Proceedings of the 29th Ann. Int'l Symp. Computer Architecture, pp. 271–280 (2002)
11. Liu, Z., Chen, Y.-Y., Chen, H.-Y.: A Vectorization of FIR Filter Supporting Arbitrary Coefficients Length and Data Types. Aca Electronica Sinica 41(2), 346–351 (2013)
12. Rodriguez V, P.: A radix-2 FFT algorithm for modern single instruction multiple data (SIMD) architectures. In: Proc. 2002 IEEE International Conference on Acoustics, Speech and Signal Processing (ICASSP 2002), vol. 3, pp. 3220–3223 (2002)
13. Gou, C., Kuzmanov, G., Gaydadjiev, G.N.: SAMS: Single-Affiliation Multiple-Stride Parallel Memory Scheme. In: Proceedings of the Workshop on Memory Access on Future Processors: a Solved Problem, Ischia, Italy, pp. 350–368 (May 2008)
14. Texas Instruments, C64x Fixed-Point DSPs Bench-marks, http://www.ti.com/lsds/ti/dsp/c6000_dsp/c64x/benchmarks.page

An Analytical Model for Matrix Multiplication on Many Threaded Vector Processors

Yongwen Wang*, Jun Gao, Bingcai Sui, Chengyi Zhang, and Weixia Xu

School of Computer, National University of Defense Technology, 410073, China
yongwen@nudt.edu.cn

Abstract. Vector can enhance peak performance while multi-threading can improve efficiency. MTV is a new architecture that combines the two to achieve both high computing performance and high throughput. Matrix multiplication is the kernel of many scientific applications. A parallel matrix multiplication algorithm is presented and an analytical performance model is built. Based on the model, the performance of MTV was evaluated and critical configurations are given to guide the design of MTV processors..

Keywords: Multi-thread, Vector, Microarchtiecture, Matrix multiplication.

1 Introduction

Microprocessor designers used to exploit instruction level parallelism (ILP) to improve the performance of a single thread, using techniques such as multiple instruction issue, out-of-order issue, and aggressive branch prediction[1]. However the emphasis on single-thread performance has shown diminishing returns because of the limitations in terms of latency to main memory and the inherently low ILP of applications. This has led to an explosion in microprocessor design complexity and made power dissipation a major concern[2].

Vector and multi-threading are very important techniques in the area of computer architecture and programming model. Vector processing was first used for HPC, such as the early Cray machines. General purpose microprocessors then extended SIMD-style vector instructions to enhance performance, such as VIS[3], HPC-ACE[4], AVX[5], AltiVec[6] etc. The best advantage of vector is that it can improve peak performance without increasing the complexity of control logic. Vector processing has became the mainstream technique for HPC. The multi-threading approach increases application performance by improving throughput, the total amount of work done across multiple threads of execution. This is especially effective in workloads with large amounts of thread level parallelism[7] A multi-thread microprocessor can achieve the same throughput as a single-thread microprocessor by running multiple tasks in parallel at much lower frequency.

---

* This work is supported in part by National Natural Science Foundation of China under grants 61170045.

W. Xu et al. (Eds.): NCCET 2014, CCIS 491, pp. 12–19, 2015.

The combination of Multi-threading and vector techniques makes MTV. MTV means Many Vector Threads. It can enhance both throuput and computing performance.

Matrix multiplication is the kernel algorithm for many scientific and engineering applications[8], many high performance libraries have been developed to optimize matrix multiplication. In order to evaluate MTV, the performance of matrix multiplication should be first evaluated.

In this paper, an matrix multiplication algorithm is described and an analytical performance model is built. The performance of MTV is evaluated based the presented model.

The rest of the paper is organized as follows. Section 2 describe the microarchitecture and principle of MTV processor. Section 3 describes the matrix multiplication algorithm. Section 4 demonstrates the analytical performance model. Section 5 evaluates the performance of MTV and gives some typical configurations for balanced performance. Conclusions are given in section 6.

2   MTV: Many Threaded Vector Processor

The MTV processor core is a RISC-like processor core. However, it has multiple hadware thread, and each thread has a independent context, including PC, general purpose register file, floating point register file, vector register file and system status registers. From a programmer's point of view, each thread is a complete processor.

There are specialized vector processing unit in the MTV core, which handles SIMD-style instructions. Instructions from different threads can be executed concurrently. If a load instruction from one thread is blocked, calculation instruction from another thread can be scheduled and executed. In this way the the instruction pipeline can be full filled and the latency of memory access is hidden.

Multiple or man MTV core can be integrated in on MTV processor chip. The diagram of a MTV chip is shown in Fig. 2. In a typical scenario, a chip can

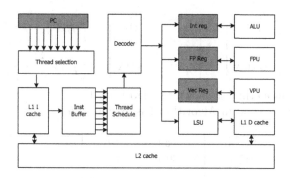

Fig. 1. Diagram of a MTV core

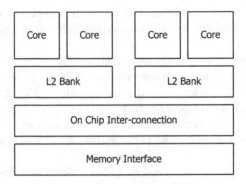

Fig. 2. Diagram of a MTV processor

integrate 64 MTV cores, and each core can support SIMD-8 fused multiply-add operations and generate 16 results per cycle. The chip could achieve 1 Tflops performance at 1 GHz.

MTV has memory hierarchy with special data placement requirements. Scalar data can be saved in L1 cache while vector data can only be kept in the L2 cache. Firstly,the capacity of L1 cache is small while the vector data is big. The precious L1 resource can be saved for the scalar data in this way. Secondly, vector data are not very sensitive to access latency because the latency can be well hidden by multiple threads.

3   Matrix Multiplication Algorithm

Parallel algorithm is used to achieve high performance of matrix multiplication. Ld_B-1ton-SIMD block matrix multiplication algorithm[9] is used in this paper.

Suppose A is a $m \times k$ matrix and B is a $k \times n$ matrix. The product of $A \times B$ is a $m \times n$ matrix, namely C. A can be partitioned to $M \times K$ sub-matrixes. B can be partitioned to $K \times N$ sub-matrixes. the partition $C = A \times B$ is shown in equation 1.

$$\begin{bmatrix} C^{11} & \dots & C^{1N} \\ \vdots & \vdots & \vdots \\ C^{M1} & \dots & C^{MN} \end{bmatrix} = \begin{bmatrix} A^{11} & \dots & A^{1K} \\ \vdots & \vdots & \vdots \\ A^{M1} & \dots & A^{MK} \end{bmatrix} \times \begin{bmatrix} B^{11} & \dots & B^{1N} \\ \vdots & \vdots & \vdots \\ B^{K1} & \dots & B^{KN} \end{bmatrix} . \qquad (1)$$

The calculation method is shown in Algorithm 1.

The matrix calucation in Algorithm 1 is explained as

$$\begin{bmatrix} \overline{a_{0,0}}\ \overline{a_{0,1}} \dots \overline{a_{0,7}} \\ a_{1,0}\ a_{1,1} \dots a_{1,7} \\ \vdots\quad \vdots\quad \vdots\quad \vdots \\ a_{7,0}\ a_{7,1} \dots a_{7,7} \end{bmatrix} \times \begin{bmatrix} b_{0,0}\ b_{0,1} \dots b_{0,7} \\ b_{1,0}\ b_{1,1} \dots b_{1,7} \\ \vdots\quad \vdots\quad \vdots\quad \vdots \\ b_{7,0}\ b_{7,1} \dots b_{7,7} \end{bmatrix} = \begin{bmatrix} \overline{c_{0,0}}\ \overline{c_{0,1}} \dots \overline{c_{0,7}} \\ c_{1,0}\ c_{1,1} \dots c_{1,7} \\ \vdots\quad \vdots\quad \vdots\quad \vdots \\ c_{7,0}\ c_{7,1} \dots c_{7,7} \end{bmatrix} .$$

Algorithm 1: Block matrix multiplication algorithm

(1)   All the threads start calculation simultaneously.
(2)   Each thread load the related sub-matrix A^{IJ} to L2 cache.
        the sub-matrix will reside there until no further access.
(3)   Each thread load the related sub-matrix C^{IT} to L2 cache.
(4) B^{JQ} are loaded to L2 cache
(5)   For each C^{IT}, the multiplication is equivalent to

$$\left[C^{IT} \right] = \left[A^{I1} \dots A^{IP} \right] \times \begin{bmatrix} B^{1T} \\ \vdots \\ B^{PT} \end{bmatrix}$$

(6)   Each tread fetches continuous n elements for column j of
        matrix A to make a new matrix.
(7)   Each thread fetches a element from row j of matrix B and
        broadcast it to make a new matrix.
(8)   Each thread multiply the above to matrix and get the con-
        tinuous n partial product of column j of matrix C. add the
        products will get the partial sum of matrix C.
(9)   return to step 2, untill all the matrix finished.

4   Analytical Performance Model

For the matrix multiply given in Algorithm 1, A^{IJ} is a $m_c \times k_c$ matrix and
resides in the L2 cache, which. C^{IQ} is a $m_c \times n$ matrix and B^{JQ} is a $k_c \times n$
matrix. The total amount of calculation should be $(2 \times m_c \times k_c) \times n$. And the
total amount of memory access should be $m_c \times k_c$ for matrx A, $k_c \times n$ for matrx
B and $m_c \times n$ for matrix C.

4.1   Memroy Bandwidth Model

If the memory bandwidth of each core is B_C, The number of thread in each core
is T, then the time to load partitioned matrix A to L2 cache is:

$$\frac{m_c \times k_c \times T \times 8}{B_C} . \tag{2}$$

The time to load B to L2 cache is

$$\frac{2 \times m_c \times n \times T \times 8}{B_C} . \tag{3}$$

The time to load C to L2 cache is

$$\frac{k_c \times n \times T \times 8}{B_C} . \tag{4}$$

The data movement time of a single core is the sum of equation 2, 3 and 4,
as shown in equation 5.

$$T_{mem} = \frac{(m_c \times k_c + (2 \times m_c + k_c) \times n) \times T \times 8}{B_c} . \tag{5}$$

The amount calculation for $C = A \times B$ is

$$2 \times m_c \times k_c \times n \times T . \tag{6}$$

If the peak performance of a single core is D_C, then the calculation time is show in equation 7.

$$T_{comp} = \frac{2 \times m_c \times k_c \times n \times T}{D_C} . \tag{7}$$

In order to achieve the highest performance, the time of memory access should be totally hidden by the time of calculation.

$$T_{comp} =< T_{mem}. \tag{8}$$

Combined with equation 5 and 7, it shows that

$$\frac{1}{8} \times \frac{2 \times m_c \times k_c \times n}{m_c \times k_c + (2 \times m_c + k_c) \times n} \times \frac{B_c}{D_c} \geq 1 . \tag{9}$$

n is the number of columns of matrix C, which is usually a big number. Matrix A doesn't have as a aggressive requirement of memory bandwidth. the bigger m_c and k_c are, the less bandwidth is required. When $2 \times m_c = k_c$, the request of memory bandwidth is the least.

In the equations above, there are tree factors: the first factor $\frac{1}{8}$ is a constant, the second factor is the ratio of computation to memory access in algorithm, namely CMR. The third factor is the ratio of memory bandwidth to computing performance in hardware. Putting them all together, we get the following equation.

$$B_c \geq \frac{D_C \times 8}{CMR} . \tag{10}$$

Equation 10 indicates the he relationship between the hardware calculation-memory ratio and algorithm calculation-memory ratio.

4.2   Memory Latency

The discussion assumes that the memory latency is complete hidden by computation. How ever, it is not always true. the extra memory access time is discussed in this section.

When a new inner loop computation is started, vector data access will certainly not hit L2 cache. For matrix A, the total miss counts is

$$\frac{n_c}{n_r} \tag{11}$$

The total miss counts of matrix B is

$$\frac{m_c}{m_r} \times \frac{n_c}{n_r} \ . \tag{12}$$

The total miss counts of matrix C is

$$\frac{m_c}{m_r} \times \frac{n_c}{n_r} \ . \tag{13}$$

Suppose the latency from memory to L2 cache is L_{m2c} and the latency from L2 cache to register file is L_{c2r}, and the extra memory access time which can not be hidden by computation is

$$T_{extra} = (L_{m2c} + L_{c2r}) \times (1 + 2 \times \frac{n_c}{n_r} \times \frac{m_c}{m_r}) + L_{c2r} \times \frac{n_c}{n_r} \ . \tag{14}$$

4.3   L2 Size

Since A reside in L2 cache, half of L2 cache size is used by A and the other have is used by B and C. Thus the size of L2 cache should be

$$m_c \times k_c \times 2 \times T \times 8 \ . \tag{15}$$

5   Evaluation

We use calculation efficiency to evaluate the performance of matrix multiplication, which is defined as

$$\eta = \frac{T_{com}}{T_{com} + T_{extra}} \ . \tag{16}$$

The baseline configuration of the MTV processor is shown in table 5.

Table 1. Baseline MTV processor configuration

Items	Configurations
Number of cores	64
Number of threads per core	4
NUmber of elements per SIMD	4
Number of vector register	32
Latency from l2 cache to register	8
Latency from memory to L2 cache	100

We first stduy the size of L2 cache, which is shown in table 5. The vector data are saved in L2 cache. The size of L2 cache has a great impact on the efficiency. The bigger l2 is, the higher the efficiency is.

Table 2. Baseline MTV processor configuration

L2 cache size	value of m_c	value of k_c	Computing Efficient
256KB	64	64	70.28%
512KB	64	128	82.54%
1024KB	128	128	82.56%
2048KB	128	256	90.44%
4096KB	256	256	90.45%
8192KB	256	512	94.98%

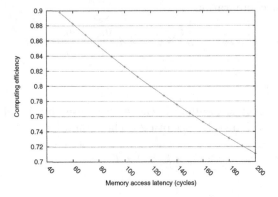

Fig. 3. The impact of memory access latency

Table 3. Balanced Memory bandwidth configurations

Peak performance	512GFlops	1TFlops	2TFlops	4TFlops
Number of cores	64	64	128	128
Thread per core	8	8	8	8
SIMD width per core	4	8	8	16
L2 cache size	1MB	1MB	2MB	2MB
Bandwidth	76GB/s	142GB/s	200GB/s	368GB/s

The memory latency also has a great impact on the computing efficiency. The shorter the memory access time is, the higher the efficiency, as shown in Fig. 5.

Another metric that impact the computing efficiency is memory bandwidth. Table 5 show the memory bandwidth requirements to get the balanced computing efficiency for different configurations

6   Conclusions

MTV improves both peak performance and actual performance by executing vector computation from multiple threads. In this paper, we presented a analytical model to evaluate the performance of matrix multiplication and give some typical configurations for given performance target.

References

1. Rau, B.R., Fisher, J.A.: Instruction-level parallel processing: History, overview, and perspective. Journal of Supercomputing 7 (1993)
2. Badulescu, A.M., Veidenbaum, A.V.: Power-efficient instruction fetch architecture for superscalar processors. In: Proceedings of the Parallel and Distributed Processing Techniques and Architectures (2002)
3. Weaver, D.L., Germond, T.: The SPARC Architecture Manual. SPARC International, Inc. (1994)
4. Maruyama, T., Yoshida, T., Kan, R., Yamazaki, I., Yamamura, S., Takahashi, N., Hondou, M., Okano, H.: SPARC64 VIIIfx: A new-generation octocore processor for petascale computing. IEEE Micro 30, 30–41 (2010)
5. Seiler, L., Carmean, D., Sprangle, E., Forsyth, T., Abrash, M., Dubey, P., Junkins, S., Lake, A., Sugerman, J., Cavin, R., Espasa, R., Grochowski, E., Juan, T., Hanrahan, P.: Larrabee: a many-core x86 architecture for visual computing. ACM Transaction on Graphics 27, 1–16 (2008)
6. IBM: PowerPC Microprocessor Family: AltiVec Technology Programming Environments Manual (2004)
7. Kongetira, P., Aingaran, K., Olukotun, K.: Niagara: A 32-way multithreaded sparc processor. IEEE Micro 25, 21–29 (2005)
8. Dongarra, J.J., Croz, J.D., Hammarling, S.: An extended set of FORTRAN basic linear algebra subprograms. ACM Transactions on Mathematical Software 14, 1–17 (1988)
9. Liu, J., Chi, L., Xie, L., Wang, Y., Gan, X., Feng, H., Hu, Q.: A peak performance model for matrix multiplication on general-purpose dsp. Journal of Hunan University 40, 148 (2013)

HMCPA: Heuristic Method Utilizing Critical Path Analysis for Design Space Exploration of Superscalar Microprocessors

Fangyan Qin, Lei Wang, Yu Deng, Yongwen Wang, and Tianlei Zhao

National University of Defense Technology, Changsha, China
qinfangyan1213@163.com, leiwang@nudt.edu.cn

Abstract. Microprocessor design space exploration at-tempts to determine the optimal parameter conguration to satisfy target requirements within limited time. Current mainstream superscalar microprocessors typically use out-of-order execution and fully utilize instruction level parallelism. However, the increasing complexity of superscalar microprocessor design leads to ever big design space, which poses a challenge to the determination of the optimal design point. To address this problem, this paper proposes a heuristic method utilizing critical path analysis (HMCPA) to perform design space exploration of superscalar microprocessors. Profiling a program running on a simulator enables the program dependence graph to be built by using the detailed information generated during the simulation. The critical path of the dependence graph can then be obtained and further analyzed to determine the performance bottleneck under current design conguration. Based on the information of the performance bottleneck, design space exploration can fnally be conducted efficiently. Experimental results show that compared with the traversal and simulated annealing methods, HMCPA can effectively reduce the number of design points that need to be explored, as well as determine the optimal conguration quickly.

Keywords: superscalar microprocessor, simulator, critical path, performance bottleneck, design space exploration.

1 Introduction

The improvement in integrated circuit technology and the increasing number of transistors in microprocessor chips have significantly enhanced the performance and structure complexity of microprocessors, as predicted by Moore's law. This condition makes microprocessor design challenging because of the difficulty in balancing the resources of superscalar microprocessors. Modern processors fully use instruction level parallelism to process hundreds of instructions in flight. During its lifetime, an instruction may go through such events as cache misses, branch mispredictions, reorder buffer stalls, and data dependence hazards [1]. Such matters could degrade the performance of microprocessors. So it's a main job for microprocessor designers to design a balanced microprocessor with appropriate resources and the best performance.

W. Xu et al. (Eds.): NCCET 2014, CCIS 491, pp. 20–35, 2015.

The performance of a microprocessor is always assessed based on the running time of benchmark programs. Considering the lack of real microprocessors, RTL, and FPGA models in the early stage of microprocessor design, designers could only evaluate performance by using models reflecting architecture characteristics [2]. So, the widely used method is to run benchmark programs on models to obtain the performance information.

Design space exploration concentrates on finding the optimal parameter configuration to satisfy target requirements within limited time, but the increase in design space and design complexity lends difficulty to this process [3,4]. Traditional techniques use simulators to emulate the processor structure and obtain the performance value of the design points in design space, then to identify which design point is good enough. However, it is not enough for the entire design process because of two main drawbacks. First, the long simulation duration leads to that many simulation is not enabled, which necessitates the use of search methods to accelerate the process of identifing the optimal design point. Research shows that more than two months are required to identify the best design point for the SPEC 2000 benchmarks for a design space consisting of 2000 design points [5]. Second, the microprocessor design cannot be solely based on simulations because of the coarse-grained simulation results that cannot intuitively identify the performance bottleneck of the processor, which is the most primary factor degrading the performance. Thus, how the parameters affect the performance is difficult to quantify.

Thus, effective and extensive design space exploration with limited time and resources are challenging problems for microprocessor designers. Numerous studies have focused on microprocessor performance analysis [1,6,7,8] and design space exploration [5,9,10]. The main problem of these methods for design space exploration is that they do not leverage insights as to how the different design parameters influence the design performance, so there remains great space for more effective design space exploration.

In order to perform the design space exploration more effectively and faster in the early stage of microprocessor design, this paper proposes a heuristic method utilizing critical path analysis (HMCPA) that combines the modeling, simulating, and theoretical analysis approaches. Critical path is a concept in project management that represents the longest path, and is the progress activity sequence that determines the project duration. Even small floating incidents in the critical path could directly affect the earliest possible completion time of the entire project.

By modifying the simulator, the technique obtains fine-grained profiling information of the program execution, which is used to build the dependence graph. We can calculate the critical path in the dependence graph to gain insights into and determine the performance bottlenecks of a superscalar microprocessor. Then according to these bottleneck information, change the corresponding parameter to guide the search of optimal design point.

This technique proposed in this paper enables a deeper analysis of the microprocessor architecture and figuring out the key parameter degrading the performance. Compared to earlier works, we use the information of performance bottlenecks to guide the seach of design point. That the corresponding parameter of the current design point can be changed based on the performance bottleneck analysis to obtain a new design point which popularly has a better performance. It avoids redundant iterations for design space exploration, such that the randomness in choosing a new design point can be reduced to accelerate design space exploration.

We have implemented all the tools in the proposed design space exploration flow, and the preliminary experiments show that this method can effectively perform the design space exploration by reducing the number of iterations.

The remainder of this paper is organized as follows. Background and related works are introduced in section 2. Section 3 provides an overview of the HMCPA method. Key techniques and design space exploration method are described in detail in section 4 and 5 respectively. Section 6 discusses the experimental results. Finally, we conclude this paper and discuss future work in section 7.

2   Background and Related Work

2.1   Background

Conventional simulation-based techniques run programs to obtain coarse-grained informantion, which is not very helpful for design improvement. Prior research showed that utilizing critical path analysis can solve this problem to a certain extent [11,12]. This analysis abstracts the execution of a program with a dependence graph, which shows the program execution process and is a systematic notation in processor performance analysis. In the dependence graph, every operation is represented by a node, whereas the data and control information are intuitively reflected by the edges. Our early work has used colored Petri Net to model processors and analyze the performance bottleneck [13].

2.2   Related Work

Simulators are often used in research on the performance of a microprocessor because these devices can be built easily and accurately reflect the execution of a real microprocessor. M5 [2], simplescalar [14], GEMS [15] and GEM5 [16] are popular microprocessor simulators.

The microprocessors design space contains a large number of design points with different parameter configurations that may result in performance differences. A detailed description of design pace exploration techniques is discussed in [17].

Conventional techniques are usually simulator-based to assess the performance of the current design to identify whether the parameter configuration currently meets the performance requirement, such as [2,18,19,20]. To perform the design space exploration, the traversal method can be used to simulate every design point in the design space to identify the one with the best performance. This methed can obtain the global optimum at the big cost of time for enumerating all design points. To solve the problem of long simulation time, researchers have exploited many search algorithms for more effective design space exploration, which can be conducted through random walk [21], simulated annealing method [19], and genetic algorithms [9] etc. In 1986, the random walk method was first used to model checking by West [22], as well as to guide design space exploration in paper [9]. The advantage of random walk is that most design points in the design space can be feasibly visited. But this method is incomplete and often misses corner cases because of randomness, such that the final result may not be of great accuracy. P. Laarhoven and E. Aarts used simulated annealing method to search for the optimum in the global space while avoiding being trapped in a local optimum without traversing the whole design space [18]. S. Eyerman proposed a genetic local search algorithm for design space exploration [9], which outperforms all other search algorithms in terms of accuracy.

Although these search algorithms perform more efficient and faster design space exploration for reduced iterations or increased accuracy, it still takes a considerable amount of time to perform the design space exploration [23]. The main reason is that they do not leverage insights as to how different parameters of a computer system interact to increase or degrade performance at a given point and treat the computer system as a "black-box". Thus, these techniques lack guidance for design improvement, such that a large amount of time is still needed for design space exploration.

3 Overview of HMCPA

This paper proposes the HMCPA method for the design space exploration of superscalar microprocessors to overcome the disadvantages of conventional search techniques. Its main purpose is to accelerate the design space exploration by getting rid of the randomness of choosing design points. The procedure for HMPCA consists of six steps.

Step 1: Analyzing the microprocessor architecture described by the simulator, and then build its pipeline model. Step 2: Running benchmark programs on the simulator to obtain the simulator output. Step 3: Extracting the detailed profile information from the simulator output, then build a model of program dependence graph with the message of the microprocessor's parameter configuration. Step 4: Obtaining the critical path via ctirical path computation. Step 5: Dividing the critical path into different parts to identify the performance bottleneck. Step 6: Design space exploration is performed. The design space is determined firstly, and the parameter configuration of the microprocessor was changed on the basis of the performance bottleneck, such as changing the pipeline structure, resources, or delay of functional units. Then the simulator is reconstructed for another run. The above steps are performed repeatedly until the optimal parameter configuration is identified.

This technique mitigates the limitation of selecting the design point randomly, which can reduce the design points should to be searched, namely reduce the number of iterations for design space exploration. This advantage provides benefits for effective design space exploration and decreases the time required for the execution of the whole design. We will introduce the key technology of this paper in the following section.

4 Key Technology

4.1 Microprocessor Model

The superscalar microprocessor model is based on the GEM5 simulator. The o3 model in it can be used to simulate out-of-order superscalar microprocessors.

Figure 1 shows the microarchitecture schematic diagram of the superscalar microprocessor pipeline used in this study, as modeled by the GEM5 simulator. This model has an issuing in-order, executing out-of-order,and committing in-order pipeline. The pipeline consists of seven stages, namely Fetch (IF), Decode (DE), Rename (RN), Issue (IS), Execute (EX), Write back (WB) and Commit (CP) The IC represents accessing instruction cache and BP represents branch prediction. The pipeline applies for a reorder buffer in RN and obtains it in IS. When the instruction is committed, it retires the reorder buffer in CP.

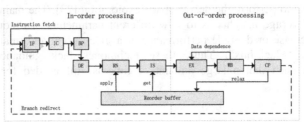

Fig. 1. Diagram of the superscalar microprocessor pipeline

We modify the GEM5 simulator and run benchmark programes on it to obtain the simulator output, which consists of the following: 1), instruction sequence of the benchmark programes; 2), time of entry to each pipeline stage; 3), message regarding the reorder buffer; 4), data dependence of instructions; 5), branch misprediction; and 6), functional units used by each instruction.

4.2   Dependence Graph Construction

4.2.1 Building the Dependence Graph
Each node of the dependence graph represents an event as an instruction enters a pipeline stage, as described in section 4.1. The attribute value of each node is the time an instruction enters a pipeline stage, which is also called the triggering time. In the pipeline, the instruction $i + 1$ cannot enter the fetch queue until the instruction i has entered, hence, a correlative edge exists from the fetch node of instruction i to that of instruction $i + 1$. If the fetch width is w, there is a correlative edge from the fetch node of instruction i to that of instruction $i+w$. Such edge is the same as that of decode, rename, issue and commit. For example, if the decode width is 3, then a correlative edge exists from the decode node of instruction i to that of instruction $i + 3$.

4.2.2 Computation of Edge Weights
The weight of an edge represents the delay from its starting node to end node. If an edge exists from node V_i to node V_j with the weight of W_{ij}, then the event V_j cannot occur earlier than W_{ij} cycles after the event V_i has occurred. For example, weight 1 from node DE_i to node DE_{i+w} represents the delay of one cycle. The weights are computed according to the rules listed in Table 1.

Table 1. Rules for weights computation

Edges	Weights
IF_i–IF_{i+1}, DE_i–DE_{i+1}, RN_i–RN_{i+1}, IS_i–IS_{i+1}, CP_i–CP_{i+1}	0 (They are set as 0.0001 in dependence graph)
IF_i–IF_{i+w}, DE_i–DE_{i+w}, RN_i–RN_{i+w}, IS_i–IS_{i+w}, CP_i–CP_{i+w}	1 (w is the width of corresponding pipeline stage)
IF_i–DE_i, DE_i–RN_i, RN_i–IS_i, EX_i–WB_i, WB_i–CP_i	3, 2, 1, 1, 1 (The delay of corresponding pipeline stage)
IS_i–EX_i	delay of functional units
WB_j–EX_j	1 (delay of data dependence)
CP_i–IF_i	1 (delay of branch misprediction)
CP_{i-w} – IS_i	1 (insufficient reorder buffer)

As previously mentioned, the simulator output contains the trigger time of every event. A node V_j has triggering time j in the dependence graph with the number of incoming edges m. All incoming edges with the weight x_n and corresponding triggering time of starting point i_n are listed. We can then obtain the arrival time $(x_n + i_n)$ of each incoming edge to node V_j. The maximum value from all arrival times is selected and

assigned to the variable T, that is, $$T = \max_{n=1}^{m}(i_n + x_n).$$ If T is less than j, an unknown

delay exists in the pipeline, and the weight of a particular edge should be modified to $x_n + (j - T)$. If T is equal to j, the aforementioned procedure is no longer needed.

4.3   Critical Path Computation

The critical path is the longest path from the starting node (fetch node of the first instruction) to the end node (commit node of the last instruction) of the dependence graph. The length of this path is the execution time of the program. We can use the following method to obtain the critical path:

First, all the connection matrix weights that describe the dependence graph are inverted. The shortest path calculation algorithm is then used to obtain the shortest path, which is called the critical path. The critical path algorithm used in this study is based on the Bellman-Ford algorithm. We have performed some modifications to support the printing of all nodes on the critical path. The algorithm is shown in Figure 2.

4.4   Performance Bottleneck Analysis

The critical path always consists of the connection relationships among the seven points IF, DE, RN, IS, EX, WB and CP. Nineteen different connection relationships exist in the model, as shown in Table 2.

```
j,k: loop variable
neis[]: gather of incoming edges to a node
nlen: number of incoming edges or outgoing edges of a node
target: nodes that have edges to the node j
nei: edge
weights[]: the weight of edges in DAG
no_of_nodes: number of nodes in DAG
dist[]: distance from each node in DAG to the source node
Q: queue to store the sequence number of nodes
source: source node of critical path

for(j=0;j<no_of_nodes,j++){
   push j into queue Q;
   initial dist[j]=infinity;
}
dist[source]=0;
while(Q not empty){
   pop j from queue Q;
   if dist[j]<>infinity
   then continue;
   neis=get_all_inbound_edges_of_node(j);
   nlen=sizeof(neis);
   for(k=0;k<nlen;k++){
     nei=neis[k];
     target=get_another_node_of_edge(nei,j);
     if(dist[target]=dist[j]+weights[nei])
     then {
        dist[target]=dist[j]+weights[nei];
        print(j);
        j=target;
     }
     else
        if(target not in queue Q)
        then push target in queue Q;
   }
}
```

Fig. 2. Critical path computation algorithm

Table 2. Constitution of critical path

Edges	Reasons for long delay
IF_i–IF_{i+1}, DE_i–DE_{i+1}, RN_i–RN_{i+1}, IS_i–IS_{i+1}, CP_i–CP_{i+1}	Branch misprediction, cache miss, insufficient reorder buffer, etc
IF_i–IF_{i+w}, DE_i–DE_{i+w}, RN_i–RN_{i+w}, IS_i–IS_{i+w} CP_i–CP_{i+w}	Insufficient width for fetch, decode, rename, issue and commit, etc
IF_i–DE_i, DE_i–RN_i, RN_i –IS_i, EX_i–WB_i, WB_i–CP_i	Inherent delay of pipeline stage, unknown delay, etc
IS_i–EX_i	Delay of functional units, insufficient functional units, etc
WB_i–EX_j	Data dependence, etc
CP_i–IF_j	Control dependence, branch misprediction, etc
CP_{i-w}–IS_i	Insufficient reorder buffer, etc

We can determine the number and total length of the 19 edges, as well as rank these edges from long to short to determine the longest edge. We can then analyze this information to identify the system performance bottleneck.

4.5   An Example

Dynamic Instruction Trace

```
        I0: R3=0
        I1: R2=5
 L1: I2: R3=R3+R2
        I3: R4=R2+R4
        I4: cmp R1,0
        I5: b L1
        I6: R3=R3+10
```

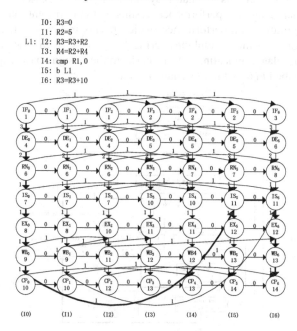

Fig. 3. Dependence graph of Dynamic Instruction Trace

The resource constraints modeld are follows: fetch width = 3, decode width = 3, rename width = 3, issue width = 4, commit width = 4, and rob size =5. One of the critical path for the dynamic instruction trace is the bold black line from fetch node of I_0 (IF_0) to commit node of I_6 (CP_6). This path has the following nodes IF_0, DE_0, RN_0, IS_0, EX_0, WB_0, CP_0, IS_5, IS_6, EX_6, WB6, and CP_6. These 12 nodes have a total weight of 13. The statistical section of the critical path is as follows: IF_i - DE_i: 3, DE_i - RN_i: 2, RN_i - IS_i: 1, IS_i - EX_i: 2, EX_i - WB_i: 2, WB_i - CP_i: 2, CP_{i-w} - IS_i: 1. As can be seen from Figure 3, in the current parameter configuration, regardless of the inherent delay of pipeline stage, because of the edge from node CP_0 to node IS_5, there are more nodes on the critical path. Contrast to Table 3, we can consider the performance bottleneck of the current design point insufficient reorder buffers, such that increasing the size of reorder buffer to seven can eliminate this bottleneck. Then the path of IF_0, DE_0, RN_0, IS_0, EX_0, WB_0, EX_2, WB_2, EX_6, WB_6, and CP_6 or the path of IF_0, DE_0, RN_0, IS_0, EX_0, EX_1, WB_1, EX_2, WB_2, EX_6, WB_6, and CP_6 are the critical paths, in which situation, the performance bottleneck is the data dependence.

5   Design Space Exploration of HMCPA

Despite having resolved the problem of traversal methods, the conventional simulated annealing method still consumes a great deal of time to explore the design space, because it only uses a single metric for design space exploration. Meanwhile, Design point selection has high randomness, which makes it impossible to ensure that the iteration is forwarded to the right direction toward the global optimum. The main drawback of these methods is that they all treat the processor as a black box, superficially analyzing the performance results without insight into the effect of structure configurations on performance, which results in low efficiency. This paper presents HMCPA, which combines critical analysis with the advantages of conventional simulated annealing(SA) to perform the design space exploration. This method is described in detail in this chapter, as the follow:

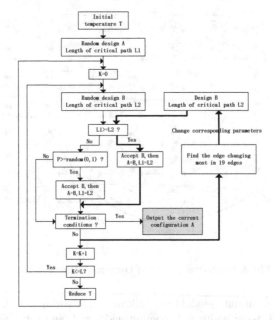

Where L is the max number of iterations per temperature, and it is 20 in this paper. This method shares the spirit of simulated annealing that it accepts a new design point with a probability. If the new design point is not accepted, the search is performed again at the current design point to get another new design point. The probability function is given as follow:

$$P = \begin{cases} 1 & \text{if } perf_{new} \geq perf_{old} \\ e^{(perf_{new} - perf_{old})/T} & \text{if } perf_{new} < perf_{old} \end{cases}$$

Where $perf_{new}$ and $perf_{old}$ respectively represent the performance of the new design point and that of the current design point. T is the temperature that is high at the beginning of the design space exploration and decreases every 20 iterations.

If the improved performance of the new design point is mainly contributed to the edge IF_i - IF_{i+w}, the fetch width may be the most critical factor degrading the performance. Changing the fetch width may also result in a significant improvement in performance. If the performance improvement of the new design point is mainly contributed to the edge from node CP_i to node IS_j, insufficient reorder buffer may be the most critical factor causing poor performance. We can then improve the design performance by increasing the size of reorder buffer.

As previously mentioned, criticality analysis can help determine the critical factor accurately, then to get the performance bottleneck at the current design point, which would be used to guid the search. This technique mitigates the limitation of the classical techniques by using only the performance value to guide the search for optimal design point.

6   Experiment and Evaluation

6.1   Experiment Platform and Implementation

The experiment hardware and software platforms are show in table 3.

Table 3. Experiment platform

Hardware platform	**Intel XEON E5540 2.53GHz, 8 cores** **Memory 40G, Cache 8192KB**
Software platform	**Linux version 2.6.18-164.el5,** **Igraph 0.7, Gem5's version 2.0** **Python 2.6.2, Gcc 4.1.2, Scons 2.3.0,** **Swig 1.3.34, Zlib 1.2.7**

This paper utilizes the languages Python and C to implement the performance analysis and design space exploration. The 12 main programs with 3100 code lines are shown in Table 4.

Table 4. Main Programs

Programs	Purpose
all_parameter.py	**Get the whole design space**
change_parameter.py	**Change the parameters of the simulator**
array.py	**Extract the time entering every pipeline stage of each instruction**
exe-delay.py	**Get the time in execute stage of each instruction**
dependent.py	**Get the message of data dependence**
mispredicted.py	**Get the message of branch misprediction**
dag.c	**Dependence graph**
bellman_ford.c	**Calculate the critical path and list out the nodes in it**
cp.c	**Calculate the number and length of 19 edges**
collect_result.py	**Write the message of 19 edges into a file**
simulated_annealing. py	**SA for design pace exploration**
critical_simulated_an nealing.py	**HMCPA for design space exploration**

6.2   Experiment Parameters and Benchmark Programs

Our design space consists of 729 design points. The design space is spanned by the independent design parameters enumerated in Table 5.

Table 5. Microarchitectural design parameters

Parameters	Value Range	Number
fetchWidth	3, 5, 7	3
decodeWidth	2, 4, 6	3
renameWidth	2, 4, 6	3
issueWidth	4,6 , 8	3
commitWidth	4, 6, 8	3
numROBEntries	8, 13, 18	3

The test programs used in this study are Laplace transform and the three core code segments of the "8 Queen" problem. We selected these programs because the overall analysis capability remains low, such that only small-scale programs can be analyzed.

6.3   Experiments Results

6.3.1 Evaluation of HMCPA

We performed an experiment on the Laplace to identify how design space exploration is conducted. The results of the HMCPA method are shown in Figure 4, where the horizontal axis represents the different design points along the design space exploration, whereas the vertical axis represents the length and constitution of the critical path. The critical path consists of 19 types of edges, then we find out the relatively longer edges that are portrayed using different paddings. The rest ones are classified under "The rest".

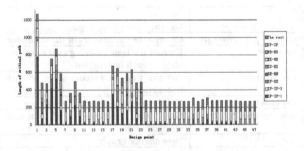

Fig. 4. The process of design space exploration by HMCPA

We can see from Figure 6 that, the length of the critical path tends to be shorter to reach an optimum, such that less iterations are required. The most critical factor affecting the length of the critical path are CP_i - IF_j (commit - fetch), WB_i - EX_j (write back - execute), EX_i - WB_i (execute - write back), DE_i - RN_i (decode - rename),

IF_i - DE_i (fetch - decode), IF_i - IF_{i+w} (fetch with a width of w), and IF_i – IF_{i+1}(fetch in sequence).

At the current design point i, the most critical factor affecting the length of the critical path is determined, and the corresponding design parameter is changed to obtain a new design point $i + 1$. Thus, the performance of design point $i + 1$ is likely to be better than that of design point i. However, the method SA chooses a new design point randomly, which cannot guarantee the design to be along the direction toward the optimal design. The HMCPA method can mitigate this disadvantage, thus reducing the number of iterations.

6.3.2   Comparison of Different Design Space Exploration Methods

This experiment compares the efficiency of different design space exploration methods, namely, the traversal method, conventional simulated annealing, and HMCPA.

Figure 5 shows a comparison of the number of iterations using different search algorithms. Figure 6 shows a comparison of the performance of the resulted optimal design point, in which a lower value indicates better performance.

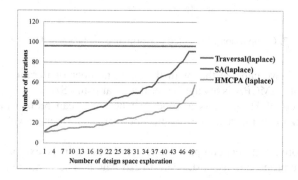

Fig. 5. Comparison of the number of iterations using simulated annealing(SA) or HMCPA

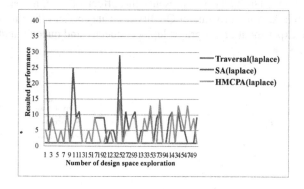

Fig. 6. Comparison of the performance of the final design point using SA or HMCPA

Figures 5 and 6 show that although we can obtain the best performance through the traversal method, the number of iterations is extremely large, thus making the implementation costly. The performance of the design points obtained by using conventional simulated annealing and HMCPA are comparable, but the number of iterations of the former is significantly bigger than that of the latter.

Then we do experiment to identify whether different methods have influence on performance. We set the number of iterations the same, using SA and HMCPA to perform design space exploration. Then census and compare the resulted performance value as Figure 7.

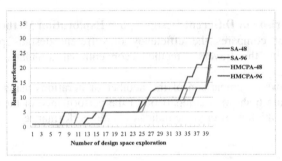

Fig. 7. Comparison of resulted performance using SA or HMCPA

From Figure 7, we can see that with the same number of iterations, the resulted performance using HMCPA is always better than that using SA.

So, the method of HMCPA is a good one not only can reduce the number of iterations but also can improve the resulted performance, then to get a better final design point.

In order to more intuitively compare the effect of design space exploration using SA and HMCPA, we propose to use a standard to estimate it. The standard is as follow:

$$Quality = perf * Num$$

Where the perf and Num respectively represent the resulted performance and number of iterations, The Quality represents the effect of design space exploration using SA or HMCPA. A lower value of Quality indicates better effect for design space exploration. We experiment on programs laplace, queen1 and queen2, and the result is shown in Figure 8.

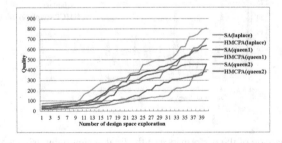

Fig. 8. Comparison of effect using SA or HMCPA

From Figure 8 we can see that, the value Quality of SA is always bigger than that of HMCPA, which indicates that the effect of design space exploration using SA is always lower than that using HMCPA. On average, HMCPA obtains 1.3x performance improvement over SA. So, using HMCPA can perform better design space exploration.

6.3.3   Study on Simulated Annealing

The simulated annealing method reduces the temperature along with the design space exploration, as well as accepts a worse design point with a lower probability. However, the initial temperature significantly affects the probability of accepting a worse design point, thus influencing the design space exploration process. Therefore, we experimented on the Laplace to analyze how different initial temperatures influence design space exploration. Figures 9 and 10 respectively show the iterations of simulated annealing with different initial temperatures.

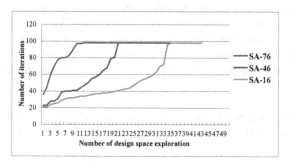

Fig. 9. Comparison of iterations with different initial temperature

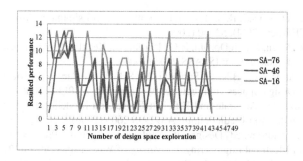

Fig. 10. Comparison of resulted performance with different initial temperature

Figure 9 shows that different initial temperatures result in different numbers of iterations. When the initial temperature T equals to 16, the number becomes minimal. And figure 10 shows that different initial temperatures have an effect on the performance of the final design point, that bigger initial temperature results in higher performance of microprocessor. So, We can thus conclude that selecting a good initial temperature can largely decrease the time for design space exploration and improve the performance of microprocessors.

7   Conclusion and Future Works

The increasing complexity of superscalar microprocessor design leads to increasing difficulty and cost for performance analysis and design space exploration.

This paper proposes a HMCPA method for the design space exploration of superscalar microprocessors. A dependence graph and critical path analysis can analyze processors in depth to identify the bottleneck in fine grain. HMCPA utilizes the bottleneck at the current design point to guide design improvement and can ensure that such improvement is forwarded to the optimum. Thus, the method can guide global optimization and accelerate design space exploration to reach the global optimal design point.

The fundamental framework for design space exploration has been completed, but a great deal of work still needs to be conducted in the future. For instance, the model for program execution is simple, which makes the analysis result inaccurate. We will modify this model and improve the analysis accuracy. We can also analyze the sub-critical path to guide design space exploration, which might improve the speed of identifying the optimal design point. The analysis capability of the algorithms in this study also needs to be improved because only small-scale programs can currently be analyzed.

Acknowledgments. We would like to thank the anonymous reviewers for providing helpful comments on this paper. This work was funded by NSF grant of China No.61402501.

References

1. Binkert, N.L., Dreslinski, R.G., Hsu, L.R., et al.: The M5 simulator: Modeling networked systems. IEEE Micro 26(4), 52–60 (2006)
2. Nagarajan, R., Chen, X., McDonald, R.G., Burger, D., Keckler, S.W.: Critical Path Analysis of the TRIPS architecture. In: ISPASS 2006 (2006)
3. E.: Ðpek, S. A. McKee, B.R. de Supinski, M. Schulz, R. Caruana. Efficiently Exploring Architectural Design Spaces via Predictive Modeling. In: ASPLOS 2006 (2006)
4. Lee, B., Brooks, D.: Accurate and Efficient Regression Modeling for Microarchitectural Performance and Power Prediction. In: ASPLOS 2006 (2006)
5. Karkhanis, T.: Automated Design of Application Specific Processors. PhD. Thesis, Department of Electrical Engineering, University of Wisconsin Madison (2006)
6. Saidi, A., Binkert, N., Mudge, T.N., Reinhardt, S.K.: Full System Critical Path Analysis. In: ISPASS 2008 (2008)
7. Salverda, P., Zilles, C.: A Criticality Analysis of Clustering in Surperscalar Processors. In: MICRO 2005 (2005)
8. Lockyer, K.G.: Introduction to Critical Path Analysis. Pitman Publishing Co., New York (1964)
9. Eyerman, S., Eeckhout, L., De Bosschere, K.: Efficient Design Space Exploration of High Performance Embedded Out of Order Processors. In: DATE 2006 (2006)
10. Lee, B., Brooks, D.: Statistically rigorous regression modeling for the microprocessor design space. In: ISCA-33: Workshop on Medeling, Benchmarking, and Simulation (June 2006)

11. Tune, E., Tullsen, D.M., Calder, B.: Quantifying instruction criticality. In: Proceedings of the 11th International Conference on Parallel Architectures and Compilation Techniques, pp. 104–113 (September 2002)
12. Fields, B., Rubin, S., Bodik, R.: Focusing processor policies via critical-path prediction. In: Proceedings of the 28th Annual International Symposium on Computer Architecture, pp. 74–85 (July 2001)
13. Wang, L., Deng, Y., Qin, F., Wang, Y., Sun, C.: Utilizing Colored Petri Net for Performance Bottleneck Analysis and Design Space Exploration of Superscalar Processors. To be appeared in ACA 2014 (2014)
14. Burger, D.C., Austin, T.M.: The SimpleScalar Tool Set, Version 2.0. Computer Architecture News 25(3) (1997)
15. Marty, M.R., Beckmann, B., Yen, L., Alameldeen, A.R., Xu, M., Moore, K.: GEMS: Multifacet's General Execution-driven Multiprocessor Simulator. In: International Symposium on Computer Architecture (2006)
16. Binkert, N., Bechmann, B., Black, G., et al.: The gem5 simulator. SIGARCH Comput. Archit. News 39, 1–7 (2011)
17. Gries, M.: Methods for evaluating and covering the design space during early design development. Integration, the VLSI Journal 38(2), 131–183 (2004)
18. Navada, S., Choudharv, N.K., Rotenbera, E.: Criticality-driven Design Space Exploration. In: PACT 2010, Vienna, Austria, September 11-15 (2010)
19. Laarhoven, P., Aarts, E.: Simulated Annealing: Theory and Applications. Springer (1987)
20. Binkert, N.L., Hallnor, E.G., Reinhardt, S.K.: Network-oriented full-system simulation using M5. In: Sixth Workshop on Computer Architecture Evaluation using Commercial Workloads (CAECW) (February 2003)
21. Spitzer, F.: Principles of random walk. van Nostrand, Princeton (1964)
22. West, C.H.: Protocol validation by random state exploration. In: International Symposium on Protocol Specification, Testing and Verification (1986)
23. Kang, S., Kumar, R.: Magellan: A Framework for Fast Muti-core Design Space Exploration and Optimization Using Search and Machine Learning. In: DATE 2008 (2008)

Low Latency Multicasting Scheme for Bufferless Hybrid NoC-Bus 3D On-Chip Networks

Chaoyun Yao[1], Chaochao Feng[1], Mingxuan Zhang[1], and Shaojun Wei[2]

[1] School of Computer, National University of Defense Technology, Changsha, P.R. China
[2] The Department of Electronic systems Tsinghua University, Beijing, P.R. China
ycy021417@163.com

Abstract. In this paper, we proposed a novel multicast routing algorithm for the 3D Bufferless Hybrid Interconnection Network to enhance the overall system performance. The proposed algorithm makes use of a single-hop and broadcast (bus-based) interlayer communication of the 3D NoC-Bus mesh architecture. Compared to the DRM_noPR multicast routing algorithm, our simulations with six different synthetic workloads reveal that our architecture using the proposed multicast routing algorithm acquires high system performance.

Keywords: NoC-Bus, 3D, multicast.

1 Introduction

While the technology continues to decrease with Moore's law, a single die can incorporate several hundreds of cores, As the number of core increases, interconnect plays a crucial role in System-on-chip design. the number of core on a single chip continues to increase for efficient utilize the transistors. Networks on chip were shown to be feasible to scale for supporting more number of cores rather than point-to-point interconnect wires or shared buses [1]. However, with the increasing cores number in the 2D plane is not an efficient way due to its long wire interconnects [2][3]. The emerging of the 3D integrated circuit that stacks several dies to reduce the long wire. The 3D integrated circuit is also an appealing way for Network on chip design. The 3D NoC architecture is widely studied in the network topology [4][5], router architecture [6][7], and routing algorithms [8][9].

The general 3D NoC architecture is simply adding two additional ports to each router for up and down directions routing. However, this architecture does not distinguish the intra-layer and inter-layer communication. And it is also not utilization the inter-wafer distance in 3D chips. Owe to increase two ports, the crossbar is more big than 2D router [10]. The 3D Hybrid architecture presented in [11] is a architecture that combination bus and packet switched. It takes advantage of inter-layer communication use bus and intra-layer communication use packet switched. In this architecture it uses a six-port router replace the seven-port router and vertical communication is just one hop to any layer on bus.

In order to run all kinds of communication applications in Multi-Processors System-on-Chip (MPSoC), fast and efficient collective communications must be supported. In an MPSoC system, the cache-coherent shared memory protocols (such as directory-based) demand to one-to-many or broadcast communications to request

W. Xu et al. (Eds.): NCCET 2014, CCIS 491, pp. 36–47, 2015.

shared data or invalidate data on different cache blocks [11]. It has been stated that only 2-5% multicast traffic in the total network traffic will have an inportant impact on system performance [11]. So, supporting multicast communication in NoC can advance system performance significantly. Several recent research and industry products trend to support multicasting in hardware implementation.

In this paper, we propose a novel multicast routing algorithm for 3D bufferless hybrid (NoC-bus) mesh architectures to enhance the overall system performance and reduce power consumption.

This proposed architecture adopts broadcast and only one hop in inter-layer (bus-based) communications to provide high-performance hardware multicast support.

The rest of paper is organized as follows. The related work is reviewed in Sect.2. Section 3 proposes the general multicast schemes in bufferless 3D mesh architecture. In Sect.4, a novel multicast routing algorithms is proposed. In Sect.5, the simulation and experimental results are presented and analyzed, followed by the conclusion in Sect.6.

2   Related Work

There are three multicast mechanisms which can be classified as unicast-based, path-based and tree-based. In unicast-based multicast scheme [12], the multicast packet is divided into many unicast packets at the source node and transmits to the destinations all by oneself. The advantage of this scheme is that can be run on the unicast routers, and the unicast routers did not require to make any changes. However, such a scheme is very low efficiency owe to the multiple copies of the same packet is injected into the network by turns. In path-based multicast scheme, the multicast packet routes the multicast packets along a path to each destination sequentially until it arrives to the last node. Low Distance multicast (LD) [13] algorithm is based on path-based method which utilized adaptive routing and optimize destination nodes order for multicast packets through the network. In tree-based multicast scheme, the multicast packet attempts to makeup a tree rooted from the source node to the destination nodes and it along the path to the destination nodes on the construction tree. The Virtual Circuit Tree Multicasting (VCTM) [14] is a typical tree-based multicast routing scheme. This routing method sends a packet to build a multicast tree before sending multicast packet. Similar as VCTM multicast scheme, two stage multicast tree construct method is proposed in [15] which consume less power than VCTM algorithm. The Recursive Partitioning Multicast (RPM) [16] divides the network into several partitions, the multicast packet replicates intermediate nodes, minimizes the packet replication time. This scheme performs better than VCTM owe to its more path diversities, but it is not carried out in hardware.

Merge the NoC to the third dimension (3D-NoC) is a widely studied topic. Feero [17] showed that 3D-NoC has the ability to reduce latency and the energy per packet by 40% by decreasing the number of hopes. The 3D-NoC can decrease 62% and 58% power consumption compare to a traditional 2D-NoC topology for a network size of N=128 and N=256 nodes, respectively, which is proposed in[5]. However, 3D mesh-based NoC architecture needs a 7×7 crossbar instead of 5×5 crossbar for the 2D mesh architecture, The 3D router is consumption much higher power than a 2D router [18]. Li et al [7] proposed a 3D NoC-Bus Hybrid mesh architecture to solution to the power consumption of the big crossbar as shown in Fig.1. It only needs one hop in vertical communication and 6×6 crossbars, this architecture is less power consumption and latency than general 3D mesh architecture. Although the bus does not allow concurrent communication in the third dimension, the dTDMA bus [7] outperforms a NoC in the vertical communication as long as the vertical link layer is less than 9.

In the open literature, there has been no work addressing bufferless multicasting for 3D hybrid NoC systems. Even multicast routing algorithms for 3D bufferless NoCs are very rare. Feng [19] proposed three bufferless multicast routing algorithms for 2D NoC architecture. They are DRM_noPR, DRM_PR_src and DRM_PR_all routing algorithms. Owe to DRM_PR_src is unicast-based multicast mechanism which increased port nodes power consumption to multiple copies of the same packet. DRM_PR_all multicast mechanism is a region partition for 2D mesh architecture, this partition way can't simple expand to 3D mesh architecture. So this paper expands DRM_noPR routing algorithms from 2D mesh architecture to 3D mesh architecture as baseline routing algorithms. In this work, we put forward a new multicast routing algorithm in 3D NoC-Bus Hybrid mesh architecture. The latency of this multicast routing algorithm bounds the DRM_noPR routing algorithm due to the single hop interlayer communication by exploiting the benefits associated with the vertical buses.

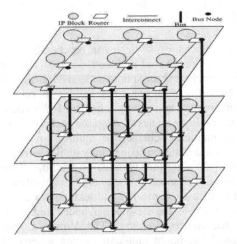

Fig. 1. 3D Hybrid NoC-Bus mesh architecture

3   Baseline 3D Bufferless Multicast Routing Algorithm

We extend the DRM_noPR multicast routing algorithm, which is a 2D plane multicast routing algorithm, to a 3D plane multicast routing algorithm. The 3D plane mesh architecture is shown in Fig.2. This algorithm is a non-deterministic path-based multicast scheme. Different from the buffer path-based multicast, the multicast packet will be routed to each destination along a non-deterministic path. When a multicast packet arrives at a router, the router always selects a destination with the minimum manhattan distance to the current router from the destination nodes. Due to the packet would be deflected away from the shortest path to the destination, the best destination nodes in the multicast will change dynamically during the routing process.

The pseudo code of this path-based bufferless 3D multicast routing algorithm is shown in Fig.3. The algorithm first collects multicast destination node IDs in the packet into an array dst_id_array (Step 1-7), second sets the first element of dst_id_array as the best candidate node ID and calculates the manhattan distance between the current node and the best candidate node (Step 8-10). Third, find the minimum manhattan distance of the best candidate node to the current node (Step 11-17). Finally, the optimal direction is calculated according to the position of the best candidate node to the current node (Step 18).

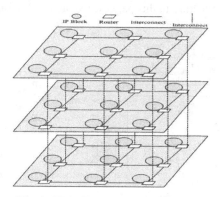

Fig. 2. 3D bufferless mesh architecture

```
Routing computation function for path-based bufferless 3D
multicast routing algorithm
Input: Multicast destination address dst_add
       Coordinate of current node (xc, yc, zc)
Output: Optimal direction set (doptimal)
1: i ← 0
2: for j in 0 to N-1 loop // N is the number of
destination
nodes in the multicast packet
3:    if dst_add[j] = '1' then
4:         dst_id_array[i] ←j
5:           i← i+1
6:    end if
7:  end loop
8:  best_candidate_id ←dst_id_array[0]
9:  (xd, yd, zd) ← get_dst_coordinate(dst_id_array[0])
10: distance← get_manhattan_distance(xd, yd, zd, xc, yc,
zc)
11: for j in 1 to i-1 loop
12:   (xd, yd, zd) ← get_dst_coordinate( dst_id_array[j] )
13:     if distance > get_manhattan_distance(xd, yd, zd,
xc, yc, zc) then
14:       distance ← get_manhattan_distance(xd, yd, zd, xc,
yc, zc)
15:       best_candidate_id ←dst_id_array[j]
16:    end if
17: end loop
18: doptimal ← get_optimal_direction (best_candidate_id,
xc, yc, zc )
```

Fig. 3. Routing computation function for bufferless 3D multicast routing algorithm

4   Proposed Multicast Strategy for 3D Hybrid Architecture

4.1   3D Bufferless Hybrid Router Architecture

The bufferless NoC architecture in this paper is extend a 2D mesh topology,

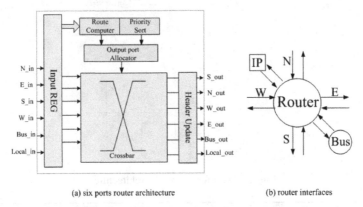

(a) six ports router architecture   (b) router interfaces

Fig. 4. 3D bufferless hybrid router architecture

Nostrum NoC [24]. Figure 4 shows the bufferless router architecture. For 3D NoC-Bus Hybrid mesh architecture, there are 6 input/output ports in each router. Each input port has only one input register, so the packet is not buffered in the router. The router adopts deflecting routing to route packets. When two or more packets compete for a common optimal port, through which leads to a shortest path to the destination, only one packet can gain the optimal port, other packet(s) will be deflected to a non-optimal port. The port allocator will sorted arriving packets in order to limit the number of misrouting packets to avoid livelock. The Priority Sort module accords the number of hops the packet has been routed in the network to acquire the optimal port, which means the most hops of the packet has the highest priority.

4.2   Routing Strategy

As discussed before, the 3D NoC-Bus Hybrid architecture makes use of vertical buses which can be provided single-hop and broadcast on interlayer communication. Our proposed multicast algorithm for the 3D NoC-Bus Hybrid architecture is based on dividing the destination set into disjoint groups (D_0, D_1, ... D_{n-1}). D_0 contains the destination nodes in the number of layer 0, Similarly, D_{n-1} contains the destination nodes in the number of layer n-1. If the multicast can inject into the network, the multicast will deflection routing in the network. When the coordinate (x, y) of the current node is equal to the destination node coordinate (x, y), then continue judge whether the current node coordinate z is equal to the destination node z. if the value of z is not equal, the multicast may acquire the bus and through it to arrive to the destination. Fig. 5 shows an example of multicasting using a same scenario for 3D mesh NoC architecture using DRM_noPR multicast routing algorithm and 3D

NoC-Bus Hybrid mesh architecture using proposed multicast routing strategy. In this example, it is assumed that for 3D mesh NoC architecture, the source node is at node 7 where the destination set is D= {5, 9, 16, 17, 24, 38, 47} and for 3D NoC-Bus Hybrid mesh architecture using our proposed multicasting strategy, the source node is at 7_0 (7_0 indicates the node labeled 7 at the layer 0) where the destination set is D={5_0, 6_2, 7_1, 9_0, 14_1, 15_1, 15_2}. For the DRM_noPR multicast routing scheme shown in the Fig.5 (a), Node 7 sends a multicast packet to nodes 5, 9, 16, 17, 24, 38 and 47. Node 24 is chosen at the first best candidate since it has the minimum manhattan distance 1 to the source node 7. After the packet is sent to node 24, node 16 is chosen as the second best candidate. Without contention, the multicast minimum latency is equal to 14 hops. The path shown in Fig.5 (a) is not the only one path since the packet may be deflected due to contention.

For the 3D NoC-Bus Hybrid mesh architecture using bus broadcast strategy, there is a great improvement in terms of packet latency for the same source node and destination set. As illustrated in Fig. 5 (b), the destination set partition method is based on the number where D= {5_0, 6_2, 7_1, 9_0, 14_1, 15_1, 15_2}. The paths to cover all destination nodes are {7_0\{7_1\}, 6_0\{6_2\}, 5_0, 10_0, 9_0, 14_0\{14_1\}, 15_0\{$15_1,15_2$\}}. In this case, the latency is equal to 7 hops (the intermediate bus transactions are not counted since they are performed in parallel with the packet traversal through other destination nodes in 2D plane). The reason for such a significant improvement is that vertical buses offering single-hop and broadcast-based interlayer communication at the same time.

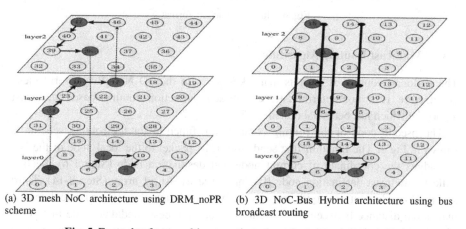

(a) 3D mesh NoC architecture using DRM_noPR scheme   (b) 3D NoC-Bus Hybrid architecture using bus broadcast routing

Fig. 5. Example of two multicast routing where the source is at node 7

4.3   Packet Format

The router supports two packet types: unicast and multicast. Figure 6 shows the format of multicast packet type. The packet fields are explained as follows:

Type field (2bits): indicate the type of the packet ("01": unicast packet; "10": multicast packet; "00"/"11": invalid packet).

Src_addr field (18 bits): denote the relative address to the source node (6 bits for row addresses, 6 bits for column addresses and the other 6 bits for layer addresses).

Dst_addr field: bit string encoding is used, the bit number is based on the number of layer and the number of node in every layer. A bit of '1' in the string means the corresponding nodes is one of destinations.

Hop_counter field (11 bits): record the number of hops the packet has been routed and used it as packet priority to avoid livelock.

Payload field: the payload has 64 bits, which can be extended to contain more bits for different application requirements.

In our multicast routing, When a multicast packet reaches a destination, the bit in the destination bit string corresponding to that destination node reset to '0', the message is copied and sent together with its header to the neighboring node in accordance with our proposed routing algorithm which will be shown in the following subsection. The hop counter field of the packet will add 1. Both of them will be completed in Fig.4 Header Update Module.

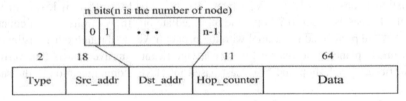

Fig. 6. Multicast packets format

4.4   Multicast Routing Algorithm

The multicast routing of packets that takes place in the 3D NoC-Bus Hybrid mesh architecture is a non-deterministic path-based deflection routing based multicast algorithm which has been elaborated in Fig.7.

The pseudo code of the routing computation function for the routing scheme is shown in Fig.7. The function first sends multicast packet to the local node or the bus by judges the coordinate of current node and destination node (Step 1-6). Second collects multicast destination node IDs into an array dst_id_array (Step 8-14). Third sets the first element of dst_id_array as the best candidate node ID and calculates the manhattan distance between the current node and the best candidate node in layer 0 (Step15-17). Forth the best candidate node with the minimum manhattan distance to the current node is found (Step 18-25). Finally, the productive direction(s) can be acquired according to the position of the best candidate node to the current node in (Step 26).

```
Routing computation function for bufferless 3D
NoC-Bus Hybrid mesh architecture
Input:  Multicast  destination  address  dst_add  and
coordinate  is  (xd,  yd,  zd),  Multicast  current  node
Coordinate is ( xc, yc, zc)
Output: Next  Hop  (Optimal  direction  set  (doptimal),
Local, Up/Down)
1: if xc =xd AND yc=yd then
2:   if zc =zd then
3:      Deliver the packet to the Local node and exit;
4:   else
5:         Send  the  packet  to  the  Up/Down  output  port
(connected bus)
         Towards the destination(s);
6:   end if
7: else
8:   i ← 0
   9:    for j in 0 to N-1 loop // N is the number of
   nodes in the architecture
10:    if dst_add[j] = '1' then
11:          dst_id_array[i] ←j
12:          i← i+1
13:      end if
14:    end loop
15:  best_candidate_id ←dst_id_array[0]
16:  (xd, yd, zd) ← get_dst_coordinate(dst_id_array[0])
17:  distance← get_manhattan_distance(xd, yd, xc, yc) //
2D plane manhattan distance
18:  for j in 1 to i-1 loop
19:    (xd, yd, zd) ← get_dst_coordinate( dst_id_array[j]
)
20:      if distance > get_manhattan_distance(xd, yd, xc,
yc) then
22:          distance ← get_manhattan_distance(xd, yd, xc,
yc)
23:          best_candidate_id ←dst_id_array[j]
24:    end if
25:  end loop
26:  doptimal ← get_optimal_direction (best_candidate_id,
xc, yc, zc )
27: end if
```

Fig. 7. Routing computation function for bufferless 3D multicast routing algorithm

4.5   Deadlock and Livelock Avoidance

Deflection routing is inherently deadlock-free due to the fact that packets never have to wait in a router. However, when a packet needs deflect, it will move further away from its destination. Thus, livelock must be avoided by limiting the number of misroutings. In our multicast routing algorithm, the multicast packets are prioritized based on its age (the number of hops already routed in the network). The age-based priority mechanism guarantees the oldest packet will first win the link arbitration and direct to its destination. Once the oldest packet reaches its destination, another packet becomes the oldest. For our 3D NoC-Bus multicast routing algorithm, bus arbiter decides on only one top priority multicast packet that can acquire the bus and through on the bus to the destination node in a cycle, the other multicast packets deflect in the 2D plane based on the age. Thus livelock can be avoided.

5   Performance Evaluation

We evaluate the performance of the proposed multicasting mechanism for the 3D NoC-Bus Hybrid interconnection network, a cycle-accurate NoC simulator developed in VHDL. The general 3D mesh architecture using extend the DRM_noPR multicast routing algorithm [19] and 3D NoC-Bus Hybrid mesh using bus broadcast multicast routing mechanism were analyzed for synthetic traffic patterns. For both architectures, Nostrum [20] router is as a baseline router structure. For the Hybrid NoC-Bus architecture, routers have 6 input/output ports and for the general 3D mesh architecture, routers have 7 input/output ports. The arbitration scheme for the switch allocator is age-based.

The performance of the network was evaluated using latency curves and the packet injection rate function. The packet latency is the time duration from when the packet is created at the source node to when the packet is delivered to the destination node. To perform the simulations, a packet generator is attached to each router and uses a FIFO to buffer the packets which cannot be injected into the network immediately due to the fact that there is no free output port to route the packet. A combination of unicast (80%) and multicast (20%) traffic was used. For the unicast portion of the traffic, we use six traffic patterns: uniform random, transpose, bit complement, bit reverse, shuffle, tornado. In uniform random traffic, each resource node sends packets randomly to other nodes with an equal probability. For transpose traffic, resource node is $(x, y, z)(!(x=y=z))$ sends package to the destination is (z, y, x). For bit complement traffic. The six-bit source node ID$\{si \mid i{\in}[0,5]\}$ sends packets to destination$\{\neg si \mid i{\in}[0,5]\}$. If the four-bit source address is $\{s_3, s_2, s_1, s_0\}$ the destination address for bit reverse traffic is $\{s_0, s_1, s_2, s_3\}$, and for shuffle traffic is $\{s_2, s_1, s_0, s_3\}$. For tornado traffic, each (radix-k) digit of the destination address Dx is a function of a digit Sx of the source address, which is $Dx = Sx+ (k/2-1) \bmod k$. For multicast packet, the destination positions are uniformly distributed.

In the experiment set, the number of destination nodes has been set to 6. The average packet latency curves for uniform random (i.e. 80% uniform random unicast + 20% uniform multicast), transpose, bit complement, bit reverse, shuffle, tornado are shown in Fig.6. It can be observed for all six traffic patterns, that 3D NoC-Bus multicast scheme achieves less average latency. The main reason is that the proposed multicasting scheme improves the maximum packet delay by utilizing the broadcast and single hop of vertical buses.

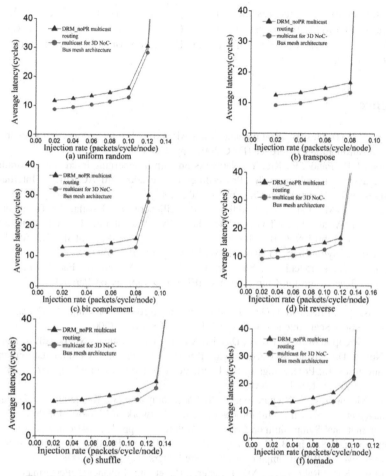

Fig. 8. Latency versus average packet inject rate with 6 multicast nodes

6   Conclusion and Future Work

In this paper, we propose an efficient multicast routing strategy for the 3D NoC-Bus Hybrid mesh architecture, thereby improving the overall NoC performance. The proposed architecture exploits a single-hop (bus-based) and broadcast interlayer communication to provide high-performance hardware multicast support. To this end, we proposed a deflection multicast routing scheme to efficiently utilize the bus broadcast function. Our simulations with different traffic profiles showed that our proposed multicast routing algorithm can achieve significant performance improvements over the DRM_noPR multicast routing algorithm. In the future, our work will be extended by introducing faulty links for proposed architecture and simulating it using a set of realistic workloads. We will also measure power consumption and area for this architecture.

Acknowledgements. This research is supported by National Natural Science Foundation of China with No. 61303066 and 61373032 and by Specialized Research Fund for the Doctor Program of Higher Education of China with Grant No. 20124307110016.

References

1. Dally, W.J., Towles, B.: Route packets, not wires: on-chip interconnection networks. In: Design Automation Conference (DAC 2001), pp. 684–689 (2001)
2. Carloni, L.P., Pande, P., Xie, Y.: Networks-on-chip in emerging interconnect paradigms: Advantages and challenges. In: Proceedings of the 2009 3rd ACM/IEEE International Symposium on Networks-on-Chip, pp. 93–102 (2009)
3. Rahmani, A.-M., Latif, K., Vaddina, K.R., Liljeberg, P., Plosila, J., Tenhunen, H.: Congestion Aware, Fault Tolerant and Thermally Efficient Inter-Layer Communication Scheme for Hybrid NoC-Bus 3D Architectures. In: Proceedings of the 5th ACM/IEEE International Symposium on Networks-on-Chip, pp. 65–72 (2011)
4. Matsutani, H., Koibuchi, M., Yamada, Y., Hsu, D.F., Amano, H.: Fat H-Tree: A Cost-Efficient Tree-Based On-Chip Network. IEEE Transactions on Parallel and Distributed Systems 20(8), 1126–1141 (2009)
5. Pavlidis, V.F., Friedman, E.G.: 3-D Topologies for Networks-on-Chip. IEEE Transactions on Very Large Scale Integration Systems 15(10), 1081–1090 (2007)
6. Kim, J., Nicopoulos, C., Park, D., Das, R., Xie, Y., Vijaykrishnan, N., Yousif, M., Das, C.: A Novel Dimensionally-Decomposed Router for On-Chip Communication in 3D Architectures. In: Proceedings of the International Symposium on Computer Architecture (ISCA 2007), pp. 138–149 (2007)
7. Li, F., Nicopoulos, C., Richardson, T., Xie, Y., Narayanan, V., Kandemir, M.: Design and Management of 3D Chip Multiprocessors Using Network-in-Memory. In: Proceedings of the International Symposium on Computer Architecture, pp. 130–141 (June 2006)
8. Ramanujam, R.S., Lin, B.: Randomized Partially-Minimal Routing on Three-Dimensional Mesh Networks. IEEE Computer Architecture Letters 7(2), 37–40 (2008)
9. Moosavi, S.R., Rahmani, A.M., Liljeberg, P., et al.: Enhancing Performance of 3D Interconnection Networks using Efficient Multicast Communication Protocol. In: 2013 21st Euromicro International Conference on Parallel, Distributed and Network-Based Processing (PDP), pp. 294–301. IEEE (2013)
10. Rahmani, A.-M., Latif, K., Vaddina, K.R., Liljeberg, P., Plosila, J., Tenhunen, H.: ARB-NET: A novel adaptive monitoring platform for stacked mesh 3D NoC architectures. In: Proceedings of the 17th Asia and South Pacific Design Automation Conference, pp. 413–418 (2012)
11. Rahmani, A.-M., Vaddina, K.R., Latif, K., Liljeberg, P., Plosila, J., Tenhunen, H.: Generic Monitoring and Management Infrastructure for 3D NoC-Bus Hybrid Architectures. In: Proceedings of the 6th ACM/IEEE International Symposium on Networks-on-Chip, pp. 177–184 (2012)
12. McKinley, P.K., Xu, H., Ni, L.M., Esfahanian, A.H.: Unicast-based multicast communication in wormhole-routed networks. IEEE Trans. Parallel Distrib. 12, 1252–1265 (1994)
13. Daneshtalab, M., Ebrahimi, M., Mohammadi, S., Afzali-Kusha, A.: Low distance path-based multicast algorithm in NOCs. IET (IEE) -Computers and Digital Techniques, Special issue on NoC 3(5), 430–442 (2009)

14. Jerger, N.E., Peh, L.-S., Lipasti, M.: Virtual Circuit Tree Multicasting: A Case for On-Chip Hardware Multicast Support. In: Proceedings of the 35th Annual International Symposium on Computer Architecture, pp. 229–240 (2008)
15. Hu, W., Lu, Z., Jantsch, A., Liu, H.: Power-efficient tree-based multicast support for networks-on-chip. In: Proc. 16th Asia and South Pacific Design Automation Conference, Piscataway, NJ, USA, pp. 363–368 (2011)
16. Wang, L., Kim, H., Kim, E.J.: Recursive Partitioning Multicast: A Bandwidth-Efficient routing for Networks-On-Chip. In: International Symposium on Networks-on-Chip (NOCS), San Diego, CA (May 2009)
17. Feero, B., Pratim Pande, P.: Performance Evaluation for Three-Dimensional Networks-on-Chip. In: Proceedings of IEEE Computer Society Annual Symposium on VLSI (ISVLSI), May 9-11, pp. 305–310 (2007)
18. Feero, B.S., Pande, P.P.: Networks-on-Chip in a Three-Dimensional Environment: A Performance Evaluation. IEEE Transactions on Computers 58(1), 32–45 (2009)
19. Chaochao, F., Zhonghai, L.U., Jantsch, A., et al.: Support Efficient and Fault-Tolerant Multicast in Bufferless Network-on-Chip. IEICE Transactions on Information and Systems 95(4), 1052–1061 (2012)
20. Millberg, M., Nilsson, E., Thid, R., Kumar, S., Jantsch, A.: The nostrum backbone-a communication protocols stack for networks on chip. In: Proc. IEEE Computer Society, Int. Conference on VLSI Design, pp. 693–696 (2004)

A Highly-Efficient Crossbar Allocator Architecture
for High-Radix Switch[*]

Mingche Lai and Lei Gao

Science and Technology on Parallel and Distributed Processing Laboratory,
National University of Defense Technology, China
{mingchelai,gaolei}@nudt.edu.cn

Abstract. The present contribution explores the allocator design for high-radix switches and implements a highly-efficient allocator PWF(Parallel WaveFront) for achieving high throughput. Based on wavefront allocator, PWF allocator realizes fast allocation within one cycle to avoid timing loop, and it proposes parallelized matching strategy on cyclical priority to supply allocation fairness as well as utilizing greedy policy to reach the maximal match number. Implemented under 32nm CMOS technology, the evaluation results of PWF hardware cost show that the area and power consumption compared to wavefront allocator are slightly increased by 32.8% and 36.8%, and the critical path delay under 8x8x8 switch is less than 0.5ns which satisfies the requirement of GHz-level frequency design for high-radix switch. By further estimating the allocation efficiency, PWF reduces the request schedule time by 61.2% and 65.7%, and increases the immediate request schedule number averagely by 38.9% and 46.7% in comparison with wavefront allocator. Then, the efficiency improvement is also revealed by the distinctly decreased average schedule time and average response time compared with wavefront and DRRM allocators, yielding apparent advantages on improving allocation performance and providing good allocation fairness.

Keywords: high-radix switch, allocator, hardware cost, allocation efficiency, fairness.

1 Introduction

Interconnection networks provide a communication framework through utilizing high-radix switches connected with multiple point-to-point links, which are the most important infrastructure in high performance computing systems. And switches are the basic building blocks of such interconnection networks and their design critically affects the performance of the whole system[1,2], as well as the application execution time[3]. In detail, high-radix switches are mainly used to guide the incoming packets

[*] This work was supported by NSFC (61103188), Natural Science Fundatuions of Hunan Province (12JJ4071) and the Specialized Research Fund for the Doctoral Program of Higher Education of China (20114307120011).

W. Xu et al. (Eds.): NCCET 2014, CCIS 491, pp. 48–58, 2015.

to the appointed output, providing with smaller packet latencies, lower cost and power consumption. However, high-radix switch design also presents challenge on achieving high throughput [4] as well as highly-efficient allocation, which could not be smoothly applied to switches with the increasing port number.

Crossbar allocator lies at the kernel of high-radix switch to determine the performance and throughput of crossbar, and is usually utilized to perform the maximal matching among inputs and outputs in terms of fairness, delay, throughput, hardware cost and scalability. And allocator implementation always represents the tradeoffs among matching quality, delay and throughput. Typical allocators like iSLIP[5], Wavefront[6], DRRM[7], appeared to reach high throughput, but they also introduced other deficiency on matching quality and delay. iSLIP is a separable allocation method that uses round-robin arbiters and performs multiple iterations with randomized priority. iSLIP allocator is widely used because they can operate within an aggressive cycle time, and could reach approach 100% throughput as well as acquire good fairness for requests. However, making arbitration decisions independently at each port degrades matching efficiency[8], and it also needs O(logN) iterations that causes unaffordable iteration times as increasing the number of switch ports, which is not feasible to implement within a single cycle. Other previous state-of-the-art proposed improved iSLIP to enhance matching strength as well as reduce network delay by decreasing iteration number[9] or extending over multiple cycles[10], still resulting in unsatisfactory matching efficiency. Wavefront allocator performs the arbitration among requests for inputs and outputs simultaneously, and it works by granting row and column tokens to a diagonal group of cells, in effect giving this group priority. Wavefront allocator also could achieve 100% throughput, and further offers significantly lower latency compared to iSLIP [11]. However, it could not provide fairness guarantees beyond ensuring that all requests are eventually served, and not necessarily find the maximum matchings[11]. Becker at al [12] proposed a speculative switch allocation mechanism based on wavefront allocator, aiming to reduce switch allocator delay but still ignore the scalability influence of switch[13], which could not suit for high-radix switches. DRRM allocator could achieve high throughput only under uniform traffic pattern but not the outburst traffic or uneven traffic, which could not apply to large scale computing systems with various traffic patterns.

In this paper, we focus on improving allocation efficiency and fairness for high-radix switch allocation logic, and present a highly-efficient allocator PWF(Parallel WaveFront) to achieve high throughput. The proposed scheme employs a greedy algorithm to implement the maximal match and generate a schedule in one cycle, and the scheme has the following characteristics:

- Parallelized execution. The arbitrations of inputs and outputs are performed in parallel, which could implement the allocation of switch in a single cycle even if extending ports or channels, such as crossbar with 16 input/output ports.
- High throughput. Each input allows multiple requests to be arbitrated simultaneously, which is helpful to improve throughput compared to sequential arbitration of ports. Besides, each output port uses greedy arbitration policy, avoiding casual selection by traditional output arbitration.

- Allocation fairness guarantees. Similarly with DRRM, the iterative schedule strategy is utilized in arbitrations of inputs and outputs, and also multiple allocator elements are designed to use diverse arbitration templates that begin match from different diagonal cells, which could avoid traffic pattern dependent starvation and supply more fair allocation.
- Slightly-increased hardware cost. As the proposed scheme provides multiple requests to be synchronously arbitrated in each input port, the number of arbiters is increased and also the hardware cost is correspondingly increased.

We first evaluate the proposed switch allocator implementation in terms of critical path delay, area and power by Synopsis Design Compiler tool, and investigate the influence of PWF allocator to key properties of switch, e.g. input/output number or channel number. Compared to wavefront allocator, the area and power are slightly increased by 32.8% and 36.8% at the worst case, but they only bring 2.7% and 3.1% increment relative to the whole switch as well as save a great deal of timing circuit. And for critical path delay, although PWF allocator generates longer critical path, it has meet the requirement for GHz-level frequency design of high-radix switch under single-cycle allocation principle. Furthermore, we also estimate the allocation efficiency and fairness by using a self-developed cycle-accurate simulator. For allocation efficiency, PWF allocator reduces request schedule time by 61.2% and 65.7% in 8x8x8 and 16x16x8 switches in comparison with wavefront allocator as increasing flit inject rate, and its immediate request schedule number is also increased averagely by 38.9% and 46.7%. And for allocation fairness, all ports in switch have almost the same average schedule time and average response time by PWF allocator with the increasing flit inject rate, which could effectively guarantee the fairness of requests to avoid starvation.

2   The Proposed Switch Allocator

The proposed switch allocator PWF is designed basing on wavefront allocator, applying to allocation of MxNxV high-radix switch by optimizing input arbitration while eliminating timing loop underlying the circuit, where M denotes the number of input ports, N describes the number of output ports and V represents the number of virtual channels at each input port. In high performance computing systems, large M, N and V are usually considered to adapt to high-radix switch, so as to yield high throughput and help with large network scalability. Here, we take 8x8x8 allocator for example to describe the architecture of our switch allocator. In Fig.1, the new allocator is composed of 8 input port arbiters and a wavefront allocator. At each input port, 8 round-robin arbitration elements are used to serve requests to different output directions. The wavefront allocation component includes 8 wavefront allocator elements and an output element. Each wavefront allocator element arbitrates one output direction and then the output element schedules request to output.

From Fig.1, each input port arbiter has 8 arbitration elements RR8x8 that use round-robin policy. As the allocator works, every input port receives requests from 8 channels, and then selects requests to 8 different output directions by the eight RR8x8 arbitration elements, each of which arbitrates one output direction from the input requests. In detail, the input arbitration element m gets requests to output port m from 8 channels and generates unique winner by round robin to allocator element. At the same time, it also receives the grant signal to output port m from wavefront allocator. As grant is valid, the input arbitration element m would return arbitration result to all channels. Since at most one bit is valid in the 8-bit grant signal, input port only returns one arbitration result from the 8 arbiter elements to all channels each cycle.

The 8-bit request generated by input port arbiter is transferred to the wavefront allocator, and is represented by request vector $r_i[j]$ that describes whether existing request on direction j from input port i. The vectors of 8 output ports are computed by greedy strategy to get maximum matching, and then 8-bit response g_i is returned to input port i. The output allocation includes 8 wavefront allocator elements, each of which receives 8-bit request vector r_i from input ports and propagates 8-bit response g_i to RR output element. These eight allocator elements employ matching templates with different highest priority, which is obviously optimized compared with conventional wavefront allocator to guarantee fairness for output port arbitration.

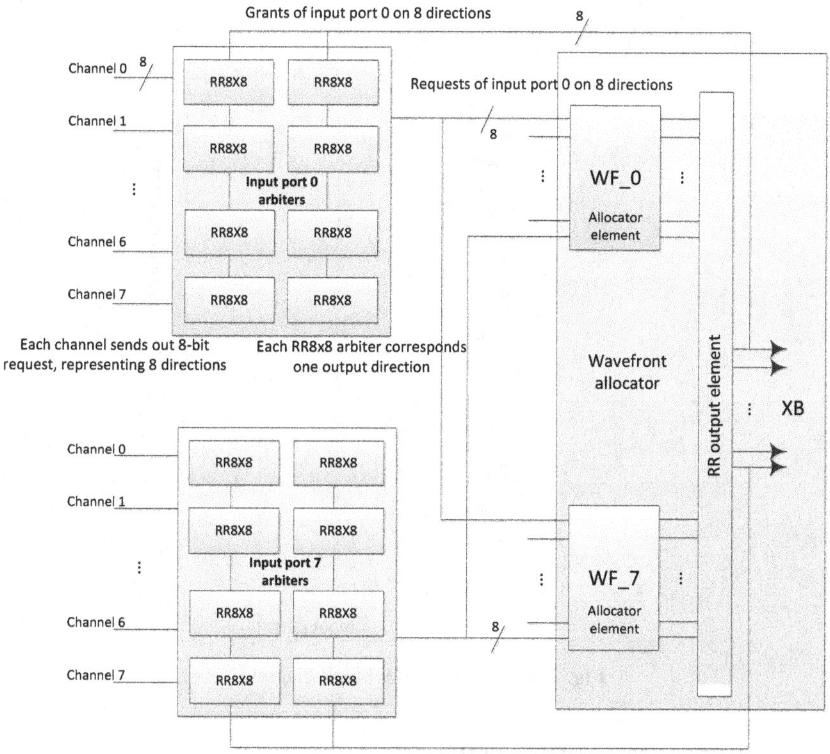

Fig. 1. Architecture of PWF switch allocator

3   Input Arbiters Structure

The input arbiter component has eight round robin arbitration elements with cyclic priority, and each arbitration element arbitrates for one output direction. Fig. 2 gives the detail of input arbiter implementation. Firstly, arbiter RR_n receives requests from eight channels applying for output direction n, and it selects unique winner. Then, all requests applying for direction n would be performed with bit-or operation by arbiter RR_n and propagated to wavefront allocator as output request signal. Thus, the output arbitration could also be executed with the output request signal while arbitrating input port. The parallelized arbitrations are helpful with quickly getting selection result as well as extending the number of ports. After the arbitration of output port by wavefront allocator, the response of asking for output direction n is sent back to arbiter RR_n. Once grant is valid, the results would also be propagated to all channels of input port.

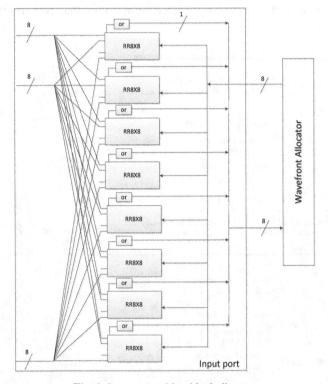

Fig. 2. Input port arbiter block diagram

4   Optimized Wavefront Allocator

The wavefront allocator works by granting row and column tokens to a diagonal group of cells. These tokens propagate in a wavefront from priority diagonal group wrapping around at the end of the array. And if a cell with a request receives both a row and a column token, it grants the request and stops the propagation of tokens.

The core component of wavefront allocator is allocator element. In the proposed switch allocator, eight different templates with maximal bisection match are designed to dynamically adjust match priority and each template has different highest-priority match, thus avoiding unfairness or starvation by fixed priority in traditional wavefront allocator. The basic idea of the proposed scheme is that the requests from all input ports are matched by the eight templates in turn, and thus it is required that each input port selects one output port while each output port selects one input port. In fact, such method utilizes a greedy strategy to implement the maximal match number.

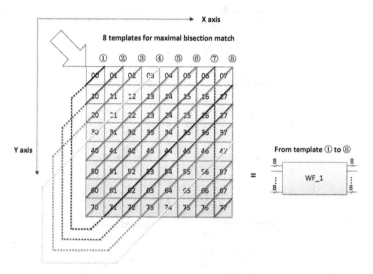

Fig. 3. 8x8 Allocator element for wavefront allocator

In Fig.3, we take 8x8 allocator for example to give the detailed allocation method, and eight colors are used to differentiate different diagonals. Each allocator element has a row token Xi and a column token Yi, and the initial placement of Xi and Yi is determined by the highest priority of match template. For example, template 1 denoted by black line decides that token $X0$, $X1$,...,$X7$ are placed at 00, 17, 26, 35, 44, 53, 63, 71 at the beginning. Then token Xi propagates along x axis positive direction and token Yi along y axis positive direction. If node (m,n) receives token Xi and token Yi simultaneously and it has request, token Xi and Yi propagation are stopped and the grant is sent back to (m,n). Otherwise, token Xi and Yi would be passed until close to the beginning position, so as to avoid timing loop.

In conventional wavefront allocator, the matching process is always from diagonal ① to ⑧, easily leading to arbitration unfairness and request starvation. Thus, the PWF allocator is designed to involve eight allocator elements, each of which starts allocation with different highest priority. For example, template one starts matching at diagonal ①, and executes the following matches ②, ③,..., ⑧; Template two initially uses diagonal ② to start match with following matches ③,..., ⑧, ①; Similarly template eight begins from diagonal ⑧, and then matches ①,...,⑦,as shown in Fig.4. As we know, fairness can be guaranteed at a certain extent by starting from a different initial diagonal every time allocation is performed, but it could not provide guarantees that all requests would eventually be served. Thus, we use eight wavefront allocator elements to compute simultaneously, and then output port employs round-robin policy to use results generated by eight allocator elements cyclically.

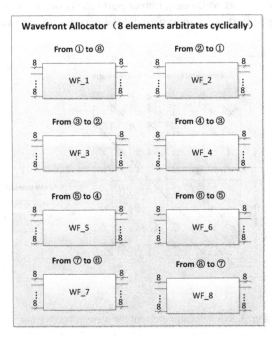

Fig. 4. Allocator elements for eight match templates

5   Experimental Results

5.1   Hardware Cost

In order to perform detailed cost evaluations and to gain insights about basic trends, we use Synopsis Design Compiler tool to find the critical path delay, the required cell area and the power consumption of the proposed PWF allocator under a commercial 32nm low-power standard cell library. The parameters CLK_UNCERTAINTY, CLK_TRAN, CLK_period and Setup/Hold time are respectively configured to be 100ps, 150ps, 600ps and 40ps.

In experiments, we configure the number of input and output ports to be 8 and 16, and the number of input channels is set to be 8 and 64, the evaluation results are shown in Fig.5 and Fig.6. As PWF allocator implements parallelized computation of multiple templates in output allocation, new allocation elements have been added compared to WF allocator and the overhead for a large deal of combinatorial circuit is correspondingly increased. But it eliminates combinatorial logic ring inherent in WF allocator and also saves the overhead of timing circuit. From the synthesis results we could find that the area and power increase by 32.8% and 36.8% at the worst case, but only bring 2.7% and 3.1% increment in high-radix switch since the logic of switch is relatively much little to the total switch. For delay, traditional WF allocator used multiple-cycle allocation, in which a single allocation was implemented in several cycles and was hard to achieve pipelining. Despite of low delay for WF allocator, it still results in allocation performance loss. The PWF allocator has relatively larger delay than that of WF allocator, but it achieves one-cycle allocation, favoring to improve allocation efficiency. In 8x8x8 switch, the delay of PWF is less than 0.5ns, satisfying the requirement for GHz-level frequency switch design.

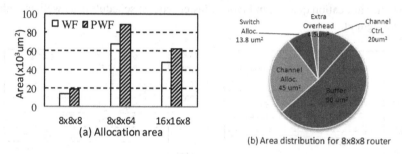

Fig. 5. Comparisons of area for PWF and WF allocators

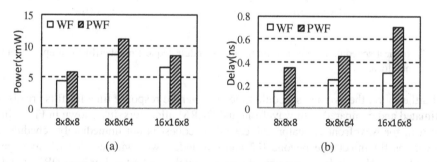

Fig. 6. Comparisons of power(a) and delay(b) for PWF and WF allocators

5.2   Performance Evaluation

We evaluate the allocation impact of proposed allocator on switch performance under Yarc[14] structure by using a self-developed cycle-accurate simulator. In experiment, we mainly consider 8x8x8 and 16x16x8 switches for estimation, in which the random traffic pattern is applied and each input generates 40000 pseudo-random requests. Besides, the flit number for one packet is randomly selected from 1 to 6, and the flit inject rate is ranged from 0.5 to 1.

We estimate the allocation efficiency of presented allocation scheme in terms of request schedule time and immediate schedule request number. The request schedule time records the total cycle number from sending the first request to responding the last request, and the immediate schedule request number gives the statistical number of the requests which are immediately responded by the allocator. The evaluated results are demonstrated in Fig.7. With the increased flit inject rate, the request schedule time of switch with PWF allocator is greatly decreased compared to that of wavefront-based switch, and the decrement reaches 61.2% and 65.7% respectively under 8x8x8 and 16x16x8 switches. That's because PWF allocator achieves allocation within a cycle in comparison with multi-cycle implementation in wavefront allocator. On the other hand, the immediate schedule request number is also increased by 38.9% and 46.7% averagely relative to wavefront allocator, as wavefront needs to consume more cycles for responding requests even though the requests may be scheduled immediately and PWF only needs one cycle. Apparently, the PWF allocator could acquire better allocation quality, in favor of faster request scheduling as well as higher packet throughput.

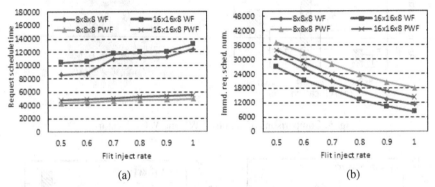

Fig. 7. Request schedule time(a) and immediate schedule request number(b) for proposed and wavefront allocators

Furthermore, the average schedule time and average response time for flits are also estimated and compared with wavefront and DRRM allocators, just shown in Fig.8. In Fig.8(a), for wavefront allocator, the case that request is not immediately scheduled appears as flit inject rate beyond 0.7 and 0.6 under two switches, and the average schedule time sharply increases with the incremental inject rates. For both DRRM and PWF allocators the above case appears only when inject rate exceeds 0.9 and 0.8, and the average schedule time for PWF is less than that of DRRM under the same inject rate since PWF utilizes greedy policy to reach the maximal request match number. In Fig.8(b), similar conclusion could be drawn that the average response time of proposed allocator goes up slowly and is much less than that of wavefront and DRRM allocators. Wavefront consumes more cycles for each allocation and DRRM is hard to acquire the maximal bisection match, but PWF could attain the maximal match number among input requests and output response. Thus compared with wavefront and DRRM allocators, the average schedule time of PWF is reduced by 64% and 15%

for 8x8x8 and 16x16x8 switches, and the average response time is decreased by 60% and 21%. Therefore, the PWF allocator could effectively shorten request wait time and avoid request to be starvation, yielding distinct advantages on improving schedule performance and achieving good allocation fairness.

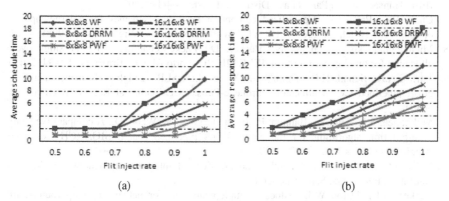

(a)   (b)

Fig. 8. Average schedule time(a) and average response time(b) for three allocators

6   Conclusions

In this paper, an allocation scheme for high-radix switches is presented focusing on the efficiency and fairness of switch allocation logic, and it has the characteristics of low delay, high throughput and good fairness. First, the evaluation results for hardware cost show that the area and power increase 32.8% and 36.8% in comparison with wavefront, only bringing 2.7% and 3.1% increment for the whole switch. And the critical path delay satisfies the requirement for GHz-level frequency switch design. Then, by evaluating the allocation efficiency with a self-developed cycle-accurate simulator, the request schedule time of PWF is reduced by 61.2% and 65.7% under 8x8x8 and 16x16x8 switches as increasing flit inject rate, and the increments of immediate request schedule number reach 38.9% and 46.7% averagely. Similarly, the average schedule time and average response time are also distinctly improved, exhibiting better allocation efficiency and providing schedule fairness guarantees.

References

1. Kim, J., Dally, W.J., Towles, B., Gupta, A.K.: Microarchitecture of a high-radix router. In: 32nd Annual International Symposium on Computer Architecture, pp. 420–431 (2005)
2. Wang, K.F., Fang, M., Chen, S.Q.: Design of a tile-based high-radix switch with high throughput. In: 2011 International Conference on Networking and Information Technology, pp. 277–285 (2011)
3. Sanchez, D., Michelogiannakis, G., Kozyrakis, C.: An analysis of interconnection networks for large scale chip-multiprocessors. ACM Transactions on Architecture and Code Optimization 7(1), 4:1–4:28 (2010)

4. Soteriou, V., Ramanujam, R.S., Lin, B., Peh, L.S.: A High-Throughput Distributed Shared-Buffer NoC Router. Computer Architecture Letters 8(1), 21–24 (2009)
5. McKeown, N.: The iSLIP Scheduling Algorithm for Input-Queued Switches. IEEE/ACM Transactions on Networking 7(2), 188–201 (1999)
6. Tamir, Y., Chi, H.-C.: Symmetric Crossbar Arbiters for VLSI Communication Switches. IEEE Transactions on Parallel and Distributed Systems 4(1) (1993)
7. Chao, H.J., Park, J.S.: Centralized contention resolution schemes for a large-capacity optical ATM switch. In: Proc. IEEE ATM Workshop, Fairfax, Virginia (May 1998)
8. Michelogiannakis, G., Jiang, N., Becker, D.: Packet chaining: efficient single-cycle allocation for on-chip networks. In: IEEE MICRO, Porto Allegre, Brazil, pp. 83–94 (2011)
9. Jafri, S.A.R., Sohail, H.B., Thottethodi, M., et al.: asSLIP: a high-performance adaptive-effort pipelined switch allocator. Purdue e-Pubs, ECE Technical Reports (October 28, 2013)
10. Mukherjee, S.S., Silla, F., Bannon, P., Emer, J., Lang, S., Webb, D.: A comparative study of arbitration algorithms for the alpha 21364 pipelined router. SIGARCH Computer Architecture News 30, 223–234 (2002)
11. Dally, W.J., Towles, B.: Principles and practices of interconnection networks. Morgan Kaufmann Publishers, San Francisco (2004)
12. Becker, D.U., Dally, W.J.: Allocator implementations for network-on-chip routers. In: Proc. of 2009 ACM/IEEE Conference on High Performance Computing, Networking, Storage and Analysis, pp. 1–12 (2009)
13. Mora, G., Flich, J., Duato, J., Baydal, E., López, P., Lysne, O.: Towards an Efficient Switch Architecture for High-Radix Switches. In: ACM/IEEE Symposium on Architectures for Networking and Communications Systems, San Jose, CA, December 3-5 (2006)
14. Scott, S., Abts, D., Kim, J., Dally, W.J.: The BlackWidow High-radix Clos Network. In: Proc. of the International Symposium on Computer Architecture (ISCA), Boston, MA (June 2006)

FPGA Implementation of FastICA Algorithm for On-line EEG Signal Separation

Dongsheng Zhao, Jiang Jiang, Chang Wang, Baoliang Lu, and Yongxin Zhu

School of Microelectronics,
Shanghai Jiaotong University,
Shanghai, China
zhaodongsheng@ic.sjtu.edu.cn,
{jiangjiangdr,willy,zhuyongxin}@sjtu.edu.cn, blu@cs.sjtu.edu.cn

Abstract. Fast independent component analysis (FastICA) is an efficient and popular algorithm to solve blind source separation (BSS) problems. FastICA is widely used to identify artifact and interference from their mixtures such as electroencephalogram (EEG), magnetoencephalography (MEG), and electrocardiogram (ECG). In this paper, we propose a Scalable Macro-pipelined FastICA Architecture (SMFA) which aims to exploit architectural scalability and temporal parallelism. The SMFA has strong data processing ability for on-line EEG signals and is capable of coping with different types of input data. The FastICA algorithm based on the proposed SMFA is implemented on a field programmable gate array (FPGA). It's a key module of an ongoing project which aims to evaluate human's fatigue degree on-line from EEG. Experimental results demonstrate the effectiveness of the presented FastICA architecture as expected.

Keywords: FastICA, on-line, scalable, macro-pipelined, FPGA.

1 Introduction

Fast Independent Component Analysis (FastICA) is a statistical method used to separate signals from an unknown mixture without any prior knowledge about the source signals. This method has been applied in many fields like speech processing, image processing and biomedical signal processing [1]-[3], such as EEG, MEG and ECG. Some applications need on-line signal processing such as noise canceling, the famous cocktail-party problem and EEG signal analysis. However, ICA is usually limited to only process off-line because of the intensive computation.

Several FPGA implementations of the ICA algorithm have been proposed in succession. Huang and Hung [4] proposed an implementation of Infomax ICA algorithm on FPGA applied in EEG signal processing. Van and Wu [5] provided an energy-efficient FastICA design with an early determination scheme for eight-channel EEG signal separation. Kim et al. [6] proposed the FPGA implementation of the ICA algorithm constructed by the adaptive noise canceling (ANC) module for 2-channel speech enhancement. Nordin, Hsu and Szu [7] proposed an implementation of

W. Xu et al. (Eds.): NCCET 2014, CCIS 491, pp. 59–68, 2015.

FastICA algorithm on FPGA applied in hyper-spectral (HIS) image processing. Du et al. [8] proposed the parallel ICA (pICA) algorithm and the corresponding FPGA implementation on a pilchard board. The parallel ICA based on FastICA divides the process into several sub-processes to achieve the single program multiple data parallelism. Charoensak and Sattar [9] proposed an efficient FPGA hardware architecture for the realization of a real-time BSS. The FPGA design implemented the modified Torkkola's BSS algorithm for audio signals based on ICA.

However, related papers published in recent years mainly focus on designing a particular architecture for specific input data type. This paper proposes a scalable macro-pipelined FastICA architecture (SMFA), which has high scalability in on-line ICA applications, such as EEG signal processing.

This paper is organized as follows. The background of the FastICA algorithm is introduced in Section II. Section III describes FPGA implementation of SMFA. Experimental results and discussions are presented in Section IV and conclusions are made in the last section.

2   Background of the FastICA Algorithm

2.1   Algorithm of FastICA

Most of blind source separation (BSS) researches so far focus on the case of mixtures. Assume that the mixed signal X is defined as $X = AS$, A is an unknown full-rank mixing matrix. The goal of ICA algorithm is to recover the unknown source S by estimating matrix A. The basic FastICA algorithm should have the following steps [10]:

1. Preprocess the measured signal to reduce complexity.
2. Choose the random initial vectors w_m, w_m is the column vector of separating matrix W.
3. Calculate $w_m = E\{Z(w_m^T Z)^3\} - 3w_m$ in parallel.
4. $W \leftarrow (WW^T)^{-1/2}W$, then get the orthogonal matrix W.
5. Divide W by its norm. If WW^T is not close enough to 1, go back to step 2.

If there are n-independent components to be separated, then each converging result of the FastICA algorithm w is one of the columns in separating matrix W. The estimated independent component s_est can be expressed as

$$s\_est = w^T Z \tag{1}$$

and $s\_est = (s\_est_1, s\_est_2, \ldots, s\_est_n)^T$.

During the whole calculation, most of the calculation time is spent on the latter four steps which contain complex massive matrix calculations, so we implement these calculations on FPGA.

2.2   Scalability Consideration for On-line ICA

Fig. 1 is the illustration of on-line ICA process for EEG signal. As can be seen, the sliding window size is T. Assume that the sampling rate is f and the channel of the input signal is four. In T seconds, $4 \times T \times f$ -point data is regarded as a set to be sent to the ICA model each time, then updating $4 \times T \times f$ -point data in T' seconds, the final result is composed of the output of the ICA model in T' seconds each time. In this case, T, T' and f may change according to different types of input data, thus the ICA model should also meet these requirements.

The scalability requirement of the on-line ICA lies in two aspects. First, the ICA module should be capable of coping with different type of input data, it should be noted that the size of input data is determined by both T and f. Second, the demand of on-line data processing ability varies in different systems, which results in different size of sliding window, this means that the computation time of the ICA module should be flexible to satisfy the demand of different situation.

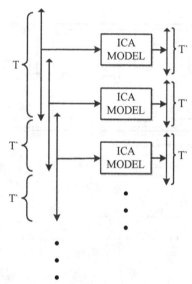

Fig. 1. Illustration of on-line ICA process

3   FPGA Implementation

In this section, the FPGA implementation of the FastICA based on the proposed SMFA is introduced, as shown in Fig. 2. It is designed for separating mixed signal which is four channels sampling simultaneously. The SMFA mainly consists of three modules: the memory control unit (MCU), the updating unit (UU) and the symmetric orthogonalization unit (SOU).

Without loss of generality, we use 256 samples per channel to demonstrate the control flow of the SMFA. First, the input data are sequentially distributed into four local memories (LM) and each LM keeps one fourth of the input data. The backup LM is used to store the updating data. Second, data is transferred from LM to the processing element ring (PER) to perform updating processing. Processing elements (PEs) are grouped to be a stage and the whole PER has four stages. The number of PEs can scale up or down according to specific needs. Third, the processed data from the UU is sent to SOU to make the matrix orthogonal. Different from sequential orthogonalization like Gram-Schmidt, through symmetric orthogonalization, the column vector of the orthogonal matrix can be calculated in parallel. Fourth, data produced from the SOU is written back to memory to prepare for the next round of iteration. Then, through the convergence checking unit, the convergence can be detected. Once meeting the convergence threshold or reaching the maximum iteration, the computation process will be terminated. Otherwise, processed data goes back to UU and restart calculating again. Finally, the separated signals are obtained, data in LM should be updated and then the next round of computation will be started if the updated data is ready.

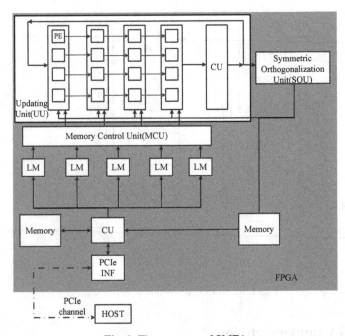

Fig. 2. The structure of SMFA

3.1   MCU

MCU is designed to manage the input data and data transmission between LM and PER. Since input data is equally distributed into four LMs, each LM consist a 4×64 matrix. The backup LM is used to store the updated data. The configuration of memory control unit depends on the input data.

As the size of input matrix is determined by both T and f, and different T or f may lead to different size of matrix in each LM, so the number of iteration number of PER should make the corresponding change. Besides, when T' changes, we may need to adjust the number of stages, this can also lead to the change of the iteration number of PER. So, MCU should be reconfigured properly to coordinate with the PER unit.

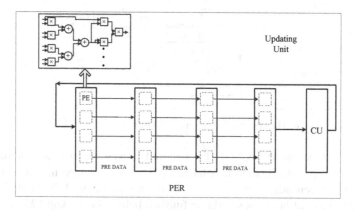

Fig. 3. The structure of PER

3.2   UU

The main task of UU is to get the separating matrix W by calculating $w_m = E\{Z(w_m^T Z)^3\} - 3w_m$, w_m is the column vector of separating matrix W. To exploit architectural scalability and temporal parallelism, macro-pipelined architecture is adopted to perform complex matrix calculation.

All PEs are calculating at the same time, which exploits the temporal parallelism. Each PE, which includes multiple floating point multipliers and accumulators, calculates the product from the current separating matrix W and source data, then accumulates the intermediate result from the previous PE.

Assume that the number of pipeline stages in a PE is s, so the total number of pipeline stages of the PER is $4 \times s$. Four PEs are grouped into a stage. There are four stages which are organized as a macro-pipelined ring topology. The PER and the LM are working in pairs. The LM feeds source data to the PER and the PER makes all of the floating point operation. The structure of PER is shown in Fig. 3.

Since stages are organized as a ring, it is capable of supporting different matrix sizes. If the input data type such as T, T' or sampling rate f has changed, PER can still come to the correct result by setting the right iteration number. Besides, the architecture is scalable since the number of stages and the number of PEs in each stage can easily scale up or down [11].

3.3   Symmetric Orthogonalization Unit

Unlike UU, during the process of each iteration, the size of the matrix send to SOU is the same, so the main concern of this unit is how to reuse modules, such as the matrix multiplication module (MMM) and the symmetric orthogonalization module (SOM). As shown in Fig. 4, the output of MMM can be used by both the SOM and the convergence detecting module (CDM), and both of these modules are calculating at the same time to increase the throughput of this unit.

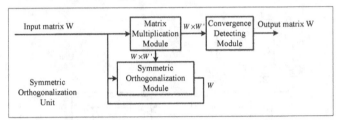

Fig. 4. The structure of Symmetric Orthogonalization Unit

Assume the input matrix is $4 \times n$, the one-unit processing unit takes about $2 \times n$ cycles and the orthogonalization unit takes 1102 cycles for each iteration. The max iteration number depends on the accuracy of the result we need. It should be noted that the calculation of iteration should be finished before the backup LM is filled up, that is

$$(2 \times n + 1102) \times N / f < T' \tag{2}$$

$$T \times f < X \tag{3}$$

where N is the iteration number, f is the calculation frequency of FPGA and X is the size of backup LM.

In summary, the SMFA is of high flexibility. By the collaboration of LM and PER, the PE number of this architecture is also capable to scale up or down according to the type of input data and demand of system.

4   Experimental Result and Demonstrations

As shown in Fig. 5, the proposed SMFA is implemented on Virtex 6 FPGA board. It's a key module of an ongoing project which aims to determine human's fatigue degree on-line from EEG signal.

First, the EEG signal is collected from brain by sensors. Then, after the process of amplifier, filter and ADC, the mixed EEG signal is sent to the FPGA board to perform signal separation by the FastICA implementation based on the SMFA. It is an important part of EEG on-line noise reduction and artifact removal. The output of FPGA is sent to mobile phone or PC through Bluetooth module for further processing, such as fatigue-related feature extraction and fatigue estimation algorithm. The whole system is aimed to evaluate the driver's fatigue degree in a car.

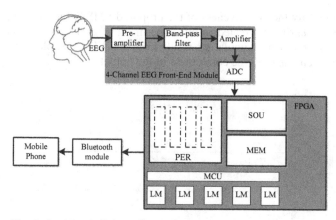

Fig. 5. An driver's fatigue degree detecting system based on EEG

Table 1. Time consumption

	Input data size			
	4*10240	*4*20480*	*4*40960*	*4*81920*
PC computation time (ms)	93.42	279.1	426.1	684.4
FPGA cycles	428,298	835,658	1650,378	32798,818

Table 2. Resource usage of Virtex 6 xc6vlx240t FPGA

Logic Utilization	Used	Utilization
Slice Registers	160629	53%
Slice LUTs	132811	88%
Block RAMS	10	2%
DSP48E1s	440	57%

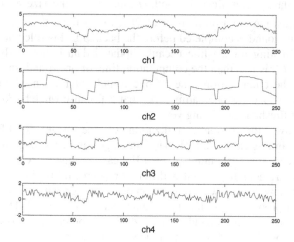

Fig. 6. Mixed signals

In order to verify the effectiveness of the proposed SMFA, four mixed signals with a linear mixed matrix are created in our experiment. Fig. 6 shows 4-channel mixed signals. Fig. 7 shows the simulation result from the FPGA implementation of the SMFA, which demonstrates the correctness of the output.

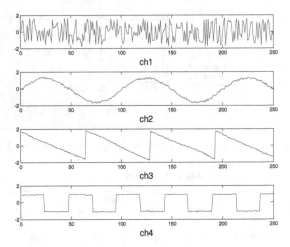

Fig. 7. SMFA separated result

We use 4-lane generation 1 PCI-E in DMA mode to transmit data to FPGA which runs at 200 MHz, for which the bandwidth is 500MB/s. As input data is less than 2MB, so it may cost less than 4ms in data transmission. Table 1 and Fig. 8 shows the time consumption of PC and FPGA under different size of input data. Software simulation runs on a PC with a Intel Core i3 quad core at 3.4GHz, 8 GB DDR3 RAM. The OS is, 64-bit win7, and the version of matlab is 7.11.

The demonstration of scalability of the SMFA is as follows. As we can see, the size of input data is determined by both T and f, if the size of input data has changed, we adjust the iteration number of PER to get the correct result. Besides, if calculation of one round is completed before the backup LM is filled up, then the PER has to stop calculating for a while because updated data is not ready, this is what happens when T' is less than the computation time of one round. In contrast, if T' is greater than the computation time of one round, then we need to scale up the number of PE to reduce the calculating time, that is because when backup LM is filled up, PER has not finished calculating yet.

Table 2 shows the resource utilization of the Virtex 6 FPGA for our implementation. In this case, the PER has four stages and each stage has four PEs. It should be noticed that the number of PEs can change according to different performance requirement, thus result in different resource utilization.

Table 3 is presented to show a comparison of our design with other works on ICA. The speed of our proposed design is faster than that of [4], [5], [6]. The time spent on preprocess of FastICA is not included in our design as preprocess is only a small part of the whole process. It should be noticed that the sampling rate can change coordinate with different situation.

Table 3. Comparison with other on-line ICA implementation

	Ref [4]	**Ref [5]**	**Ref [6]**	**This work**
Application	EEG	EEG	Speech	EEG
Algorithm	INFOMAX	FastICA	FastICA	FastICA
Channel	4	8	2	4
Sampling rate (Hz)	64	N/A	16K	10K
Speed (MHz)	68	100	50	172
Computation time (s)	N/A	0.29	0.003	0.0025

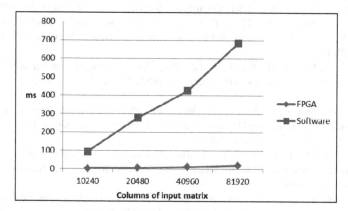

Fig. 8. Time consumption

5   Conclusions and Future Works

In this paper, we present an FPGA implementation of FastICA algorithm based on the proposed SMFA, which greatly reduce the computation time, it is at least 40 times faster for the several sets of data used in the experiment. As the computation time is less than the size of sliding window, so the proposed SMFA can meet the demand of on-line requirements.

More importantly, the proposed SMFA has high flexibility as it can cope with different type of input data. As the number of PEs can directly affect time consumption of the algorithm, this architecture also has high scalability because the number of PEs can scale up or down according to specific requirements.

In the future, we are planning to further enhance our FPGA implementation to make it capable to applications with more than 4-channel, such as 8-channel and 16-channel. Furthermore, the SMFA is suitable for a wide range of applications. The following applications can be mapped to this architecture: Biomedical signal processing, Noise canceling, Imaging processing.

Acknowledgment. This work is supported by the National Science Foundation of China (Grant No. 61373032), and the Science and Technology Commission of Shanghai Municipality (Grant No. 13511500200).

References

1. Lee, T.W.: Independent component analysis. Springer US (1998)
2. Hyvärinen, A., Karhunen, J., Oja, E.: Independent component analysis. John Wiley & Sons (2004)
3. Cichocki, A., Amari, S.: Adaptive blind signal and image processing. John Wiley, Chichester (2002)
4. Huang, W.C., Hung, S.H., et al.: FPGA implementation of 4-channel ICA for online EEG signal separation. In: Biomedical Circuits and Systems Conference, BioCAS 2008 (2008)
5. Van, L.-D., Wu, D.-Y., Chen, C.-S.: Energy-Efficient FastICA Implementation for Biomedical Signal Separation. IEEE Transactions on Neural Networks 22(11), 1809–1822 (2011)
6. Shyu, K.-K., Lee, M.-H., Wu, Y.-T., Lee, P.-L.: Implementation of pipelined FastICA on FPGA for real-time blind source separation. IEEE Trans. Neural Netw. 19(6), 958–970 (2008)
7. Nordin, A., Hsu, C.C., Szu, H.H.: Design of FPGA ICA for hyperspectral imaging processing. In: Aerospace/Defense Sensing, Simulation, and Controls. International Society for Optics and Photonics (2001)
8. H., D., Qi, H., Peterson, G.D.: Parallel ICA and its hardware implementation in hyperspectral image analysis. In: Defense and Security. International Society for Optics and Photonics (2004)
9. Charoensak, C., Sattar, F.: Design of Low-Cost FPGA Hardware for Real-time ICA-Based Blind Source Separation Algorithm. EURASIP J. Adv. Signal Process 2005(18), 3076–3086 (2005)
10. Hyvärinen, A., Oja, E.: A fast fixed-point algorithm for independent component analysis. Neural Computation 9(7), 1483–1492 (1997)
11. Jiang, J., Mirian, V., Tang, K.P., Chow, P., Xing, Z.: Matrix Multiplication Based on Scalable Macro-Pipelined FPGA Accelerator Architecture. In: 2009 Int. Conf. Reconfigurable Comput. FPGAs, pp. 48–53 (December 2009)

FPGA Based Low-Latency Market Data Feed Handler

Liyuan Zhou, Jiang Jiang, Ruochen Liao, Tianyi Yang, and Chang Wang

School of Microelectronics, Shanghai Jiao Tong University, No.800, Dongchuan Road,
200240 Shanghai, China
{Zhouliyuanat,unremem,yangziwang520@}gmail.com,
{jiangjiangdr,liaorc}@sjtu.edu.cn

Abstract. Financial market data refers to price and trading data transmitted between financial exchange instruments and traders. Delivery of financial market feeds requires massive data processing with ultra-low latency. FAST protocol is a financial technology standard for compressing data stream during network transmission. This paper presents the design and implementation of a hardware accelerator for financial market data in FAST protocol. We propose a parallel data decoding architecture for field analysis process, which is the key feature in our design. The decoder of this work is able to parse and filter FAST format messages, and with an additional parallel structure compared with typical handlers, achieving a 40% speedup on decoding time compared to previous attempts. The filter function is reconfigurable for various user preferences and further protocol updates. Test under massive source data indicated an average latency of 1.6μs per message.

Keywords: Market data handler, low latency, FAST, FPGA.

1   Introduction

The Financial Market Data is price and trade related data reported to customers by trading venues. Instruments like stock exchange provide the customers with real time information concerning their investments in equities, fixed income products, derivatives and currencies.

Transmission of market data between traders and exchanges is highly time sensitive, also the collection and distribution of information to various traders need massive throughput of data stream, requiring an execution system with large bandwidth and high processing performance.

The delay of delivery from exchange to traders would be critical[1], for trading is based on analyzing the historical trends from financial data. A data feed handler with low latency would be significant to traders, for acquiring analyzed results and making decisions ahead of time leads to dominant position in market.

Currently, market data handlers in financial exchange institutions are composed of specialized software systems combined with FPGAs (field programmable gate arrays) designed to process financial data. Typical feed handler includes client and server side applications, server accepts connection from the client and distributes financial data of

W. Xu et al. (Eds.): NCCET 2014, CCIS 491, pp. 69–77, 2015.

particular format. While the extensity of stock exchange data proliferates, we need feed handler systems able to compute messages in the scale of gigabytes per second.[2] We propose a feed handler with low latency which would shorten the respond time in financial market exchange.

Conventional data feed handlers based on software platforms exerts their arithmetic performance on general purpose processors, in which incoming data are passed through PCI by peripheral device and stored in cache(memory) for processing. [3]Additional latency is inevitable due to operating system cost as well as software algorithms running on CPU. For example a market data feed handler solution based on IBM PowerEN processor achieved an average latency of 6.7μs for OPRA v2 feed.[4]

Specialized hardware systems are typical in today's market data feed handlers. ASIC (Application Specific Integrated Circuits) is a commonly used category for low latency oriented hardware acceleration. But financial market data format protocols frequently updates, making it necessary to promote system designs that can sustain customized modifications. [5] Compare to ASIC design, FPGA meets the requirement with reconfigurable character, saving the cost involved in design and fabricating flow for ASIC devices.[6]

This paper introduces the design of a FPGA based hardware able to decode standard FAST (FIX Adapted for Streaming) format financial data feeds, with higher bandwidth surpassing current design in latency under equivalent hardware resources. Our design enhanced the method of splintering fields in FAST data messages, which makes it possible for decoder to process multiple field data in parallel. This parallel structure is applied in order to maximum the throughput, the decoder has multiple bytes input of source data and parse the message in parallel.

2   Previous Works

Previous works include hardware designs on FPGAs for financial data feeds handler.

Gareth W. Morris, David B. Thomas and Wayne Luk built a low latency market data processor, their design pushed messages directly into memory by DMA, eliminated the extra latency caused by operating system. Their design was implemented on Celoxica AMDC accelerator card incorporated Xilinx Virtex5 boards. The work supports 5.5 million message per second, with a latency of 26us. [7]

Christian Leber, Benjamin Geib and Heiner Litz in University of Heidelberg Germany, developed FPGA based processor for high frequency trading. Their work enables Ethernet UDP level decoding and transmit FAST format data. The approach achieved low latency 4 times better than previous software based platform. [8]

Robin Pottathuparambil and his partners in University of North Carolina developed financial data handler to decode ITCH format data in NASDAQ exchange. HDL and impulse C were used to code hardware platform on FPGA, their work demonstrated a latency of 2.7us surpassing the CPU equivalent latency of 38us. [9]

The previous works designed and implemented the hardware decoder which outperforms the software feed handlers. However the parallelism of the decoders were not fully exploited. Their works mainly focus on data transmission latency from Internet to memory and memory to user applications. Their achievements efficiently speed up the receiving process of market data. But in fact, FAST data decoder still can be improved to lower the latency of decoding process. This paper focuses on the core module for FAST data decoding with a suggesting parallel structure, aiming to accelerate decoding process of fast data handler.

3   Proposed Feed Handler Architecture

3.1   System Level Overview

In order to parse and decode the input FAST format financial market message. The design allow receiving data from Ethernet by package directly to registers for processing. Decoder, the core module of the system, read multiple bytes per cycle and parse the message in low latency. Processing results are stored in memory for users.

System includes Ethernet and DDR2 instantiations working as interfaces between memory devices and the main logic. The decoder module consists of 4 stages in pipeline, working in parallel to parse the receiving data.

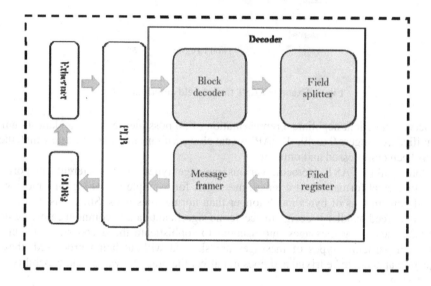

Fig. 1. Feed handler top module overview

3.2   FAST Protocol

The decoder is composed of several parts to parse an incoming message according to the special structure of FAST format data. FAST messages are wrapped in standard format defined as 'block', a block consists of multiple messages, with block header and tail indicating version, size, and timestamp. Messages are classified into types in categories, token as ASCII codes. Term 'field' is the component of different types of messages. Field types and values are expected to experience trivial changes among consecutive messages, making the FAST protocol effective, compressing the identical fields to abridge extra transmission costs. Figure 2 shows a typical type of data (category A as example), each line indicates a certain type of field. The decoder functions as decompressing the fields that are discarded during the compressing process.

Field Name	Length (bytes)
Message Header	4
Security Symbol	5
Reserved	1
Expiration Block	3
Strike Price Denominator Code	1
Strike Price	4
Volume	4
Premium Price Denominator Code	1
Premium Price	4
Trade Identifier	4
Reserved	4
Total Length:	35

Fig. 2. Example FAST format field description [10]

Server and client negotiate a representation of 50 possible fields in the data stream, identified as integers 0 to 49. 'PMAP' is sent along with user data to indicate which the fields been compressed and omitted.

Note that in FAST protocol, various message types under different categories contain special format of extra length messages, for example a chatting type message would contain tens of bytes much longer than normal messages. Since this decoding module in feed handler is design to accelerate significant data in common cases, we do not take these long messages into account to sophisticate the decoder architecture. Although particular types of messages are skipped without being processed, these objection appears to be trivial and does not affect the practical values and capability of this design.

3.3   LLP (Low Latency Parallel) Decoder

The LLP Decoder functions as a parser restoring the compressed fields according to the indication of PMAP field. The Block Decoder is the preprocessing of source data, breaking down the messages in a block and make verifications on additional information. Block decoder extracts PMAP and user data for the following levels. Field Splitter works as translating PMAP information and producing signals indicating particular fields to be restored. Receiving results from field splitter, Field Registers will either hold their values when found been compressed or be updated with new field values when found not been compressed. Additionally, signal indicating an end of message is passed on all along to call for a output of message, when this happens, Message Framer make a push of registers to store the message into memory for users' consideration.

In order to further improve the overall performance of the handler, Block Decoder and Field Splitter are design in parallel structure which read multiple bytes in one clock cycle. Pile of registers will cache the input since incoming data in one cycle may contain arbitrary combinations of messages. FAST messages fields are typically limited in 4 bytes thus processing these fields in parallel will shorten the execution cycles for a single message.

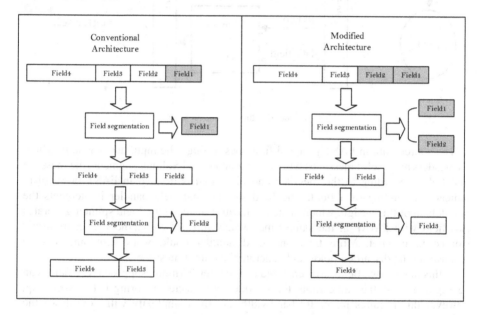

Fig. 3. Modified Structure to promote parallel decoding

Figure 3 shows the parallel structure compare with a typical decoder. Suppose we attempt to decode message with arbitrary length in a field splitter, only one field could be detected in one clock cycle, however when the length of message is limited, we may be able to separate more than one field in a single clock cycle. When message is longer, e.g. Field 4 in Figure 3, only one filed could be executed. For financial data in FAST protocol, most all types of messages are within 8 bytes, and a large percentage of them are no more than 4 bytes, therefore the modified structure in Figure 3 are supposed to bring increased overall throughput.

Figure 4 depicts the pipeline and parallel field handler architecture of decoder module.

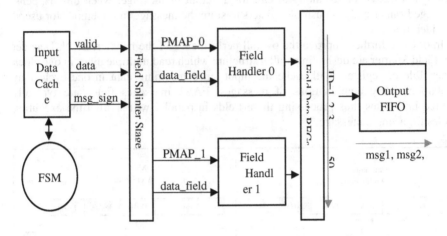

Fig. 4. Decoder module architecture

The source data in FAST protocol first goes through the input data cache in which the headers and useful messages will be separated. Field Splinter segments the message into fields according to the message end bit which is defined in FAST protocol to indicate the ending of a field. The field splinter and field handler implements the parallelism of this design, which is the main cause of speed up. Field splinter generates two field with PMAP at the same time, which allows two handlers' execution and storage in parallel. More than one field handler could work simultaneously to reconstruct the discarded fields and generate the output message.

In this design two fields are generated at once, furthermore, suppose more fields can be segmented at the same time, the decoder is expected to bring better speed up, however this requires larger IO bandwidth and the complexity will slow down the frequency of decoder module.

3.4   Peripheral Modules

The entire design also includes Ethernet module, memory module.

Data acquired from Ethernet will first be stored in DDR memory, DMA instantiation helps Ethernet data transmission into FPGA memory. Feed handler fetches data from memory, decoding results are stored in another part of memory for users.

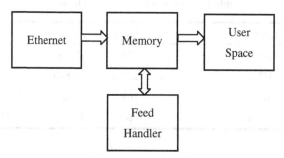

Fig. 5. System peripheral modules

4   Implementation and Performance Evaluation

4.1   Implementation Platform

To evaluate the real time performance and cost of the proposed architecture, we implemented the proposed architecture on a Xilinx Virtex-5 XC5VLX50T board. On board clock frequency is 125MHz. VHDL coding is completed under development environment Xilinx ISE 14.3. Feed handler architecture applied pipelined and logic in each stage was carefully optimized to meet the timing restrictions of 8ns. Ethernet instantiation is realized using Xilinx Lwip in 100M mode. 125MHz DDR2 memory is used as local memory. To evaluate the performance, the latency was counted from receiving source data from Ethernet to writing the parsed output into memory. Considering parallel structure could only be effective under massive data processing, we calculate the average latency by processing large amount of messages generated from PC side in FAST format.

As an emulation of source data, PC side data generator establishes TCP connection over Ethernet with FPGA and sends the randomly generated data in FAST format as the input for testing.

4.2   Implementation Results and Resource Utilization

By optimizing pipeline stages and module logic to restrain the timing of each cycle, we ultimately achieved a global clock period of 7.51ns. This restriction allows a full utilization of on board frequency. Table 1 shows the resources utilization of Xilinx Virtex-5 board.

Table 1. Resources Utilization on board

Slice Logic Utilization	Used	Available	Utilization
Number of Slice Registers	759	28,800	2%
Number of Slice LUTs	2,249	28,800	7%
Number of occupied Slices	768	7,200	10%
Number of bonded IOBs	264	480	55%

4.3   Comparison with Previous Works

Our testing shows an average processing latency of 340ns per message, considering the latency of writing output data into memory, an overhead of 400ns makes an average latency of 740ns. Compare with the hardware acceleration design in previous works (Figure 6), we see that this parallel architecture with multiple input increased the overall performance of market data feed handler by 3-6 times.

Figure 6 shows a comparison of message decoding latency with previous works. The latency is measured as an average time consumption of executing a single message.

Table 2. Results comparison with previous works

Design	Latency	FPGA Platform	Year
This work	760ns	Xilinx Virtex 5 LX110T FPGA	2013
Morris and Thomas	4us	Celoxica AMDC accelerator	2009
		Card;	
		Xilinx Virtex 5 LX110T FPGA	
Leber and Geib	2.6us	Xilinx Virtex-4 FX100 FPGA	2011

Testing results showed that parallel structure increased the overall performance since FAST messages consist of mainly short length fields, which motivated us the design modification to parallel structure. When fields within message input buffer frequently appear, the parallel structure reduced overall throughput efficiently.

5   Conclusion and Future Works

This paper introduced the design and implementation of a financial market data feed handler on FPGA. Aiming at achieving the hardware acceleration in place of software platform, the feed handler system functions as a parser of format messages coming from the Ethernet stream. This work is based on FAST protocol, a technology standard developed by FIX Protocol Ltd., specifically aimed at optimizing data representation on the network. It is used to support high-throughput, low latency data communications between financial institutions. FAST protocol offers compression capabilities for the transmission of massive market data feeds. Currently there are open source implementations of FAST specifications based on C and Java, a variety of software or hardware based design permit us to evaluate our work and reach evidence in latency proofing the practical value of this work.

To achieve hardware handler with lower latency and higher throughput to fully utilize the Ethernet bandwidth, the design was implemented in parallel structure which allows multiple byte length input from Ethernet. This structure proposed an improvement on latency compared to conventional designs and made further efforts on hardware acceleration device for low latency financial data feed handler.

Acknowledgement. This work is supported by the National Science Foundation of China (Grant No. 61373032), and the Science and Technology Commission of Shanghai Municipality (Grant No. 13511500200).

References

1. Chlistalla, M., Speyer, B., Kaiser, S., et al.: High-frequency trading. Deutsche Bank Research, 1–19 (2011)
2. Leber, C., Geib, B., Litz, H.: High Frequency Trading Acceleration using FPGAs. In: 2011 International Conference on Field Programmable Logic and Applications, pp. 317–322. IEEE Press (2011)
3. Leber, C., Geib, B., Litz, H.: High frequency trading acceleration using FPGAs. In: 2011 International Conference on Field Programmable Logic and Applications (FPL). IEEE (2011)
4. Pasetto, D., et al.: Ultra low latency market data feed on IBM PowerENTM. Computer Science-Research and Development 26(3-4), 307–315 (2011)
5. Morris, G.W., Thomas, D.B., Luk, W.: FPGA accelerated low-latency market data feed processing. In: 17th IEEE Symposium on High Performance Interconnects, HOTI 2009. IEEE (2009)
6. Pottathuparambil, R., et al.: Low-Latency FPGA Based Financial Data Feed Handler. In: 2011 IEEE 19th Annual International Symposium on Field-Programmable Custom Computing Machines (FCCM). IEEE (2011)
7. Morris, G.W., Thomas, D.B., Luk, W.: FPGA accelerated low-latency market data feed processing
8. Leber, C., Geib, B., Litz, H.: High frequency trading acceleration using FPGAs. Field Programmable Logic and Applications (FPL)
9. Pottathuparambil, R., et al.: Low-Latency FPGA Based Financial Data Feed Handler. Field-Programmable Custom Computing Machines (FCCM)
10. http://www.opradata.com/specs/
    OPRA_Binary_Part_Spec_1.1_091912.pdf

FPGA-Based Real-Time Emulation for High-Speed Double-Precision Small Time-Step Electromagnetic Transient System

Jianxing Li[1], Chunhui Ding[1], Guanghui He[1], and Qing Mu[2]

[1] School of Electronic Information and Electrical Engineering,
Shanghai Jiao Tong University, Shanghai, China
{lijianxing,dingchunhui,guanghui.he}@sjtu.edu.cn
[2] China Electric Power Research Institute, Beijing, China
muqing@epri.sgcc.com.cn

Abstract. Real-time emulation of electromagnetic transient (EMT) system involves huge computation task and requires low latency. In this paper, a Field Programmable Gate Array (FPGA)-based EMT system is proposed for small time-step emulation. This system takes advantage of fully pipelined computing structure and can support the simulation of a large-scale power grid with various types of components. Moreover, by employing our proposed node injected current accumulation (NICA) structure, the current vector updating problem in large-scale grid that involves large computation is solved, and the small time-step latency which normally takes about 10μs is brought down to only 2μs. Finally, a specified power grid system is emulated on FPGA that can support up to 74 three-phase buses with only 2μs latency for each time-step. The emulation result is also compared to other similar designs and shows the superiority of our system.

Keywords: electromagnetic transient system, small time-step, Field Programmable Gate Array (FPGA), node injected current accumulation (NICA).

1 Introduction

Real-time EMT simulation aims at achieving a stable and efficient power system analysis and on-line dynamic security assessment. It can simulate the dynamic response of an actual power system within one time-step and complete the data transfer. Many researches have focused on making time-step smaller. The simulation time-step of large EMT system is brought down to about 10μs as frequency response range of electronic devices increases greatly [1]. Smaller time-step requires higher computing speed, lower latency and accurate numerical methods, and greater power grid scale makes the computation task even tougher. The simulation of large-scale power grid system in small time-step still remains a problem. Real-time simulation systems mostly use parallel processor and high-speed DSP chips [7-8]. But traditional general purpose processor and DSP cannot meet the need of high-frequency

W. Xu et al. (Eds.): NCCET 2014, CCIS 491, pp. 78–88, 2015.
© Springer-Verlag Berlin Heidelberg 2015

component simulation. To solve this problem, many dedicated real-time EMT simulators, such as ARENE [2], Real Time Digital Simulator (RTDS) [3] and RT-LAB, have been employed to achieve real-time simulation. In addition, more and more studies have focused on using FPGA as the core simulator hardware for the high efficiency, high-precision, low latency characteristics of new electronic devices [7].

RTDS is based on high-speed processor, and it is a combination of advanced computer hardware and comprehensive software. But the simulation scale is limited by the number of RTDS racks, which is at high cost and its scalability is relatively low. In [4], an impedance relay is implemented on RTDS, but the simulation scale is small and cannot be configurable. A co-simulation system is built in [5] using both FPGA and RTDS. A two port buck converter is modeled on an FPGA and interfaced with the small time-step environment in RTDS using a travelling wave model. But it is a small-scale system and element type is fixed. A method proposed in [6] uses RT-LAB with standard multi-core CPU and FPGA Chips to simulate Modular Multilevel Converter (MMC), which can achieve large-scale simulation but cannot support various components. A large-scale EMT simulation proposed in [7]. 3-FPGA and 10-FPGA real-time hardware emulation of a three-phase 42-bus and 420-bus power system is implemented using detailed modeling of various system components. But it is based on IEEE single-precision floating-point whose precision cannot meet with the accuracy requirement of long term iteration. Moreover, time-steps for these systems are up to 11.55µs and 36.12µs on the 3-FPGA and the 10-FPGA designs respectively, which is too long for real-time simulation. Likewise, a system in [8] which consists of 15 transmission lines, 4 generators and 8 loads is realized on FPGA with a time-step of 12µs running at 80MHz clock frequency. The latency is also relatively long compared with our design.

To better achieve the accuracy and real-time requirement of EMT simulation, here we propose a FPGA-based EMT emulation system which uses double-precision floating point computation and brings down time-step to 2µs. It is a large-scale system that can support up to 74 three-phase bus, 3 transmission line, 200 R-L-C components, 24 single-phase two-winding transformer, 60 breakers (including maximum 6 coupled switches) and several current and voltage sources. The number of these components is also configurable.

The paper is organized as follows: Section 2 describes the theory of EMT simulation. Section 3 describes the proposed small time-step system and its operation flow. Section 4 introduces the problem of node injected current accumulation and its solution in our system. Section 5 presents the hardware emulation result. Finally, conclusion is given in section 6.

2   Electromagnetic Transient Simulation System

Electromagnetic transient simulation can be concluded as solving time domain response of the power system, including the mathematical model of the system itself and numerical algorithms adapted with it. Its mathematical model includes two categories: one is the constraint equations, namely Kirchhoff Current Law (KCL) and

Kirchhoff Voltage Law (KVL) depended by topology; The other is voltage-current relation equation decided by characteristics of each component of the system. The later one is difficult in forming and less efficient than the first one in regard to large-scale simulation. In our proposed system the first mathematical model is employed, and now take an inductance branch in Fig.1 as an example to illustrate the model.

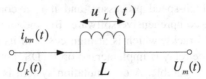

Fig. 1. Single inductance branch

Its basic differential VA equation is given as:

$$u_L(t) = U_k(t) - U_m(t) = L\frac{di_{km}(t)}{dt} .$$ (1)

Take differential operation to both sides of (1), the equation becomes:

$$di_{km}(t) = \frac{1}{L}u_L(t)dt .$$ (2)

Then use trapezoidal integration to (2) for a small time-step Δt:

$$i_{km}(t) = I_{hist}(t - \Delta t) + \frac{1}{R}[u_k(t) - u_m(t)] .$$ (3)

Where

$$I_{hist}(t - \Delta t) = i_{km}(t - \Delta t) + \frac{1}{R_L}[u_k(t - \Delta t) - u_m(t - \Delta t)], \ R_L = \frac{2L}{\Delta t} .$$

From equation (3) we can get the Norton equivalent circuit form of this inductance branch shown in Fig.2.

All small time-step equivalent model of electronic components can be built in this way. Then KCL and KVL constraint equation are used to get node simultaneous equation:

$$[G][U]=[I] .$$ (4)

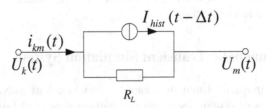

Fig. 2. Norton equivalent inductance branch

In equation (4), [G] is the conductance matrix in n×n, (n is the number of independent nodes in the circuit); [U] is the node voltage vector; and [I] is the injected current source vector and it should be calculated every time-step.

The operation of EMT simulation system in every small time-step can be concluded as:

1. Solving the injected current source vector from previous node voltage vector and voltage-current relation equation of components.

2. Selecting new conductance matrix if any switch operation happens which changes the system topology.

3. Solving new node voltage vector from $[U]=[G]^{-1}[I]$ as input for the next time-step.

3   Proposed EMT Emulation System

Our proposed EMT emulation system will be introduced in this section. It is a large-scale small time-step system which can support the emulation of maximum 74 three-phase buses, and its latency for every time-step is within 2μs. Moreover, all of the computation is in 64-bit IEEE floating point format, which guarantees the accuracy of long term iteration.

All initial data is transferred from server to FPGA memory before the emulation begins, and so does the conductance matrix. The number of conductance matrix depends on the number of coupled switches that can affect the topology [9]. In our system up to 6 coupled switches can be supported, which means 2^6 =64 conductance matrix in maximum size of 64×64.

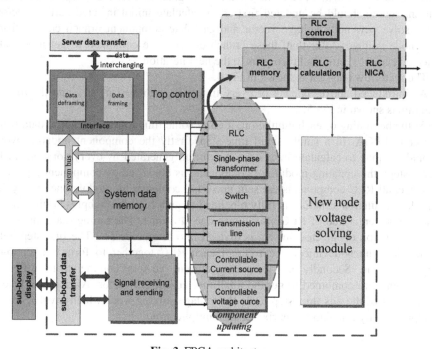

Fig. 3. FPGA architecture

The number of emulated components is configurable, and it could be set by users to simulate different power networks. The system structure on FPGA is shown in Fig.3.

There are several main sub-modules.

A. Top control

Top control module gives main control signals to other function modules such as starting signal, data reading signal and end simulation signal.

B. Component updating module

Component updating module is classified by component type (painted pink in Fig.3). For instance, RLC and switch belongs to two independent calculating modules. These calculating modules are fully pipelined to achieve high throughput. Each component updating module consists of 4 sub-modules as is shown in Fig.3, including Memory, Control module, Calculating module and Node Injected Current Accumulation (NICA) module which will be explained in detail in Section 4.

C. New node voltage solving module

Solving new node voltage vector by $[U]=[G]^{-1}[I]$. And the new voltage vector will become input for component updating module in next iteration.

D. System data memory

Storing important system data which occupies great memory space, such as conductance matrix and updated voltage vector during each iteration.

E. Signal receiving and sending module

Receiving control signal from users to change state of the system dynamically, and transfer specified data to display board to monitor the system operation. When all initial data is ready in FPGA, the emulation begins. In first time-step, voltage and current source should be updated first as to calculate initial injected current vector. Then solve new node voltage vector and calculate component branch current from new node voltage. After that, these branch currents are combined to get new node injected current vector, and then goes to the next iteration.

The total flow diagram is shown in Fig.4.

As introduced above, latency of every time-step is limited in 2µs, and the timing diagram is shown in Fig.5.

At the beginning of each emulation, it takes some time to transfer initial data from server to FPGA. In a single small time-step, firstly the component updating work should be done to calculate injected node current generated by every component. In our system, the updating module of components is classified by component type. For instance, all RLC components are sent into RLC computation module one at a cycle, and the calculation structure is fully pipelined to gain high throughput. So the output injected current value of RLC also comes one at a time. The timing diagram shows that calculation of injected current is divided into two processes. The first step is to accumulate the node injected current of each RLC together to form a temporary current vector. Secondly all temporary current vectors coming from different components are combined to get the total injected current vector. After that it take s almost half of the 2µs time-step to do the voltage solving work which involves huge computation by calculating matrix-vector multiplication.

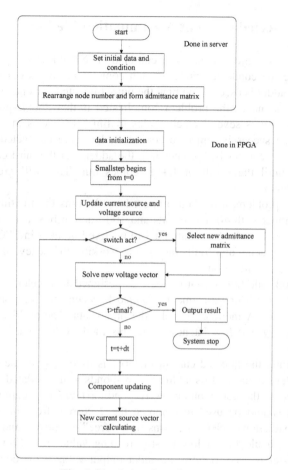

Fig. 4. Simulation flow diagram

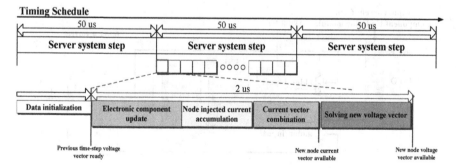

Fig. 5. Timing diagram of proposed system

4   Node Injected Current Accumulation Method

The process of node injected current accumulation (NICA) needs special strategy to deal with, since the connected node of each component comes out randomly. A 3-stage pipelined adder is used to combine the output injected currents which update the same node. What makes the problem complicated is that double-precision floating point addition requires several clock cycles to finish (3 cycles in our design). For example, if three successive injected current I_1, I_2, I_3 are connected with the same node, the first two current I_1, I_2 comes into the adder, but the third current I_3 should wait 3 cycles until the result of $I_1 + I_2$ comes out. This will greatly affect the computation latency.

To solve this problem, a method proposed in [8] turns the floating point number into a fixed number with 40 integer bits and 100 fraction bits, and then the addition can be finished in 1 cycle. But adding a 140-bit fixed number in FPGA in one cycle creates great logic delay and limits the system working frequency, and it also affects accuracy in long term iteration.

In our method, additional control logic is designed to accelerate the calculating process. Moreover, a storage element is added between the Component Calculation module and the NICA module to cache the input data. The problem can be solved both with accuracy and low latency using this method. The hardware structure is shown in Fig.6.

In this structure, the injected current memory is used to store the injected current value from adder output, and its address corresponds to the updated node number of injected current. If the adder output corresponding memory location is not empty, then the adder should be used to combine the 2 current from memory and adder output. In this situation, adder state turns from "free" to "busy", and the read enable signal of FIFO should be set low to stop reading value from FIFO into adder. A temporary register is used to store the adder output value if the combination action takes places, since data coming from memory takes 1 cycle delay. The data flow diagram is shown in Fig.7.

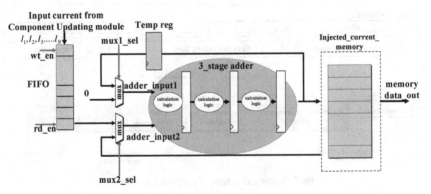

Fig. 6. NICA structure

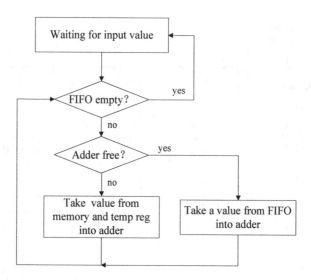

Fig. 7. Data flow diagram of current accumulation

The latency of current accumulation module come form 3 parts: input delay, FIFO delay and calculation delay.

Since all of our component updating modules are pipelined, input currents are sent into FIFO one by one. Assuming that N is the number of a certain kind of component, then the input delay equals the component number N.

The second part of delay comes from FIFO. As said before, the elements in FIFO will be blocked if adder is in "busy" state. So the delay of FIFO depends on how many cycles adder is used to do the combination of current from memory and temporary register. Each coupled nodes will cause a delay. For instance, if input current I_1, I_2, I_3, I_4 correspond to node "3","1","4","3" respectively, then I_1 and I_4 need to be combined and will cause the adder "busy" later. The worst delay case is that every input node is coupled (for instance, all current correspond to the same node), then when the last input comes into FIFO, there are N/2 values in FIFO that are blocked before. The last input should wait N cycles to be read from FIFO. So the longest FIFO delay should be N.

The last delay part comes from calculation delay of adder which counts from the time the last input is sent into adder. Since adder is in 3 stages, the pipelined data in each adder stage need to be combined in some case, and that requires additional control logic and delay. The worst delay case is described in Fig.8.

In Fig.8, the same color symbols the same updated node, and it shows that the worst case of calculation delay is 13 cycles since the last input was sent into adder.

Total latency= input delay+ FIFO delay +calculation delay= 2N+13 cycles

When this special strategy is not applied, total latency=N×(adder delay + memory output delay)= 4N cycles.

In our proposed system there are 40 R-L-C components for each updating module, and the total time saved by NICA structure is 42%. The saved time by our proposed system becomes even more significantly as the number of components increases.

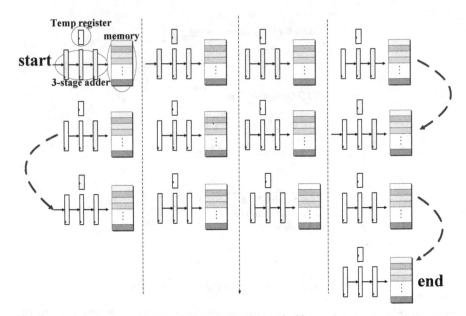

Fig. 8. Calculation delay of adder

5   Emulation and Implementation Results

The FPGA-based real-time emulation system is implemented on Xilinx Virtex-7 690T Development Board. Table 1 shows the total resource utilization.

The consumption of Block Ram mainly comes from conductance matrix (37%). And our system has the margin to support even more conductance matrix. The usage of LUT mainly comes form control and calculation logic, and its 69.7% occupancy guarantees the smooth place and route on our development board. DSP consumption attributes to the use of double-precision floating point multiplier in our huge computation task.

Table 1. Total resource utilization

Block Ram	Register	LUT	DSP
50.6%	24.6%	69.7%	75.1%

Table 2. Performance comparison

EMT emulation system	[7]	[8]	**This work**
Time-step (μs)	11.55	12	2
Emulation scale	42 three-phase bus	16 three-phase bus	74 three-phase bus
Clock frequency	100MHz	80 MHz	125MHz

The performance of our proposed system is also compared to similar design presented in [7] and [8] respectively. The comparison results are shown in Table 2.

Time-step of our system is limited in 2μs, while in [7] and [8] time-step is 11.55μs and 12μs respectively. Moreover, the emulation scale supported by our system is 74 three-phase bus, which is over 1.5 times that of [7] and 4 times that of [8]. The clock of our system also runs at higher frequency, indicating lower path delay in the design. Table 2 shows that the time-step of our proposed EMT emulation system is only about 16%~20% that of other designs while supporting larger emulation scale.

6   Conclusions

In this paper we proposed a double-precision FPGA-based EMT emulation system for real-time simulation. With fully pipelined structure and modular division design according to component type, the system is scale-configurable and can support up to 74 three-phase buses. Furthermore, to handle the huge computation task caused by node current vector updating and avoid long latency, the NICA structure is employed. It brings down the computation latency significantly and finishes the task in high accuracy. The emulation result shows that the system time-step latency is only 2μs, which is far below the 10μs time-step requirement for large-scale EMT simulation system. Compared with other similar designs, our proposed EMT emulation system shortens the time-step by 80% while supporting even larger simulation scale.

Acknowledgements. This work is supported by National Natural Science Foundation of China under Grant No.61306026.

References

1. Dufour, C., Jalili-Marandi, V.: Real-Time Simulation using Transient Stability, ElectroMagnetic Transient and FPGA-based High-Resolution Solvers. In: 2012 SC Companion on High Performance Computing, Networking, Storage and Analysis (SCC), pp. 283–288. IEEE (2012)
2. Etxeberria-Otadui, I., Manzo, V., Bacha, S., Baltes, F.: Generalized average modelling of FACTS for real time simulation in ARENE. In: IEEE 2002 28th Annual Conference of the IECON 2002 (Industrial Electronics Society), vol. 2, pp. 864–869 (2002)
3. Wang, B., Dong, X., Bo, Z., Klimek, A., Caunce, B., Perks, A.: RTDS environment development of ultra-high-voltage power system and relay protection test. In: Power Engineering Society General Meeting, pp. 1–7. IEEE (2007)
4. Ouellette, D.S., Geisbrecht, W.J., Wierckx, R.P., Forsyth, P.A.: Modelling an impedance relay using a real time digital simulator. In: Eighth IEE International Conference on Developments in Power System Protection, vol. 2, pp. 665–668 (2004)
5. Meka, R., Sloderbeck, M., Faruque, M.O., Langston, J., Steurer, M.: FPGA model of a high-frequency power electronic converter in an RTDS power system co-simulation. In: IEEE Electric Ship Technologies Symposium, pp. 71–75 (2013)

6. Wang, C., Li, W., Belanger, J.: Real-time and faster-than-real-time simulation of Modular Multilevel Converters using standard multi-core CPU and FPGA chips. In: IECON 39th Annual Conference of the IEEE Industrial Electronics Society, pp. 5405–5411 (2013)

7. Chen, Y., Dinavahi, V.: Multi-FPGA digital hardware design for detailed large-scale real-time electromagnetic transient simulation of power systems. IET Generation, Transmission & Distribution 7(5), 451–463 (2013)

8. Chen, Y., Dinavahi, V.: FPGA-based real-time EMTP. IEEE Transactions on Power Delivery 24(2), 892–902 (2009)

9. Dufour, C., Jalili-Marandi, V., Belanger, J.: Real-Time Simulation using Transient Stability, ElectroMagnetic Transient and FPGA-based High-Resolution Solvers. In: 2012 SC Companion High Performance Computing, Networking, Storage and Analysis (SCC), pp. 283–288. IEEE (2012)

Nodal-Analysis-Based FPGA Implementation for Real-Time Electromagnetic Transient Emulation System

Xiaozhang Gong[1], Tianyi Yang[1], Xing Zhang[2], and Guanghui He[1]

[1] School of Electronic Information and Electrical Engineering,
Shanghai Jiao Tong University, Shanghai, China
{taimgp,unremem,guanghui.he}@sjtu.edu.cn
[2] China Electric Power Research Institute, Beijing, China
zhangxing@epri.sgcc.com.cn

Abstract. Electromagnetic transient (EMT) simulation of power systems is widely applied in the planning, design, and operation of modern grid. However, large-scale real-time EMT simulation requires significant computational power and is difficult to achieve small simulation timestep. A field-programmable gate array (FPGA)-based configurable EMT emulation system is proposed in this paper. A parallel nodal algorithm with pipelined double-precision floating-point calculation is designed to achieve high accuracy and small timestep. In addition, a novel nodal equation calculation (NEC) structure is designed to save area and latency. Moreover, the NEC module is reused to merge the nodal current vectors, which further improves the emulation scale of the system. The proposed real-time EMT emulation system on FPGA achieves a timestep of 2us and can emulate a configurable power network up to 74 nodes.

Keywords: electromagnetic transient simulation, FPGA, real-time, nodal analysis.

1 Introduction

Electromagnetic transient (EMT) simulation has always played a significant role in the development of power system. It calculates the dynamic response of the electrical networks with arithmetic computation and is finding wide ranging applications in high voltage direct current transmission (HVDC), flexible alternating current transmission systems (FACTS), and voltage source converters (VSC)[1].

The traditional electromagnetic transient program (EMTP) was first proposed by Dommel in 1969[2].Since it is widely adopted and well developed, several commercial EMTP-based software packages offer a wide variety of simulation capability. However, with the rapid increase of network size and more high frequency electrical devices, the transient simulation requires the higher computational power. To accurately capture higher frequency transients, the simulation timestep is required to decrease to less than 5us [1], which is really a great challenge to current simulators.

W. Xu et al. (Eds.): NCCET 2014, CCIS 491, pp. 89–98, 2015.

Recent years, multi-DSP, multi-RISC, or PC-clusters are used to accomplish the real-time EMT simulation. This relies on the fundamental premise that a big power network can be divided into smaller subsystems and be computed concurrently [1]. Commercial real-time digital simulators such as RTDS [3] and PC-cluster simulators based RT-LAB use parallel processing techniques by utilizing the computational power of DSPs or PCs to simulate complex power systems. However, sequential computation and cost of extra communication latency are still problems of these systems.

Owing to the fast developments of VLSI technology and advanced EDA tools, field programmable gate arrays (FPGAs) are becoming the target processors of many applications [5][6][7]. This is because the FPGA has intrinsic parallelism and tremendous computational resources. Therefore, FPGA-based real-time EMTP becomes highly attractive.

Related work by Yuan Chen *et al* in [6] is a basic realization of electromagnetic transient simulation on FPGA. But the supported network size is relatively small and the timestep is only 12us. Their later work focus on the large-scale electromagnetic transient simulation using multiple FPGAs [7].They implement an up to 420-bus power system at a time-step of 36.12us, in which the time-step is relatively long.

To improve the performance of current FPGA-based simulators, we design a real-time EMT emulator with accurate modeling of more high frequency no-linear devices such as IGBTs and diodes. The emulator is based on a paralleled EMT algorithm with deeply pipelined computations using double-precision floating-point number representation. The initial data of the network is configured through a fiber from host computer. Implemented EMT emulation system on Xilinx Virtex-7 FPGA achieves a timestep of 2us and can emulate a network size up to 74 nodes.

The nodal equation calculation (NEC) is the central module of the simulator which determines the system's performance. The NEC contains two matrix-vector multiplications and should be well designed to save area and latency. There are several structures involved in matrix calculation such as the macro-pipelined systolic structure [8], the tree-traversal method [9], and the processing elements (PE) array [10]. The works in [10] identify two basic methods for multiply-accumulate operation, the tree-traversal method and the striding method. However, their design requires two memories at a size of α^2 and a very complex controller to schedule the add operation. Here, α is the latency of the pipelined adder. Based on this, later works focus on the matrix's sparse property or the I/O bandwidth of this universal architecture [8]. These designs are all based on complex controllers and buffers. None of them is suitable for NEC because of their relatively long latency and control complexity. To improve the performance of the central NEC module, a linear array with optimized PEs is used and results show an improvement both in area and latency.

The rest of this paper is organized as follows. In section 2, the EMT system and the nodal analysis algorithm are discussed. Section 3 presents the proposed FPGA-based EMT emulator. The central NEC unit is outlined in Section 4. Then, the implementation results and performance comparison are described in Section 5. Finally, a conclusion is drawn in Section 6.

2   The EMTP System and Nodal Analysis Algorithm

2.1   EMTP Theory

Most of the EMT programs use the nodal analysis to solve the time domain transient response of power electric systems because of its high-accuracy and low computation time [1]. They adopt discrete models to characterize different elements, which is based on Dommel's models in [2] .

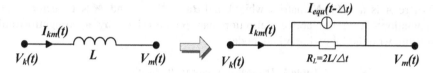

Fig. 1. Inductance branch and its equivalent circuit

The EMT computation process is as follow:
1). Use an appropriate integration method, transform the differential equation of each component's characteristics into a discrete accompanying model, which is shown in Fig.1.
2). Set up the power network based on the discrete models. Adopt the nodal analysis method to form the nodal voltage equation.
3). Calculate the nodal voltage using the nodal admittance matrix and the discrete nodal current vector.
4). Using the calculated new node voltage to update all the element models in the system. Then, the transient simulation goes on by repeating step 3 and step 4.
For a network with N nodes, the nodal equation can be formed as follows:

$$Y \times U = I \qquad (1)$$

Here Y is the system nodal admittance matrix; U is the vector of N node voltages; and I is the vector of N current sources.

Ho *et al* [4] propose a modified nodal approach to increase the capacity of processing voltage sources. If set A of N nodes have unknown voltages, and the other B nodes connected to voltage sources with known value, thus, the equation (1) becomes:

$$\begin{bmatrix} Y_{AA} & Y_{AB} \\ Y_{BA} & Y_{BB} \end{bmatrix} \times \begin{bmatrix} U_A \\ U_B \end{bmatrix} = \begin{bmatrix} I_A \\ I_B \end{bmatrix} \qquad (2)$$

Then the unknown voltages can be solved by calculating the following linear algebraic equation:

$$U_A = Y_{AA}^{-1} \times (I_A - Y_{AB} U_B) \qquad (3)$$

For real-time EMTP simulators, the Y_{AA}^{-1} matrix is pre-calculated for all possible switch state combinations and stored in local memory.

2.2   The Nodal Analysis Algorithm

The calculation of the nodal equation (3) is the kernel of the whole EMT emulation system. The NEC requires two matrix-vector multiplications. The latency and area of this module, to a large extent, determine the final performance of the transient emulater.

In general, the standard matrix multiplication $B = A \times V$ is defined as follows:

$$B_i = \sum_{k=0}^{N-1} A_{i,k} \times V_k \tag{4}$$

Where A is a $M \times N$ matrix, while V and B are $N \times 1$ and $M \times 1$ vectors. The computations from the above definition can be described by a straightforward algorithm with the following pseudocode:

Table 1. The matrix-vector multiplication

```
for (i=0 ; i <M ;i=i+1)
  {
    B[i] = 0;
    for (k=0 ; k <N ;k=k+1)
        B[i] = B[i] + A[i,k]V[k] ;
  }
```

All the computation above should be conducted in double-precision floating point format. These arithmetic calculations can be easily done on FPGAs using the built-in resources such as DSP48 slices in pipelined architecture. Unfortunately, using pipelined floating-point units for data accumulation on FPGA may cause data hazards, for the add function can't get done in one clock cycle. So, how to deal with this accumulation is an important and difficult task to accomplish the NEC operation.

3   FPGA Architecture for Real-Time EMT Emulation

To speed up the EMT computation process discussed above, we propose a parallel architecture to decrease the simulation timestep without sacrificing accuracy. The top-level architecture of the FPGA-based real-time EMT emulator is shown in Fig.2. It is consists of six main subsystems: elements modeling system, NEC, system memory, breakers action and matrix selection, main controller, and interface units.

Before the system starts the EMT computation, upper simulation server sends the network topology and element parameters to the FPGA emulator through Rocket I/O transceiver. In every EMT simulation timestep, firstly, the Breaker Action unit analyze the state of switches. If the network topology is changed by breakers, the Matrix Selection unit selects the new Y_{AA}^{-1} and Y_{AB} matrix from the System Memory. Secondly, the nodal equation is computed. Lastly, different kinds of power electrical elements are updated parallelly using the new voltage U. Device types include linear element, transformer, voltage and current source, transmission line, switch, and other user defined elements. The calculation of $Y_{AB}U_B$ is also done in this phase after all the sources are updated.

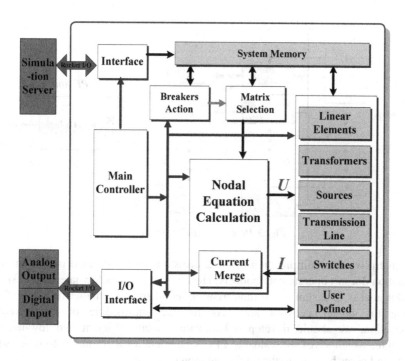

Fig. 2. The top-level architecture of the proposed emulator

Because all the electrical elements are processed concurrently in different units, each of them outputs a nodal current vector. The Current Merge unit is responsible for the merge computation for these current arrays. Moreover, to save area and FPGA computational resources, the Current Merge unit is implemented through reusing the existing hardware of the Nodal Equation Calculation unit.

All the electrical elements units are pipelined and can accept one element at a clock cycle. If some type element is of great number, the corresponding process unit is duplicated. This improved parallelism further improves the emulation speed.

4   The Nodal Equation Calculation (NEC) Unit

4.1   Proposed NEC Structure

A liner array of process elements (PE), each consist of a multiplier and an novel accumulation logic (AC logic), is used to perform the NEC. As shown in Fig.3, the rows of matrix A are sent to the PEs each value per cycle, simultaneously, value of vector V is sent sequentially to another input of all PEs. Therefore, every PE outputs one value of B. In each PE, the multiplication is done firstly, then, the result data is transferred to the accumulation logic. A novel AC logic is proposed to improve the total latency. Assuming the latency of the AC logic is k, size of matrix A is $m \times n$, then the total latency is $n + \alpha + k - 1$ with an α-stages multiplier. Thus, the performance of this architecture totally depends on the internal AC logic.

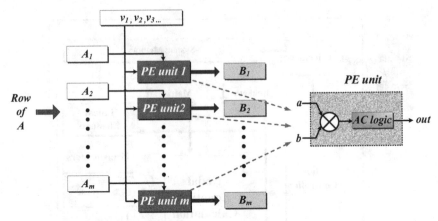

Fig. 3. Proposed NEC structure

The matrix-vector multiplication of NEC deals with a size-limited matrix and the computation doesn't operate continuously. However, it requires low latency and small area. Our goal is to design a real-time transient emulator at a smaller timestep while covering the bigger network size. As for the sub-module of matrix-vector multiplication, we should develop a hardware resource-efficient and low-latency architecture, which saves the valuable FPGA computational resources to other sub-modules and gives benefits to the total emulation timestep.

In order to overcome these design problems, a new structure is proposed to handle the accumulation task. As shown in Fig.4, the AC logic is consist of one floating-point adder, one 64bits register along with some control logic.

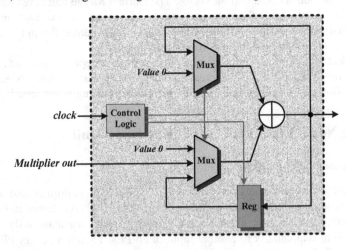

Fig. 4. Proposed AC logic

In each NEC, the previous multiplier sends one input value to this AC logic at each clock cycle, defined as $m_1, m_2, m_3 \dots m_n$. When m_1 arrive, the α stages pipelined adder is empty, and m_1 is added with a value 0. After α cycles, $m_1 + 0$ is on the adder's output while $m_{\alpha+1}$ arrives upon the input. Then $m_1 + 0$ is looped back and added with $m_{\alpha+1}$. As this goes on, when the last value is delivered into the adder, all m_i are reduced to α strading-add value. The α value are $m_1 + m_{\alpha+1} + m_{2\alpha+1} \cdots$, $m_2 + m_{\alpha+2} + m_{2\alpha+2} \cdots$,$m_3 + m_{\alpha+3} + m_{2\alpha+3} + \cdots$,... , $m_\alpha + m_{2\alpha} + m_{3\alpha} + \cdots$. Then the remaining task is to add the α value up. Table 2 illustrates how the last α value add together using an $\alpha = 3$ example, where s_1 is used to represent $m_1 + m_{\alpha+1} + m_{2\alpha+1} \cdots$, and s_2 represents $m_2 + m_{\alpha+2} + m_{2\alpha+2} \cdots$,and so on .

As illustrated in Table 2, the accumulation latency is 10 while the adder's α is set to 3. If the multiplier delay α_{mul} is set to 5, the total NEC latency is n + 13.

Usually, for an α stages adder, the beginning state is that the α stride value in the α stages of the pipelined adder. In worst case, $\alpha - 1$ add operations are needed to add them together. Then the worst latency is $\alpha + (\alpha - 1) * \alpha = \alpha^2$. However, there are usually more overlaps of the $\alpha - 1$ add operations owning to the pipelined logic, so the total latency $\leq \alpha^2$.

Table 2. The accumulation strategy

Clock Cycle	Adder Stage 1	Adder Stage 2	Adder Stage 3	Register	Output
0	s_2	s_1	0	0	
1	s_3	s_2	s_1	0	
2	0	s_3	s_2	s_1	
3	$s_1 + s_2$	0	s_3	s_1	
4	0	$s_1 + s_2$	0	s_3	
5	0	0	$s_1 + s_2$	s_3	
6	$s_1 + s_2 + s_3$	0	0	s_3	
7	0	$s_1 + s_2 + s_3$	0	s_3	
8	0	0	$s_1 + s_2 + s_3$	s_3	
9	0	0	0	s_3	$s_1 + s_2 + s_3$

4.2   The Reuse Technique Of NEC Unit

Notice than there are two matrix-vector multiplication operations in equation (3). Firstly $Y_{AB}U_B$ is calculated, then $Y_{AA}^{-1} \times I_A{}'$, where $I_A{}'$ means $I_A - Y_{AB}U_B$. It is obvious that the two matrix-vector multiplications can be done using the same NEC unit at different time. Extra multiplexes and control logic are added to the current PE array to schedule the two multiplications.

Another significant reuse technique is the merge computation of different nodal current vectors. In our FPGA-based EMT emulator, different electrical devices are modeled in different modules and updated simultaneously, each producing a current vector with a depth of n. Here, "n" is the node number of simulated network. The mergence is also an accumulate operation, and can be calculated by reusing the double-precision adders of the NEC structure. A tree accumulation structure is used to merge these current vectors.

As illustrated in Fig.5, the liner PE array is reconstructed into an accumulation tree. If there are eight current vectors defined as $I_1, I_2, ..., I_8$ and each I is a current vector of n nodes. At clock cycle $i(0 < i < n)$, $I_1[i], I_2[i], ..., I_8[i]$ are sent to the new PE structure. After $n + 3\alpha$ clock cycles, the total nodal current $I_{total}[i]$ is produced. Through this reuse technique, we not only speed up the nodal current merge operation but also save a great amount of hardware resources.

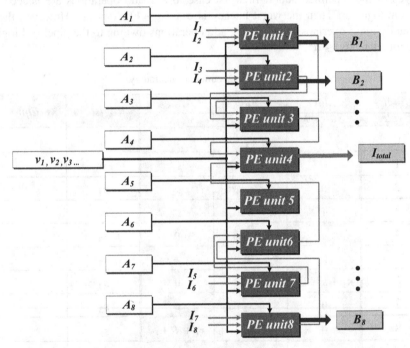

Fig. 5. Reuse of the NEC unit

5   Performance Analysis

Each PE of the NEC unit has a multiplier and an adder, both in double precision floating-point format. The characteristics of the pipelined adder and multiplier are shown in Table 3. Both of them can run at about 246 MHz.

For EMT emulators, the latency and the area used are two dominant metrics to evaluate the design. A smaller latency ensures the decrease of the simulation timestep. The less hardware area saves FPGA resources for the EMT system to cover a more complex grid.

Table 3. Characteristics of adder and multiplier on FPGA

Operation	Latency	Area Lut /Reg /Dsp			Clock Speed(MHz)
Multiplier	5	131	223	13	246.7
Adder	3	699	302	0	246.1

The proposed AC logic largely improves the performance of the NEC unit. Table 4 compares our AC logic with previous work[9][10]. Results show that our design has a much smaller latency and resource usage.

Table 4. Comparison with related works

Design	FCBT[9]	SSA[10]	This Work
Adders	2	1	1
Buffer Size	$3\lceil \log n \rceil$	$2\alpha^2$	1
Latency for n inputs	$\leq 3n + (\alpha - 1)\lceil \log n \rceil$	$\leq n + 2\alpha^2$	$\leq n + \alpha^2$

The FPGA-based real-time EMT emulator was implemented on a Xilinx VC709 Development Board, and results are shown in Table 5. Each EMT step consumes 250 clock cycles. So the simulation timestep is 2us at a clock frequency of 125MHz. The system supports up to 200 linear elements and 60 high frequency switches. As shown in Table 5, the NEC module utilizes the most FPGA logic resources.

Table 5. FPGA implemented results

Module	Lut	Dsp	Memory
EMT System	301940(69.7%)	2704(75.1%)	24.6%
NEC	127480(29.4%)	832(23.1)	0

6   Conclusion

In this paper, an FPGA-based real-time electromagnetic transient emulator with low simulation timestep has been presented. The proposed architecture can support arbitrary power network with six types of electrical elements. Using a parallel nodal analysis technique with pipelined computation, the simulation timestep is decreased to 2us, while the supported network size can be up to 74 nodes. Meanwhile, a novel nodal equation calculation structure is employed to perform the matrix-vector multiplication with low latency. Moreover, the reuse technique of NEC unit for nodal current mergence further saves FPGA resources. The implemented system on FPGA exceed related systems in network size and simulation timestep.

Acknowledgments. This work is supported by National Natural Science Foundation of China under Grant No.61306026.

References

1. Gole, A.M.: Electromagnetic transient simulation of power electronic equipment in power systems: challenges and solutions. In: IEEE Power Engineering Society General Meeting (2006)
2. Dommel, H.W.: Digital computer solution of electromagnetic transients in single and multiphase networks. IEEE Trans. Power App. Syst. 88(4), 388–399 (1969)
3. Kuffel, R., Giesbrecht, J., Maguire, T., Wierckx, R.P., McLaren, P.: RTDS—A fully digital power system simulator operating in real time. In: Communications, Power, and Computing. Conference Proceedings, vol. 2, pp. 300–305. IEEE (1995)
4. Ho, C.W., Ruehli, A., Brennan, P.: The modified nodal approach to network analysis. IEEE Trans. Circuits and Systems 22(6), 504–509 (1975)
5. Myaing, A., Dinavahi, V.: FPGA-based real-time emulation of power electronic systems with detailed representation of device characteristics. IEEE Transactions on Industrial Electronics 58(1), 358–368 (2011)
6. Chen, Y., Dinavahi, V.: FPGA-based real-time EMTP. IEEE Trans.Power Del. 24(2), 892–902 (2009)
7. Chen, Y., Dinavahi, V.: Multi-FPGA digital hardware design for detailed large-scale real-time electromagnetic transient simulation of power systems. IET Generation, Transmission & Distribution 7(5), 451–463 (2013)
8. Wenqi, B., et al.: A reconfigurable macro-pipelined systolic accelerator architecture. In: International Conference on Field-Programmable Technology (FPT), pp. 1–6. IEEE (2011)
9. Zhuo, L., Prasanna, K.: Sparse Matrix-Vector Multiplication on FPGAs. In: Proceedings of the 2005 ACM/SIGDA 13th International Symposium on Field-Programmable Gate Arrays, pp. 63–74 (2005)
10. Zhuo, L., Prasanna, K.: High-Performance Reduction Circuits Using Deeply Pipelined Operators on FPGAs. IEEE Trans. Parallel and Dist. Sys. 18(10), 1377–1392 (2007)

Low Complexity Algorithm and VLSI Design of Joint Demosaicing and Denoising for Digital Still Camera

Liang Hong, Wei Jin, Guanghui He, Weifeng He, and Zhigang Mao

School of Microelectronics,
Shanghai Jiao Tong University,
Shanghai 200240, China
hongliang@icrd.com.cn,
{kings2005,guanghui.he,hewf,maozhigang}@sjtu.edu.cn

Abstract. In this paper, we propose a low complexity algorithm to jointly demosaic and denoise Bayer format image, which combines the Hamilton and Adams (HA) method for interpolation and Epsilon filter for noise removal. Instead of using a 5x5 filtering window, one 7x1 horizontal Epsilon filter and one 1x3 vertical Epsilon filter are adopted in our method, which reduces hardware cost significantly while keeps high performance. Simulation results show that our proposed algorithm improves the mean PSNR performance of image by 1 dB compared to the algorithms treating these two processes independently. Furthermore, only 4 line buffers are consumed, and simple logic operators including adders and shifters are used for computation. For real-time implementation, a 5 stage pipelined VLSI architecture with 24 kb SRAM for line buffer is presented. The prototype of the joint processor is verified with Xilinx FPGA device and consumes about 36.6K gates for computational logic after synthesis with TSMC 90nm technology. The joint processor achieves a throughput of 6 Gbps at 250 MHz.

Keywords: Bayer CFA, Joint, Demosaic, Denoise, Algorithm, VLSI Implementation.

1 Introduction

Modern digital still cameras (DSCs) use a color filter array (CFA) to sample the original color. Bayer format is widely used in CFA [1]. In a Bayer format image, the number of Green (G) color components are twice as that of Blue (B) and Red (R). To recover the other two missing color components for each pixel, interpolation (also called demosaicing) is adopted in digital cameras. Besides interpolation, denoising is another critical process since the output of image sensor usually has signal-dependent noise [2].

To interpolate the missing colors and remove the noise, many demosaicing [3-5] and denoising [6], [7] algorithms are proposed. These conventional works treat these two processes as independent of each other. For CFA interpolation, a high performance VLSI implementation is proposed in 2006 [8], which can be used as a processing unit for practical cameras. Some image or camera processors also implement the CFA interpolation algorithm [9]. However, performing these two processes independently is not the best for image quality.

W. Xu et al. (Eds.): NCCET 2014, CCIS 491, pp. 99–107, 2015.
© Springer-Verlag Berlin Heidelberg 2015

In order to further improve the image quality, a unified method was proposed to perform joint demosaicing and image denoising [2]. The joint algorithm is more effective than treating them independently [2]. D. Paliy et al. presented an approach using LPA-ICI (Local Polynomial Approximation using Intersection of Confidence Interval rule) for both interpolation and denoising [3]. L. Condat proposed a joint approach using frequency analysis to reconstruct the luma and chroma channels of the image [10]. Unfortunately, these joint algorithms obtain the improved performance at the expense of high computational complexity and storage consumption. They are very hard to be applied in the real-time chips.

Motivated by the advantages of performing demosaicing and denoising jointly, we propose a novel algorithm of joint demosaicing and denoising in this paper. Our algorithm combine the interpolation adopting Hamilton and Adams (HA) [4] algorithm and denoising using Epsilon filter [6] together. A 5 stage pipelined VLSI architecture with 36.6K logic gates and 4 line buffers is proposed for implementation. To the best of our knowledge, this is the first VLSI architecture for joint demosaicing and denoising reported in the open literature.

The reminder of this paper is organized as follows. Section 2 presents our joint demosaicing and denoising algorithm. In Section 3, we show the details of VLSI implementation of our method. Simulation and implementation results are shown and compared with other methods and architectures in Section 4. Finally we conclude our paper in Section 5.

2   Proposed Joint Demosaicing and Denoise Algorithm

This section presents the details of our proposed joint demosaicing and denoising algorithm. The whole process is divided into six steps to show our methods for recovering the missing colors and removing the noise as shown in Figure 1. The proposed algorithm interpolates the missing colors and removes the noise for Bayer

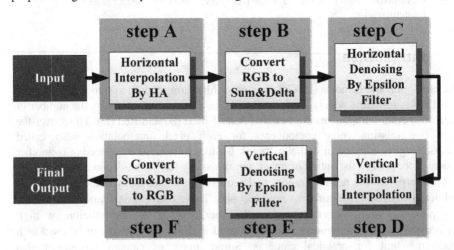

Fig. 1. Process overview of our proposed algorithm

format image. The noise for CCD and CMOS image sensor is modeled by the sum of a Gaussian component and a signal-dependent Poissonian component [3, 10]. However, the problem can be simplified to AWGN model since homomorphic nonlinear transformation can be employed for variance stabilization [10].

The first step is horizontal interpolation. If the current pixel is Red or Blue, the missing Green pixel is calculated in only horizontal direction for less hardware cost according to the rules of Hamilton-Adams (HA) algorithm [4] as follows.

$$\hat{G}_{i,j}^h = \frac{1}{2}\left(G_{i,j-1}^h + G_{i,j+1}^h\right) + \frac{1}{4}\left(2R_{i,j}^h - R_{i,j-2}^h - R_{i,j+2}^h\right) \qquad (1)$$

where (i,j) is the position of current pixel in the whole image, and superscript h means horizontal direction.

Similar to formula (1), if the current pixel is Green, the computation of missing Red/Blue pixel is interpolated as:

$$\hat{R}_{i,j}^h = \frac{1}{2}\left(R_{i,j-1} + R_{i,j+1}\right) + \frac{1}{4}\left(2G_{i,j} - G_{i,j-2} - G_{i,j+2}\right) \qquad (2)$$

Blue pixel is calculated in identical way. Note that the pixels in Bayer CFA only contain either Blue and Green or Red and Green in each row. So the result of estimation for Red/Blue channel is an interleaved matrix, i.e. one row Blue and one row Red.

Considering the high correlation between the G channel and R/B channel, combining the G channel information with R/B channel information will help to improve the quality of restoration image. The sum and difference of Green value and Red/Blue value are calculated after the first interpolation. The transformation is listed as follows.

$$\begin{pmatrix} \widehat{\Phi}_{g,r}^h \\ \widehat{\Delta}_{g,r}^h \end{pmatrix} = \begin{pmatrix} 1 & 1 \\ 1 & -1 \end{pmatrix} \begin{pmatrix} G \\ \hat{R}^h \end{pmatrix} \qquad (3)$$

Formula (3) shows the transformation when the current pixel is originally Green. $\widehat{\Phi}_{g,r}^h$ is the sum of Green color and Red color, while $\widehat{\Delta}_{g,r}^h$ is the difference of Green color and Red color.

After merging the Green and Red/Blue information, Epsilon Filter [6] is adopted as denoising method because of its simplicity and high efficiency. This method improves the primary average filter for Gaussian noise by giving a zero weight to the neighbor pixel when the difference between this pixel and current pixel is larger than a previous set threshold ε (which means this pixel in not 'relevant' to the current pixel; otherwise, it means 'relevant' to). The best effect ε value is relevant to the noise strength of image. The formula for this filter is given as follows:

$$y(k) = \Phi_{\varepsilon,M}[x(k)]$$
$$= x(k) + \sum_{i=-M}^{M} a(i)F(x(k+i) - x(k)) \qquad (4)$$

where x represents pre-denoising data, y represents post-denoising data, k is the current pixel index, and M represents the number of horizontal neighbor pixel used for average filter.

In equation (4), $a(i)$ represents the filter coefficient and equals to the reciprocal of the number of pixels relevant to current pixel. Function $F(x)$ is defined as (5). In our algorithm, the best denoising effect ε value corresponding to typical noise strength of image is set through simulation.

$$F(x) = \begin{cases} x \ (if \ |x| < threshold \ \varepsilon) \\ 0 \ (else) \end{cases} \tag{5}$$

After denoising in horizontal direction, the full image of G±R/B information ($\tilde{\Phi}^h$ and $\tilde{\Delta}^h$) are interpolated since the first interpolation step only recovers one missing color. The interpolation is performed via vertical direction at the second time. For simplicity, linear interpolation is used as follows.

$$\tilde{\Phi}^h_{g,r}(i,j) = \frac{1}{2}(\tilde{\Phi}^h_{g,r}(i+1,j) + \tilde{\Phi}^h_{g,r}(i-1,j)) \tag{6}$$

$$\tilde{\Delta}^h_{g,r}(i,j) = \frac{1}{2}(\tilde{\Delta}^h_{g,r}(i+1,j) + \tilde{\Delta}^h_{g,r}(i-1,j)) \tag{7}$$

For Blue channel, the interpolation is the same. For Green pixel, the pixel value is obtained according to formula (8).

$$\tilde{G} = \frac{1}{2}(\tilde{\Phi}^h + \tilde{\Delta}^h) \tag{8}$$

After obtaining the full G±R and G±B image, Epsilon filter is used for the second time denoising. However, this time the convolution filter is performed in vertical direction for previous interpolation data. The purpose of this step is to reduce the noise introduced by the second interpolation, and also make the image smoother in vertical direction.

Finally, the sum and delta domain values are converted back into RGB values. For Green pixel, the final Green pixel value is obtained after the second Epsilon filter.

For Red pixel, the final Red pixel value is given as

$$\tilde{R} = (\tilde{G} - \tilde{\Delta}^h_{g,r}) \tag{9}$$

Where $\tilde{G}$ and $\tilde{\Delta}^h_{g,r}$ are the Green value and delta value after the second Epsilon filter. The green and delta values are used to recover the red pixel rather than sum and delta value because the green pixels contain more information, which will help produce more accurate result. For blue pixel, the same computation is adopted.

3   VLSI Architecture and Implementation

Based on the presented algorithm, we propose a VLSI architecture (the joint processor) for hardware implementation as shown in Figure 2. The architecture for this joint processor has 4 line Bayer image buffers and a 5-stage pipeline. The blue lines are control signals, and black lines are data stream. The main controller determines the pipeline schedule, which is shown in Figure 3. The pipeline stage consumes 19 cycles totally. A 4-line buffer is used to store the previous four line pixels, while the current line pixels are directly input to Interpolate 1 module. After one cycle delay, the current input pixel updates the content of one line of the 4-line buffer.

The 5-stage pipeline includes Interpolate 1 module, Sum Delta module, Epsilon filter 1 module, Interpolate 2 module, and Epsilon filter 2 module. Interpolate 1 module and Epsilon filter 1 module process pixels in horizontal direction, and Interpolate 2 module and Epsilon filter 2 are similar to them while process pixels in vertical direction. The Sum Delta module is used to calculate the summation and difference (delta) between Green channel and Blue/Red channel. The architecture of Line Buffer, Interpolate 1 and Epsilon filter 1 are shown in Figure 4. For Interpolate 1 and Epsilon filter 1 module, there are 5 duplicate structures and one for each line. Five lines are processing in parallel when demosaicing and denoising in horizontal.

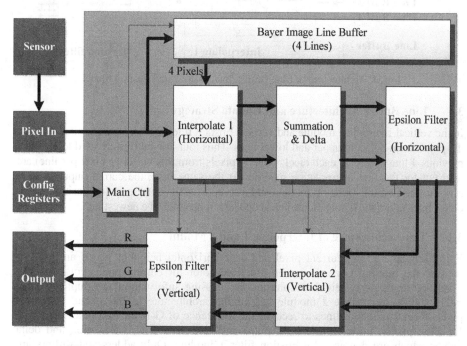

Fig. 2. Proposed VLSI architecture for joint demosaicing and denoising

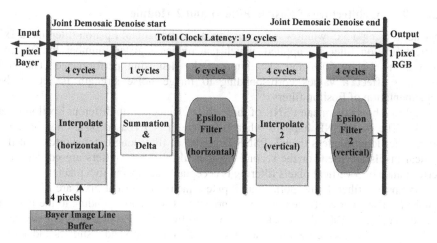

Fig. 3. Pipeline stage schedule of proposed architecture

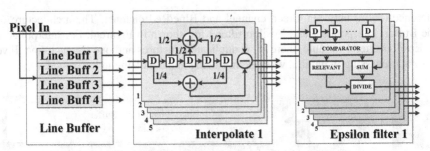

Fig. 4. Architecture of Line Buffer, Interpolate 1 and Epsilon filter 1

3.1   Line Buffer Architecture and Update Strategy

In the vertical Interpolate module and vertical Epsilon filter module, current pixel will use the pixels from adjacent upper and lower lines. Thus four line buffers are used to store the previous 4 line pixels. In each clock cycle, 4 pixels from this buffer (1 pixel per line) are read out for the first interpolation module. At the same time, the current input pixel is given to the first interpolation module and also updates the corresponding position of the oldest line. When the whole oldest line is updated, it becomes the newest line.

3.2   The Architecture of Interpolate 1 and 2 Module

For Interpolate 1, the current pixel and four horizontal neighbor pixels are used to recover the missing Green color or Blue/Red color for current pixel. For boundary pixels of image, the neighbor columns for missing information are duplicated for interpolation. Interpolate 2 module has similar architecture to Interpolate 1; it uses pixels from 2 neighbor lines to recover the difference of G-B for Red pixels and G-R for Blue pixels; meanwhile, Green pixels are recovered from summation and delta values which are denoised by Epsilon filter 1 module. Only adders and shifters are used in these two modules.

3.3   The Architecture of Epsilon Filter 1 and 2 Module

Instead of using a 5x5 window for denoising, a 7x1 horizontal Epsilon filter and a 1x3 vertical Epsilon filter are applied, which can reduce registers number for filtering from 25 to 10 by 60% and also improve the denoising performance. The best denoising effect ε values corresponding to image noise strength is set in the implementation of Epsilon filters.

Table 1. shows the mean PSNR of three color channels with different Epsilon filter lengths. The best PSNR happens when filter length is 7 (based on 24 test images). When filter length is less than 7, PSNR degrades as filter length get shorter. But if 5 vertical pixels are used for the second Epsilon filter, 8 line buffers are needed. The performance of 3 vertical pixels filtering is acceptable compared to 5 pixels.

For Epsilon filter 1, the horizontal 7 pixels including current pixel are filtered for denoising. The filter coefficient is the reciprocal of 1 to 7 corresponding to the number of relevant pixels. A divider with a fixed dividend from 1 to 7 is designed. For dividend of 1, 2 and 4, shifters are used for realization, while for 3, 5, 6 and 7 shifters and adders are used, which saves hardware cost. Epsilon filter 2 has similar architecture to Epsilon filter 1; it uses 3 vertical pixels for denoising. The same method is used for divider.

4   Results and Performance Analysis

A test image set including 24 Kodak images* is used to test different cases of image content. The Gaussian noise with zero mean and variance $\sigma = 12.75$ (for range from 0 to 255 image data) to each image are assumed.

Table 2. shows the comparisons of our joint method with other reported methods on some typical images. In the last row, the mean PSNR (Peak Signal Noise Ratio) values are obtained based on the average PSNR of all 24 test images.

Compared to method 1 and method 2, our algorithm improves PSNR about 0.7 dB, 1.6 dB, 0.7 dB and 0.6 dB, 1.5 dB, 0.5 dB in R, G, and B channel respectively. For few images (such as Kodim 8 and 23), PSNR of R and B may be lower than method 1 and method 2. The reason may lie in the high-frequency region (see the windows and tiles of Kodim 8) which is easy to produce mixer fuzzy boundaries.

Table 1. PSNR with Different Epsilon Filter Lengths

PSNR/dB	Filter length		Filter length		Filter length	
	H [a]	V [b]	H	V	H	V
	7	5	5	5	7	3
R	29.61		29.46		28.5	
G	30.61		30.32		29.8	
B	29.85		29.71		28.6	

a. Horizontal Epsilon filter length   b. Vertical Epsilon filter length

Table 2. Comparisons of Demosaicing and Denoising Quality with PSNR for 24 Images

PSNR/dB	Method 1**: HA[4]+Epsilon[a]			Method 2***: DLMMSE[5] +Epsilon[a]			This work		
Kodim	R	G	B	R	G	B	R	G	B
2	26.4	27.1	27.0	26.2	26.9	26.7	29.0	31.4	30.1
5	26.7	27.5	27.0	27.0	27.6	27.3	26.9	27.9	27.1
7	28.0	28.3	28.2	27.9	28.4	28.2	29.6	30.9	29.7
8	24.5	25.0	24.7	24.9	25.2	25.1	24.5	26.5	24.5
13	25.0	25.5	25.1	25.7	26.0	25.8	25.8	26.4	25.8
17	29.8	29.9	29.6	29.9	30.1	29.8	29.9	31.0	29.7
19	28.2	28.5	28.4	28.5	28.9	28.7	27.9	29.4	27.8
23	31.1	31.3	31.3	31.2	31.4	31.3	30.4	32.2	30.6
Mean	27.8	28.2	28.0	27.9	28.3	28.1	**28.5**	**29.8**	**28.6**

a. The Epsilon filter here uses a 5x5 window for denoising.

---

* Kodak Lossless True Color Image Suite. Available: http://r0k.us/graphics/kodak/
** Method 1 uses Epsilon filter for denoising and HA for interpolation separately.
*** Method 2 uses Epsilon filter for denoising and DLMMSE (Directional Linear Minimum Mean Square-Error) for interpolation separately.

Table 3. Performance Comparisons

Methods	[8][a]	[10][b]	[3][b]	[9][a]	[2][b]	This work
Image Quality (PSNR)	27.95	32.56 (σ=10)	30.4 (σ=12.75)	N/A	30.06 (σ=10)	28.98
Line Buffer Required	3	13	N/A	9	11	4
Technology	0.35 um	-	-	0.35 um	-	90 nm
Gate Count	10 k	-	-	675 k (Total)	-	36.6 k
Max. Speed (MHz)	40	-	-	100	-	250
Power(mW)	200	-	-	278 (Total)	-	15.3
Normalized Gate Effi.[c] (gate/pixel)	0.08	-	-	2.50 (Total)	-	0.09

a. Only including interpolation   b. No VLSI implementation

c. Normalized gate efficiency = Gate Count * (Technology / 90nm) / pixel format

Table 3. gives the performance comparison results of different algorithms and/or VLSI implementations. The mean PSNR of this work is obtained from the average of mean PSNR of R, G, and B channel in Table 2. Our method has some performance loss compared to other joint demosaic and denoise algorithms in [2, 3, 10], which have no VLSI implementation and consume more line buffers than this work. We compare our hardware results with other works which implemented VLSI for interpolation. The gate count and normalized gate efficiency of [9] are the results of the whole image processor, which are much bigger than others. The work of [8] only implements interpolation without denoising, resulting in less line buffer and gate count than our work. The normalized gate efficiency of our work is almost the same as [8]. As a result, our joint processor can achieve a good performance-complexity tradeoff for real cameras.

In our design, the buffer depth is 768 and width is 8 bit, so the total RAM size is 24 kb with 4 line buffers. After synthesis with TSMC 90nm technology, the total computational logic gate count is 36.6K. The joint processor can achieve a throughput of 6 Gbps with 15.3 mW power consumption (only includes computational logic without line buffer) at maximum frequency 250 MHz. The prototype of this processor is implemented and verified in Xilinx Vertex-5 XC5VLX50T FPGA, the computation circuit uses 1361 slices, 1901 slice registers and 3844 LUTs. The highest resolution output of the joint processor is 5-frames/s with 4928x3264 pixels. The design is all parameterized, which makes our joint processor is easy to be expanded to large pixel format for modern digital still cameras and smart phones.

5   Conclusion

In this paper, we proposed a novel low complexity joint algorithm and its VLSI implementation of both demosaicing and denoising for Bayer image in digital still cameras. This algorithm combines the HA method for interpolation and Epsilon filter for noise removal. The image quality is improved by 1 dB compared to the algorithms treating these two processes independently. To save hardware cost, the joint processor is implemented without using any multiplier or divider. In addition, only 4 line buffers are consumed, which makes our joint processor a practical implementation for DSCs. Moreover, a five stage pipelined structure is proposed for the real-time chip. It uses a 24 kb on chip SRAM and 36.6K gates for computational logic. The joint processor can achieve a throughput of 6 Gbps at 250 MHz.

Acknowledgements. This work is supported by National Nature Science Foundation of China under Grant No. 61306026.

References

1. Bayer, B.E.: Color imaging array, US Patent 3 971 065 (1976)
2. Hirakawa, K., Parks, T.W.: Joint demosaicing and denoising. IEEE Transactions on Image Processing 15, 2146–2157 (2006)
3. Paliy, D., Katkovnik, V., Bilcu, R., Alenius, S., Egiazarian, K.: Spatially adaptive color filter array interpolation for noiseless and noisy data. International Journal of Imaging Systems and Technology 17, 105–122 (2007)
4. Adams Jr, J.E., Hamilton Jr, J.F.: Adaptive color plane interpolation in single sensor color electronic camera, ed: U.S. Patents 5 506 619 (1997)
5. Zhang, L., Wu, X.: Color demosaicking via directional linear minimum mean square-error estimation. IEEE Transactions on Image Processing 14, 2167–2178 (2005)
6. Matsumoto, M., Hashimoto, S.: Noise Reduction and Edge Enhancement Based on Band-Pass Epsilon-filter. In: International Conference on Information Management and Engineering, ICIME 2009, pp. 111–115 (2009)
7. Katkovnik, V., Egiazarian, K., Astola, J.: Adaptive window size image de-noising based on intersection of confidence intervals (ICI) rule. Journal of Mathematical Imaging and Vision 16, 223–235 (2002)
8. Hsia, S.C., Chen, M.H., Tsai, P.S.: VLSI Implementation of low-power high-quality color interpolation processor for CCD camera. IEEE Transactions on Very Large Scale Integration (VLSI) Systems 14, 361–369 (2006)
9. Doswald, D., Hafliger, J., Blessing, P., Felber, N., Niederer, P., Fichtner, W.: A 30-frames/s megapixel real-time CMOS image processor. IEEE Journal of Solid-State Circuits 35, 1732–1743 (2000)
10. Condat, L.: A simple, fast and efficient approach to denoisaicking: Joint demosaicking and denoising. In: 2010 17th IEEE International Conference on Image Processing (ICIP), pp. 905–908 (2010)

A Slide-Window-Based Hardware XML Parsing Accelerator

Linan Huang, Jiang Jiang, Chang Wang, Yanghan Wang, and Yan Pei

School of Microelectronics, Shanghai Jiao Tong University
Shanghai, China
{huanglinan,jiangjiangdr,willy,wangyanghan,taessicap}@sjtu.edu.cn

Abstract. Nowadays, XML is playing an extremely important role in various fields such as web services and database systems. However, the task of XML parsing is generally known as bottleneck in related applications since it takes a general processor dozens of cycles to process every single character of XML file. As a result, software XML parsing is of poor performance and hardware accelerator is an appropriate alternative to perform efficient XML parsing. Until now, some hardware XML parsers with good performance have come to the world. In order to further improve XML parsing performance, we propose a slide-window-based XML parsing accelerator (SWXPA) which introduces data-level parallelism and implement our design on a Xilinx Virtex-6 board at an average throughput of 0.33 cycle per byte (CPB) and 3.0 Gbps.

Keywords: XML Parsing, slide window, data-level parallelism, DOM, FPGA.

1 Introduction

The Extensible Markup Language (XML) has become the de facto standard for information representation. The main reasons of XML popularity include, but not limited to, its human-readable expressiveness, interoperability and platform-independence. As a result, XML is prevalent in various applications, and the operation on XML data has become an important, even necessary workload for web servers, database servers, etc. However, it is known that XML document has to be parsed before any manipulation towards it. Related studies have shown that the execution time of XML parsing takes up about 30% of the total time of web service application [1], and it has threatened the database performance severely [2].

XML parsing allows optional validation of an XML document against a Document Type Definition (DTD) or XML Schema Definition (XSD). Both DTD and XSD defines some specific information for nodes of the document. And existing XML parsing models are mainly categorized into two styles: Simple API for XML (SAX) and Document Object Model (DOM). In our design, we adopt the DOM parsing model and the SWXPA performs non-validating XML parsing. A metric of cycle per byte (CPB) is used to measure the performance.

W. Xu et al. (Eds.): NCCET 2014, CCIS 491, pp. 108–117, 2015.

The organization of this paper is as follows. Section 2 introduces the related work of XML parsers both in software and hardware community. Section 3 presents the architecture of our design. Section 4 is a detailed illustration of the SWXPA implementation. Experiment conditions and results are provided in section 5. A conclusion is made in section 6.

2   Related Work

A lot of optimizations have been developed to improve the performance of software XML parser. In 2006, based on Libxml2 XML parser, Li et al. incorporated new instructions with special hardware support for frequently used operations and reduced execution time by up to 12.7% [3]. In 2009, Lan et al. developed a Geography Markup Language (GML, GML is an application of XML in the field of geospatial information) parser based on the VTD-XML parsing model [4], which is a new open-source XML parsing model. Their experimental results showed that VTD had advantage of high throughput and low memory consumption. Since 2008, Cameron et al. presented parallel bit stream technology to XML parsing, implementing a non-validating XML parser Parabix, and demonstrated that the performance was improved to 5.76-7.395 CPB [5]. In 2012, Lin et al. parallelized Parabix, achieving a further 2× improvement in performance [6].

In hardware community, Moscola et al. purposed in 2006 a reconfigurable architecture for high-speed content-based routing and implemented a simpler XML parser for demonstration [7]. In 2009, Chang et al. developed a XML parser called RBStreX for embedded system based on SAX [8]. However, the variable parsing time is the potential drawback. Dai et al. presented in 2010 the first complete FPGA XML parsing accelerator XPA and achieved the throughput of 1 CPB [9], but it worked sequentially and still left some room for performance improvement. In 2012, Ma et al. presented multiple-thread XML parser PSDXP [10] and implemented 2-thread and 4-thread XML parsing system.

3   Architecture of Slide-Window-Based Hardware XML Parsing Accelerator (SWXPA)

The DOM-based non-validating XML parsing comprises 4 main tasks: lexical analysis, token extraction, syntax checking on XML document, and in-memory DOM tree construction.

The major difference between SWXPA and other hardware XML parser is that we make full use of one important characteristic of XML document: the valid data is delimited by delimiters, such as "<", "/", etc. and the valid characters separated by a delimiter can be processed together since they are of the same data type. As a result, it is natural to operate input data differently: for valid data, several characters can be handled in a single cycle while the delimiting characters are processed one character per cycle.

In our design, based on the speculative pipeline architecture presented in [9], the SWXPA can be fed up with 4 bytes input data every cycle. In SWXPA, before the token extraction stage, we introduce a XML data issue stage and within it, 4-byte slide window is adopted. The slide window together with the token extraction functional units helps to separate delimiters and valid data and in this way, we can operate more than one valid characters per cycle, which exploits data-level parallelism to improve XML parsing performance. The general architecture of SWXPA is shown in Fig.1. We merge the lexical analysis stage into the token extraction stage.

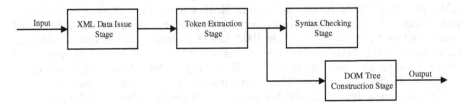

Fig. 1. General Architecture of SWXPA

The details of the XML parsing tasks will be described in the following paragraphs.

3.1   XML Data Issue Stage

XML data issue is a key stage for different operations on valid data and delimiters. A slide window combines with two stages of buffers, whose outputs are put together as a data set, plus control logic consist of the functional unit. It is capable of deciding the position of slide window from the data set and issues the data within the slide window into token extraction.

3.2   Token Extraction Stage

The valid data carried by XML document can be divided into 5 types: element name, element content, end element, attribute name and attribute content. Figure 2 is a simple example of a XML document.

XML document has the same nature of a tree structure. With a unique root element (In Fig.2 is "Customer"), each element starts by an opening tag ("<>") and finishes by a closing tag ("</>"), which may contain multiple attributes (e.g. "year", "month" and "day" for element "DateofBirth"), and each attribute has its own attribute content ("1965", "12" and "19" corresponding to "year", "month" and "day" respectively).

In the token extraction stage, XML parser receives the string sequence of XML data and extract valid tokens. At the same time, it completes the lexical analysis against the target document.

```
<?xml version="1.0" encoding="US-ASCII"?>
<Customer id="1011" >
      <Gender>Male</Gender>
      <Country>USA</Country>
      <Language>English</English>
      ...
      <Name>
            <Title>Mr</Title>
            <FirstName>Marjo</FirstName>
            <MiddleName>Akos</MiddleName>
            <LastName>Villoldo</LastName>
            ...
      </Name>
      ...
      <DateofBirth year="1965" month="12" day="19"/>
      <Address primary="yes" type="Temporary">
            <Street>832 Blossom Hill Rd</Street>
      </Address>
      <Phone>51306</Phone>
</Customer>
```

Fig. 2. A Simple XML Document

3.3   Syntax Checking Stage

According to XML syntax rules provided in XML specifications, syntax checking stage performs checking of syntax against a XML document. The basic XML syntax rules are summarized as follows.

- XML document must begin with a XML declaration (<?xml version="1.0" encoding="US-ASCII"?>).
- The root element of a XML document must be unique. Other elements are included within the root element.
- The opening tags must match with the corresponding closing tags and all elements must nest properly.
- The attribute of an element must be different with each other and the attribute content must be quoted.

Among the basic XML syntax rules, checking the nesting correctness of all elements and uniqueness of attribute within an element are the most important tasks that XML parser should achieve.

3.4   In-memory DOM Tree Construction Stage

With the help of a tree data structure, DOM-based XML parser organizes all valid data of target XML file as an in-memory DOM tree. Each node of the tree structure stands for one of the tokens. In addition to the information itself, such tree data structure requires extra pointers to save the relationships between parent, child and sibling nodes. And the DOM tree can provide inquiry function to users when the DOM tree construction is completely finished.

4   Implementation of SWXPA

Fig. 3 is the final architecture of SWXPA and the data path is shown in it. Detailed implementation of the functional units of the SWXPA will be presented in this session.

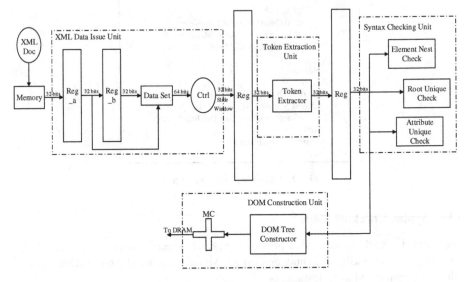

Fig. 3. The Architecture of SWXPA

4.1   XML Data Issue Unit

As mentioned in previous section, the major difference between SWXPA and other hardware XML parser is that we operate delimiters and valid data differently, which is realized with the help of XML data issue stage. This functional unit adopts two 32-bit registers (Reg_a and Reg_b in Fig. 3) to buffer the input data and the output of the buffers constitute a 64-bit data set, from which the 4-byte slide window is generated. The data set is byte addressable as Fig. 4 shows.

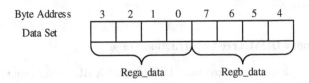

Fig. 4. Byte Address of Data Set

Generation schema of the slide window is illustrated as follows.

1. Initialize the start address of slide window to 0 and naturally the end address is 3;
2. During a cycle of operation, if no delimiter is detected in the slide window, its position remains unchanged, otherwise, we update the end address of slide window with the byte address of detected delimiter;
3. According to end address, we decide whether the new data should be pushed into data set in the next cycle. When the end address is 4, 5 or 6, Reg_a and Reg_b do not perform sampling and data set stays the same; if not, the data set is updated.
4. Finally, we calculate the start address for next cycle by equation (1).

$$\begin{cases} start\_addr = end\_addr + 1, end\_addr = 4, 5 \text{ or } 6, \\ start\_addr = end\_addr + 5, end\_addr \neq 4, 5 \text{ or } 6 \end{cases} \tag{1}$$

Fig. 5 shows the change process of slide window during SWXPA operates "<Customer id="1011">". The dotted frame is the slide window in each cycle and the processing sequence is from right to the left.

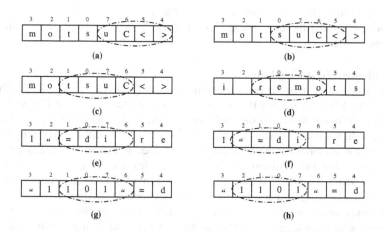

Fig. 5. Change Course of Slide Window

4.2   Token Extraction Unit

In token extraction stage, SWXPA extracts valid tokens from input data and outputs the corresponding token types according to the position of delimiters in the slide window. We employ a finite stage machine (FSM) as the core module to perform this function and the FSM is shown in Fig. 6.

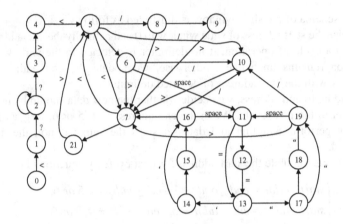

Fig. 6. The FSM in Token Extraction Stage

4.3   XML Syntax Checking Unit

The XML syntax checking stage is responsible for checking the element nesting correctness, checking the uniqueness of root element and the uniqueness of attribute within one element.

4.3.1   Element Nest Checking
A stack structure is used to perform element nesting check. Unlike XPA [9] and PSDXP [10], SWXPA pushes the 4 bytes of element name into the Element Stack every cycle. When it comes to the end element token, the incoming 4 characters are compared with the corresponding characters of stack top element poped out by order.

Besides, the important thing needs to be mentioned is that since we generate slide window according the position of delimiters, syntax checking stage gets aligned tokens sent from token extraction unit, which provides a lot of convenience for element nest checking and attribute uniqueness checking. "Aligned" means that a token is represented in several 4-byte-character form, e.g. the aligned token for "Customer" sent from token extraction stage is "Cust" and "omer", instead of "Cu", "stom", "er" or other forms.

4.3.2   Attribute Uniqueness Checking
[9] adopted Bloom Filter to realize attribute uniqueness checking and it is efficient to test if the incoming attribute name equals to previous operated ones, but when the potential false-positive happens, entire pipeline should be stalled to compare attribute names successively. In order to avoid pipeline stall problem, besides attribute stack, we add collision attribute stack as [10] did.

4.4   In-memory DOM Tree Construction Unit

DOM tree construction unit is in charge of establishing an in-memory tree in DRAM, which represents the structure of XML document, and the tree is basis of development of

DOM application programming interface. In our design, each element is called a node in the tree. Naturally, in addition to the element name itself, each node in the tree should contains pointers refer to its father node, left sibling node, right sibling node, son node and attribute list. The data structure of element name and attribute list is shown in Fig. 7.

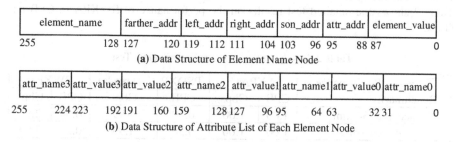

(a) Data Structure of Element Name Node

(b) Data Structure of Attribute List of Each Element Node

Fig. 7. Data Structure of DOM Tree

5   Experiments and Results Analysis

In this section, we compare SWXPA against two hardware XML parsers XPA and PSDXP demonstrated in [9] and [10] respectively. We evaluate the performance of XML parsers using both CPB and Gbps as metrics. In addition, an analysis of resource usage of our implementation is also presented.

5.1   Experimental Setup

Our design is implemented on Xilinx Virtex-6 XC6VLX240T FPGA board. To perform experimental tests conveniently, we initialize the XML document in a custom single port memory module produced by the Block ROM resources of FPGA. The SWXPA runs on 125MHZ.

5.2   Benchmarks

The benchmarks are chosen from different XML projects, each of which contains multiple test files. Table 1 lists the projects and the including test files.

Table 1. Detail Information of Benchmark

Benchmark	XML Size	Source
account234.xml	1.6KB	
mixed.xml	4KB	TPOX
custacc.xml	4.3KB	
error_sample_13.xml	8.4KB	
logic_v1.xml	68KB	QEDEQ
set_theory_v1.xml	175KB	
messageData.xml	19KB	
TestData.xml	70KB	HL7TestHarness
CodeSystems.xml	265KB	

5.3   Measurement

Both throughput and area consumption is evaluated in this section.

5.3.1   Throughput

Table 2 shows the detailed test results on the performance of SWXPA in CPB and Gbps.

Table 2. Results of Performance Experimental Tests

Performance / Benchmark	XPA		PSDXP (2 Threads)		SWXPA	
	CPB	Gbps	CPB	Gbps	CPB	Gbps
account234.xml	1.00	1.00	0.50	1.99	0.34	2.95
mixed.xml	1.00	1.00	0.50	1.99	0.33	3.03
custacc.xml	1.00	1.00	0.50	1.99	0.30	3.33
error_sample_13.xml	1.00	1.00	0.50	1.99	0.32	3.10
logic_v1.xml	1.00	1.00	0.50	1.99	0.32	3.11
set_theory_v1.xml	1.00	1.00	0.50	1.99	0.34	2.94
messageData.xml	1.00	1.00	0.50	1.99	0.35	2.82
TestData.xml	1.00	1.00	0.50	1.99	0.35	2.82
CodeSystems.xml	1.00	1.00	0.50	1.99	0.34	2.95
Average	1.00	1.00	0.50	1.99	0.33	3.00

As illustrated in Table 2, SWXPA achieves an average throughput of 0.33 CPB and 3.00 Gbps, which is almost 3 times and 1.5 times faster than XPA and two-thread PSDXP. In a single thread scenario, PSDXP achieved 1.00 CPB so as to XPA. Although in multiple-thread (more than 2) scenario, PSDXP may outperform SWXPA, SWXPA still has the potential advantage over PSDXP since our current design is a single-thread system and a N-thread SWXPA can be developed based on it, whose performance is estimated better than N-thread PSDXP.

5.3.2   Area

The device utilization of SWXPA is shown in Table 3. SWXPA uses 2% Slice Register, 5% Slice LUT and 14% Block RAM. The area consumption shown in Table 3 is not so much, leaving enough room for developing multiple-thread SWXPA on the board.

Table 3. Details of Device Utilization

Logic Utilization	Used	Utilization
Slice Register	6410	2%
Slice LUT	8838	5%
Block RAM	61	14%

6   Conclusion

In this paper, we propose an innovative slide-window-based XML parser accelerator. The key idea is that SWXPA operates one delimiting character per cycle while for valid data, SWXPA operates more than one characters (at most 4) in a single cycle, which exploits data-level parallelism to a great extent. This is achieved by the slide window technology introduced in previous section. The SWXPA is implemented on a Virtex-6 FPGA board and achieves a throughput of 0.33 CPB and 3.0 Gbps, which is a significant improvement compared with other hardware XML parser.

Acknowledgement. This work is supported by the National Science Foundation of China (Grant No. 61373032), and the Science and Technology Commission of Shanghai Municipality (Grant No. 13511500200).

References

1. Apparao, P., Bhat, M.: A Detailed Look at the Characteristics of XML Parsing. In: Proceedings of the 1st Workshop on Building Block Engine Architectures for Computers and Networks (2004)
2. Nicola, M., John, J.: XML parsing: A Threat to Database Performance. In: Proceedings of the 12th International Conference on Information and Knowledge Management (2003)
3. Zhao, L., Bhuyan, L.: Performance Evaluation and Acceleration for XML Data Parsing. In: Proceedings of the 9th Workshop on Computer Architecture Evaluation using Commercial Workloads (2006)
4. Xiaoji, L., Jianqiang, S., Jinbao, C.: VTD-XML-Based Design and Implementation of GML Parsing Project. In: IEEE International Conference on Information Engineering and Computer Science (2009)
5. Cameron, R.D., Amiri, E., Herdy, K.S., Lin, D., Shermer, T.C., Popowich, F.P.: Parallel Scanning with Bitstream Addition: An XML Case Study. In: Jeannot, E., Namyst, R., Roman, J. (eds.) Euro-Par 2011, Part II. LNCS, vol. 6853, pp. 2–13. Springer, Heidelberg (2011)
6. Dan, L., Medforth, N., Herdy, K.S., et al.: Parabix: Boosting the Efficiency of Text Processing on Commodity Processors. In: IEEE 18th International Symposium on High Performance Computer Architecture (2012)
7. Moscola, J., Cho, Y.H., Lockwood, J.W., et al.: A Reconfigurable Architecture for Multi-Gigabit Speed Content-Based Routing. In: The 14th IEEE Symposium on High-Performance Interconnects (2006)
8. Chang, C.E., Mohd-Yasin, F., Mustapha, A.K.: RBStreX: Hardware XML Parser for Embedded System. In: IEEE International Conference for Internet Technology and Secured Transactions (2009)
9. Dai, Z., Ni, N., Zhu, J.: A 1 Cycle-Per-Byte XML Parsing Accelerator. In: Proceedings of the 18th Annual ACM/SIGDA International Symposium on Field Programmable Gate Arrays (2010)
10. Jianliang, M., Zhang, S., Hu, T., et al.: Parallel Speculative Dom-based XML Parser. In: IEEE 14th International Conference on High Performance Computing and Communication & 2012 IEEE 9th International Conference on Embedded Software and Systems (2012)

Design of Fully Pipelined Dual-Mode Double Precision Reduction Circuit on FPGAs

Song Guo, Yong Dou, and Yuanwu Lei

National Laboratory for Parallel and Distribution Processing,
National University of Defense Technology,
Deya Road, 109#, Changsha, 410073, P. R. China
{songguo,yongdou,yuanwulei}@nudt.edu.cn

Abstract. This paper proposes a fully pipelined dual-mode double precision floating-point reduction circuit on the field programming gate arrays (FPGAs), which is capable of supporting one double-precision operation and two parallel single-precision operations. Through the combination of tree-traversal structure and striding mode structure, the reduction circuit can handle multiple data sets with arbitrary combination of different lengths without stall and buffer requirements, and generate in-order results. Experimental results show that the proposed reduction circuit can support the dual-mode double precision floating-point reduction at the cost of only 7% increment in the absolute latency for the double precision vector with the same length, compared with the previous single-mode double precision reduction circuits.

Keywords: dual-mode double precision, reduction circuit, multiple data sets, FPGA.

1 Introduction

Mixed precision iterative refinement, first introduced in [1] for linear solvers, has been used to improve the solutions' performance for many years, which can achieve the accuracy of higher precision data formats using the computation of lower precision formats. The vector reduction is one of the most used operations in the mixed precision iterative refinement and it can be defined as $y = x_0 + x_1 + \cdots + x_n$, where x_i is the ith element of an input vector with n elements. The common ways to support mixed-precision operation are to implement different precision floating-point arithmetic units on the FPGA chip or on FPGA and CPU separately, which result in the excessive redundant resource and communication overhead to degrade the performance.

It is advisable to design the arithmetic units supporting multiple-precision operations. In this paper, it is studied that the high performance implementation of a dual-mode double precision reduction circuit.

The most significant challenge to optimize the reduction circuit on FPGAs is the data hazard resulting from the deeply-pipelined design. For an L-stage pipelined

W. Xu et al. (Eds.): NCCET 2014, CCIS 491, pp. 118–125, 2015.

accumulator, one new item x_i has to wait for L-cycle latency until the partial sum of previous items is valid. Especially, when multiple data sets are to be reduced, there may be items from different data sets coexisting in the pipeline of the reduction circuit, and they should be distinguished to gain the correct results. Improper design will introduce the pipeline stall and consume more resources to store the partial sums, which results in the degradation of the performance and the wastage of the resource.

Up to now, many approaches have been proposed to design high performance reduction circuit, but most of these works are only for specific precision, and have many disadvantages, such as the number limitation of data sets, pipeline stall, buffer requirements, and out-of-order results. In this paper, we propose a fully-pipelined dual-mode double precision reduction circuit, which can deal with one double-precision or two parallel single-precision reduction operations. Through the combination of tree-traversal and striding mode, the reduction circuit can handle multiple data sets with arbitrary combination of different lengths without stall and buffer requirement, and generate in-order results. Experimental results show that the proposed reduction circuit can support the dual-mode double precision floating-point reduction at the cost of only 7% increment in the absolute latency for the double precision vector with the same length, compared with the previous single-mode double precision reduction circuits.

The remainder of this paper is organized as follows: the state-of-the-art FPGA designs of floating-point reduction circuit are briefly reviewed in Section II. Section III presents the architecture of the reduction circuit proposed in this paper, and the core component, dual-mode double precision adder, is illustrated in Section IV. The performance evaluation and comparison is presented in Section V. Finally, a conclusion is given in Section VI.

2   Related Work

There has been a substantial body of work in the literature to implement the high performance floating-point reduction circuit on FPGAs. However, only a few works focus on the multi-precision design [2][3][4], which are only for single data set or fixed-point format. Most of the works are optimized for double precision, which can be mainly divided into two groups from the perspective of the implementation structure.

The first one is based on the tree-traversal structure, in which the vector can be accumulated by a binary adder tree and its variants. G. R. Morris, *et al.* [5] employed a binary tree accumulator for the reduction operations, but the buffer size depends on the number and length of data sets. By replacing the redundant adders with buffers, Ling Zhuo, *et. al.* [6] proposed a scalable, stall-free floating-point reduction circuit, but the vector-length-specific buffer size and out-of-order results limits its use. Furthermore, the vector length is limited to be the power of 2. Ling Zhuo, *et al.* [7] proposes the Fully Compacted Binary Tree (FCBT) design that can reduce multiple data sets with only two floating-adders. But the buffer size required depends on the length of the data set. Yigang Tai, et al. [8] proposed a vector reduction unit with the delay buffer to store the input elements or the intermediate partial sums. But the out-of-order output make it specific for matrix operations. Miaoqing Huang, *et al.* [9] proposed a novel and modular architecture for the fully-pipelined reduction circuits, however it needs trivial storage requirement and dedicated control logic.

Another is based on the striding structure. In this group, the input vector is firstly segmented into L partial sums through an L-stage pipelined floating-point adder, and finally these partial sums are accumulated to gain the scalar result. Ling Zhuo, *et al.* proposed two striding-mode reduction circuits, Single Strided Adder (SSA) and Dual Strided Adder (DSA), to reduce multiple input sets of arbitrary sizes without pipeline stall. But the complex implementation of DSA limits its clock speed, and the SSA requires the largest buffer size. Meanwhile, the out-of-ordered result make them inappropriateness for the general case [7]. Krishna K. Nagar, *et al.* developed a double-precision floating-point accumulator with only one adder coupled to external buffering and control to dynamically schedule the inputs to the adder. However, the out-of-order output limits its broad usability [10].

3   The Overall Architecture of the Reduction Circuit

In this section, we give an in-depth insight into the overall structure of the fully-pipelined dual-mode double precision reduction circuit. As shown in Fig.1, the reduction circuit is mainly divided into two modules, accumulator and summator. The elements in the vector are streamed into the accumulator module and accumulated into L partial sums in the striding mode, where L is the pipeline stage of the adder. When the last item in the vector is accepted, the partial sums are fed into the summator module to gain the final result, and meanwhile the accumulator module can receive the elements from the new vectors.

As shown in Fig.1, the accumulator module consists of one pipelined adder. The items of the vector are streamed into the accumulator module one-by-one through the *op_in* port, and when the last item is received, the *op_last* is set, which travels down through the pipeline registers to mark the last item. The item is added to either the partial sum or zero depending on if the partial sum of the same data set with *op_in* is valid. This selection is realized using a 2-to-1 multiplexer with the signal *sel*, one for partial sum, otherwise for zero. The signal *sel* is obtained through *av* AND *ES*, where the *av* indicates the valid of the partial sum and the *ES* indicates the end of the data set. When the *ES* is set, the partial sums are no longer fed back, and fed into the summator module. The accumulator module can receive the new elements from other data vectors.

The summator module consists of $\lceil \log_2 L \rceil$ adders to form an adder chain, which add up the partial sums to generate the final output *result*. The adder chain is operated in a data-driven way. For each adder in the adder-chain, the first operand is registered in the register *rin* until the second operand is valid, and then the two operands are pushed into the corresponding adder. Note that for the single-precision mode, the elements arrive in pairs, and the zero-padding element is required, when the length of the data set is odd.

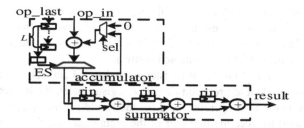

Fig. 1. Overall Architecture of the Proposed Reduction Circuit

C	X	A	S	REG	C	X	A	S	REG
1	X_0	X_0+0			9				X_0+X_4
2	X_1	X_1+0			10			$X0+X4+X1+X_5(1)$	
3	X_2	X_2+0			11				X_2+X_6
4	X_3	X_3+0			12			$X_2+X_6+X_3+X_7(1)$	
5	X_4	X_0+X_4			13				
6	X_5	X_1+X_5			14				$X_0+X_4+X_1+X_5$
7	X_6	X_2+X_6			15				$X_0+X_4+X_1+X_5$
8	X_7	X_3+X_7			16			$X_0+X_1+\cdots+X_7(2)$	

C: clock cycle   A: Accumulator   S: Summator

Fig. 2. Example of eight double precision input data elements on $L=4$

Fig.2 shows an example how the reduction circuit works from the aspect of the data present at the entry of the operator pipeline. At the first four cycles, the elements X_i are added up with zero. In the following four cycles, the partial sums X_i (i=0,1,2,3) are valid and fed back to add up with the new inputs X_i (i=4,5,6,7). After the last element X_7 enters the pipeline, the results out of the adder are fed into the summator module. The accumulator module is free and can receive elements from new vectors. In the summator module, after one clock cycle of the valid of the first operands (X_0+X_4), the two operands (X_0+X_4 and X_1+X_5) are fed into the first adder of the adder chain. At the 14th clock cycle, the sum ($X_0+X_4+X_1+X_5$) is valid, and stored into register until the sum ($X_2+X_6+X_3+X_7$) is valid at the 16th clock cycle. The two sums are fed into the second adder in the adder chain, and the final result is obtained four clock cycles later.

4   Dual-Mode Double Precision Floating-Point Adder

In this section, the architecture of the dual-mode double precision floating-point adder is presented, and then the performance is analyzed in detail.

4.1   The Architecture of Dual Mode Double Precision Floating-Point Adder

As shown in the Fig.3, an IEEE binary floating-point number consists of three fields: a sign S, a biased exponent E and a mantissa M. The sign is 1-bit for all formats. The number of bits in the exponent is 8 and 11, and the number of bits in the mantissa is 23 and 52 for single and double precision numbers, respectively. Note that only normalized data format is supported in this paper.

The architecture of the dual-mode double precision adder is shown in Fig.4, which is mainly divided into four stages: *Seg*, *MA*, *MADD*, and *Normal*. In order to support dual-mode double precision operations, the adder is segmented by the precision-based multiplexers and attached by the duplicated hardware.

As shown in Fig. 4(a), four 32-bit registers (R1, R2, R3 and R4) are used to store the operands. For the double-precision case, two register pairs, R1-R2 and R3-R4, are used to store the two 64-bit operands, and for the single-precision case, the registers R1 and R3 are used to store the first pair of the input data, and the left two registers are used to store the second pair of input data.

In the *Seg* phase (Fig.4(a)), the signs, exponents and mantissas of single- or double- precision floating-point numbers are extracted, and the correct ones are selected by four multiplexers based on the type of the operands, which is either double or single precision, indicated by the signal *ps*. The *Exp_Cal0* unit (Fig.4(b))is used to calculate the exponent difference for the double-precision data and the first pair of single precision data, where the most significant bit $S(M)$, resulting from the subtraction of the exponents of the input operands, is used to select the bigger exponent as the exponent of the result.. The *Exp_Cal1* is responsible for the calculation of the exponent difference for the second pair of single-precision data.

In the *MA* phase (Fig.4(c)), the mantissa of the operand with the smaller exponent is shifted to the alignment position with the other operand according to the exponent difference calculated by the *Exp_Cal* units.

In the *MADD* phase (Fig.4(c)), the aligned mantissas are multiplexed by the *ps*, and then fed into three 32-bit adders to implement the mantissas addition. In the double-precision case, the three adders work in the *carry-select* way. The *adder0* is used for addition of the lower 32 bits, and the *adder1* and *adder2* are used to implement the addition of left parts with the carry is 1 and 0 respectively. The results are selected by the carry bit out of the *adder0*. In the single-precision case, the adder0 and adder2 are used to implement the two mantissas addition in parallel.

As shown in Fig. 4(d), the final phase, *Norm*, consists of leading-zero-detecting (LZD for short), normalization, and rounding. The data path is duplicated to process the two single-precision operations in parallel. The LZD counts the leading zero by segments in parallel, and then adds the numbers of zero together. The norm unit is used to normalize the partial sum according to the number of the leading zero. The rounding unit adopts the near-even strategy to get the final mantissa. Finally, one double-precision sum or two single-precision sums can be gained through the *result1* and *result2* ports.

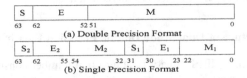

Fig. 3. The Dual-Precision Format

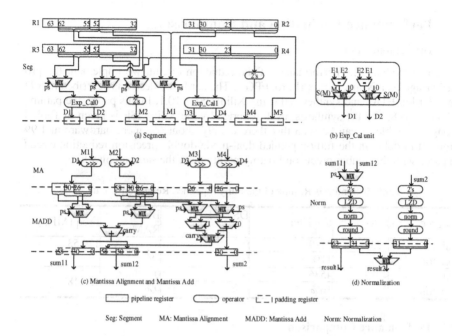

Fig. 4. Architecture of Dual-Mode Double Precision Adder

4.2   Performance Analysis

To quantitatively study the performance of the proposed reduction circuit, the reduction of a vector with n double-precision floating-point items is taken as an example. As addressed in section III, the clock cycles spent can be breakdown into two parts: the first one spent on the accumulating procedure (the first item in the formula (1)), and the second one spent on the summator procedure (the left items in the formula (1)).

Given the first part, when the length n is less than the L, it is dominated by the pipeline stage of the adder. Otherwise, it is dominated by the time spent on the items reading. The second part is much more complicated resulting from the waiting for the second operand of the adder in the adder chain. Most of the time is spent on the three pipelined adders. When the length n is greater than 4, the waiting will occur in all the three stage of the adder chain, so the clock cycles are constant. Otherwise, the waiting cycles depend on the stages where waiting occurs.

$$
cycle = \begin{cases} L + \lceil \log_2 L \rceil \times L & n = 1 \\ L + \lceil \log_2 L \rceil \times L + \sum_{i=0}^{\lceil \log_2 n \rceil - 1} 2^i & 2 \le n < L \\ n + \lceil \log_2 L \rceil \times L + \sum_{i=0}^{\lceil \log_2 L \rceil - 1} 2^i & n \ge L \end{cases} \tag{1}
$$

5   Performance Evaluation and Comparison

5.1   Implementation

In order to evaluate the performance of the reduction circuit, we implement the proposed design on a Xilinx Virtex II Pro. FPGA. The hardware design is described in RTL using Verilog HDL, and synthesized using Xilinx ISE v10.1. In this paper, the parameter L is set to 8, and the synthesis result reported by the Xilinx ISE is given in Table I. Through the table, it can be seen that there is only about 6% more hardware and 9% increment in delay in the fully-pipelined dual-mode double precision reduction circuit, compared with the double-precision floating-point one of the same architecture.

Table 1. Synthesis Results of the Fully Pipelined Reduction Circuit

Resource	Slice	Register	DSP48E1s	Block RAMs	Freq (MHz)
Double Precision	3239 23%	3119 11%	0 0%	0 0%	170.53
Dual Precision	4083 29%	4536 16%	0 0%	0 0%	155.18

5.2   Performance Comparison

The performance comparison of the proposed dual-mode double precision with the previous works is provided in Table II. In order to perform a fair comparison, a single 128-item double-precision floating-point vector is taken as the test bench. Compared with FCBT, DSA, SSA, AeMFPA, and MS DB, our reduction circuits are able to eliminate the use of Block RAMs at the cost of a slight increase in slices resource. From the perspective of the *Freq* column and *Total Latency* column, although the proposed design does not have the highest frequency, the absolute latency only increases 7%, compared with the least one. This mainly results from the dedicated self-design high-performance reduction architecture and floating-point adder component.

Table 2. Performance comparison of SSL protocol

Design	Adders	Slices	BRAM	Freq (MHz)	Total Latency		Slices × µs
					cycles	µs	
Ours	**4**	**4083**	**0**	**155**	**159**	**1.026**	**4189**
PCBT[3]	7	6808	-	165	226	1.370	9327
FCBT[3]	2	2859	10	170	≤475	≤2.794	7988
DSA[3]	2	2215	3	142	232	1.634	3619
SSA[3]	1	1804	6	165	≤520	≤3.152	5686
MFPA[5]	5	4991	2	207	198	0.957	4776
AeMFPA[5]	2	3130	14	204	198	0.970	3036
A²eMFPA[5]	2	3737	2	144	198	1.370	5120
MS DB[4]	1	1749	6	188	230	1.224	2139

6   Conclusion

A fully-pipelined dual-mode double precision floating-point reduction circuit is proposed in this paper, which is capable of supporting one double precision operation or two parallel single precision operations. Through combining the tree-traversal structure and striding structure, the reduction circuit can handle with multiple data sets with arbitrary combination of different lengths without the pipeline stall and buffer requirement, and generate in-order results. Experimental results show that the proposed reduction circuit can support the dual-mode double precision floating-point reduction at the cost of only 7% increment in the absolute latency for the double precision vector with the same length, compared with the previous single-mode double precision reduction circuits.

Acknowledgments. This work was supported by the National High Technology Research and Development Program of China under No.2012AA012706.

References

1. Bowdler, H., Martin, R., Peters, G., Wilkinson, J.: Handbook Series Linear Algebra: Solution of Real and Complex Systems of Linear Equations. Numerisc He Math. 8, 217–234 (1966)
2. Wang, X., Leeser, M.: VFloat: A Variable Precision Fixed- and Floating-Point Library for Reconfigurable Hardware. ACM Transactions on Reconfigurable Technology and Systems 3(3) (2010)
3. Neelima, K., Bharathi, M.: An algorithm for FPGA based Implementation of Variable Precision MAC unit for High Performance Digital FIR Filters. International Journal of Engineering Research and Applications 2, 670–673 (2012)
4. Tan, D., Danysh, A., Liebelt, M.: Multiple-Precision Fixed-Point Vector Multiply-Accumulator Using Shared Segmentation. ARITH 16, 12–19 (2003)
5. MoMorris, G.R., Prasanna, V.K., Anderson, R.D.: A Hybrid Approach for Mapping Conjugate Gradient onto an FPGA-Augmented Reconfigurable Supercomputer. In: Proceedings of the 14th Annual IEEE Symposium on Field-Programmable Custom Computing Machines, FCCM 2006, pp. 3–12. IEEE Computer Society, Washington, DC (2006)
6. Zhuo, L., Morris, G.R., Prasanna, V.K.: Designing Scalable FPGA-Based Reduction Circuits Using Pipelined Floating-Point Cores. In: Proceedings of IEEE 19th International Parallel and Distributed Processing Symposiums (IPDPS 2005) (April 2005)
7. Zhuo, L., Morris, G.R., Prasanna, V.K.: High-Performance Reduction Circuits Using Deeply Pipelined Operators on FPGAs. IEEE Transactions on Parallel and Distributed Systems 18(10), 1377–1392 (2007)
8. Tai, Y.-G., Lo, C.-T.D., Psarris, K.: Accelerating Matrix Operations with Improved Deeply Pipelined Vector Reduction. IEEE Transactions on Parallel and Distributed Systems 23(2), 202–210 (2012)
9. Huang, M., Andrews, D.: Modular design of fully pipelined reduction circuits on fpgas. IEEE Transactions on Parallel and Distributed Systems (2012)
10. Nagar, K.K., Bakos, J.D.: A Sparse Matrix Personality for the Convey HC-1. In: Proceeding of IEEE 19th Symposium on Field Programmable Custom Computing Machines (FCCM 2011), pp. 1–8 (2011)

Design of Cloud Server Based on Godson Processors

Chaoqun Sha[1], Gongbo Li[2,3], Chenming Zheng[1], Yanping Gao[2,4],
Xiaojun Yang[5], and Chungjin Hu[1]

[1] School of Computer and Communication Engineering, University of Science and Technology
Beijing, Beijing 100083, P.R.China
{scq,zhengcm}@sugon.com, matt.sha@gmail.com
[2] Institute of Computing Technology, Chinese Academy of Sciences, Beijing 100190,
P.R.China
[3] University of Chinese Academy of Science Beijing 100190, P. R. China
ligongbo12@mails.ucas.ac.cn, athene@ict.ac.cn
[4] Loongson Technology Co., Ltd. Beijing 100195, P.R.China
[5] Dawning Information Industry Co., Ltd. Beijing 100193, P.R.China
yangxj@sugon.com

Abstract. Compared with the existing cloud computing systems based on high-performance processors and traditional Ethernet network, a 32 Godson processors cloud computing system based on HyperTransport switch (HT switch) is presented in this paper, which uses HT switch as its interconnection fabric. HT switch makes it possible to build a high performance-cost ratio, and high performance-watt ratio cloud server based on Godson processors, to better meet the requirements of cloud computing workloads. As a key interconnection fabric used to construct the cloud server, the HT switch architecture is discussed in details. To evaluate the performance of HT switch-based multiprocessor systems, a prototyping system followed by results of performance testing is implemented.

Keywords: cloud server, Godson processors, HyperTransport, HT switch.

1 Introduction

Cloud computing systems have been playing an important role in data center. The traditional server systems are cluster of server nodes the dedicated local storage and connected over an Ethernet network. These server nodes use their directed-attached-storage as scratch/swap space and use a storage server on the Ethernet network for primary storage. In the cloud era, on one hand, optimized TCO, compute efficiency, and fastest growing server segment will grow to dominate the server. On the other hand, cloud deployment models, big data analytics, and data center virtualization are driving highly evolving parallelized workloads. The servers in large scale data centers require high performance-cost ratio and performance-watt ratio. Furthermore, Rapid growth in dense compute shows dense compute clusters are future of volume servers.

W. Xu et al. (Eds.): NCCET 2014, CCIS 491, pp. 126–139, 2015.
© Springer-Verlag Berlin Heidelberg 2015

The cloud server deployed in data center includes off-chip multiprocessor systems and chip multiprocessor systems. With the development of multi-core processor technology, the above two kinds of multiprocessor systems can coexist in cluster systems. The appreciable distinction between them is that they belong to different layers of interconnection fabric. As the high-efficiency cloud computing systems designers, we lay a strong emphasis on the researches on off-chip multiprocessor systems. Off-chip multiprocessor system has been around since the first supercomputers were constructed [1]. Conventional multiprocessing puts all of the processors on a circuit board and lets them communicate through a type of off-chip interconnect, such as traditional bus, and so on. The traces that make up this board-level connection, though, are many centimeters long and therefore must be clocked conservatively. At present, some processors have integrated on-die memory controller and HyperTransport (HT) links. All these features not only make the processor a flexible, modular, and easily connectable component for various multiprocessor configurations, but also make it feasible to construct the dense cloud server through a novel off-chip interconnect such as HyperTransport switch (HT switch).

The remainder of the paper is organized as follows. Section 2 briefly introduces the research background. Section 3 details the cloud server based on HT switch. Section 4 presents the architecture of HT Switch. A resulting prototype system is discussed in Section 5 together with the performance and the evaluation. Finally, section 6 concludes the paper and looks into future work.

2   Background

Conducted under the technologies of processors, interconnection and cloud computing workloads, we enable the research on the cloud server. The goal is to solve how to use the high performance-cost ratio, performance-watt ratio, and national security processor to build an efficient cloud server for data center.

2.1   Godson Processers Overview

Microprocessor technology is one of key technologies in IT industry, which plays an important role in the development of social economy and national security. Over the past decade, China has made great achievements in developing advanced microprocessors that meet the requirements of both civilian and security applications. Godson processors, designed by Institute of Computing Technology, Chinese Academy of Sciences, is very successful one among them. In 2010, the first multi-core CPU product in China, Godson-3A, was successfully fabricated in a 65nm CMOS process [2][3]. Godson-3A is a 64-bit MIPS64 compatible CPU consisting of four GS464 cores as Figure 1 shown [4]. Godson-3A power is about 15 Watts.

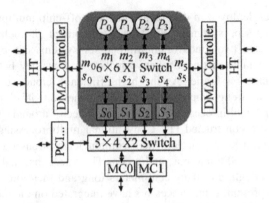

Fig. 1. Godson-3A processor architecture

The statistics illustrates that Godson-3A processors are widely used in processor family in China. The reason that systems designers have an affinity for Godson-3A processors is its innovative scalable multi-core architecture with hardware support for accelerating applications including x86 emulation. On the other hand, Godson-3A is famous for its high performance-cost ratio, performance-watt ratio, general-purpose orientation, and good ecosystem.

In fact, Godson-3A processor is a general-purpose processor with an on-die DDR3 memory controller and two HT controllers for glue-less multiprocessing. All these unique features make Godson-3A processor a great processor for cloud computing applications. HT technology defines a high-performance and scalable interconnect between processor, memory, and I/O devices [5][6]. Godson-3A extends the standard HT protocol to transfer cache coherence information across chips. The cache coherent AXI package can be packaged to HT transactions by HT controller on the sending chip, then the HT transactions are transferred to other chip through HT link, and finally these HT transactions are recovered to cache coherent AXI package by HT controller on the receiving chip. Large Cache-Coherent Non Uniform Memory Access (CC-NUMA) system can be built with Godson-3 through the hierarchical directory extension technology. The bit vector directory in each L2 cache block can treat a HT controller as a virtual core, and the HT controller can be the agent of other chips for remote memory access request.

The point-to-point HT links let Godson-3A processor connect to neighboring Godson-3A processors and other HT devices without additional support chips, and support flexible, configurable, and scalable I/O topologies using chains of I/O Tunnel and Cave devices. The low latency, chip-to-chip, and beyond interconnect HT protocol has been continuing its role as a high-performance processor interconnect, which allows the construction of larger HT fabrics. HT makes it possible to construct the efficient cloud server.

HT was originally defined as a host-centric, daisy-chained topology, with all traffic flowing from peripherals to the central processor and back. Now the specification has been expanded to allow a switch-based topology, which is most efficient for connection of multiple processors.

2.2   Motivation and Design Options

Server products based on Godson-3A processors have been developed by Dawning Information Industry Co., Ltd., such as TC2600, TC3600, and TC4600 [7]. They are all two-way servers, targeted for the high performance computing workloads, not very efficient for the cloud computing workloads. Moreover, they do not meet the requirements of high performance-price ratio, performance-watt ratio, and high density. In view of the Godson-3A processor architecture and its HT interconnects technology, a high efficient cloud server based on Godson-3A Processors is presented as Figure 2 shown, depending on the developed HT switch.

Godson-3A processors are the three series of Godson processor family. Their distinction is derived from their HT link protocols. The two HT links of Godson-3A series processors are not cHT. This means that they can not direct connect each other to construct SMP system, but its prices is the cheapest than other series. Godson-3A series processors can be used to connect I/O device such as HT I/O Hub. Based on HT switch technology to be presented in the followings and processors with noncoherent HT links integrated (e.g. Godson-3A series processors), the high performance-cost ratio cloud server will be built.

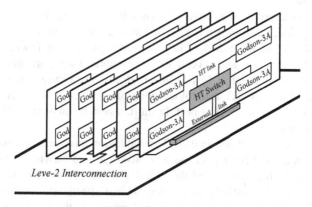

Fig. 2. Gogson-3A based cloud Serve

3   Cloud Server Based on HT Switch

The cloud server is different from some existing systems. Firstly, HT switch architecture is different. Secondly, the difference HT switch architecture decides the difference multiple processor system architecture based on them. The cloud server based on HT switch would be discussed in the followings. Each processor with its peripheral devices is an independent node, which has itself memory and I/O resources, and runs an independent OS. The cloud server lets all of processors communicate through a type of off-chip HT switch, which provides lowest possible latencies and highest throughputs.

3.1   Related Work

The HT specification revision 1.05 defines a HT switch to allow more powerful multi-processing capability [8]. A HT I/O switch can handle multiple HT I/O data streams and manage the interconnection between attached HT I/O devices. A multiport HT switch could aggregate data from multiple downstream ports into a single high speed uplink, or it can route port-to-port connections.

The HT switch function enables the connection of virtually unlimited numbers of HT devices. In addition, by switching traffic locally, the HT switch reduces latency and potential bandwidth logjams. The switch definition supports the concatenation of multiple width buses that in turn allows system designers to apply just the right amount of bandwidth in a particular section of a design. This in turn reduces overall system cost while maintaining maximum chip-to-chip I/O bandwidth. With logical partitioning and reset isolation, switch fabric fail-over is supported resulting in more robust systems. Logically, a switch appears to the system as a tree of PCI-compatible devices and bridges. A given switch can be partitioned to support several separate trees. The general model for HT switch is a set of primary ports interconnected with a set of 'n' secondary ports. Primary ports are HT Tunnel/Cave interfaces. Secondary ports are HT Host interface.

A HT switch is a multi-point, crossbar switch that, from the Host's point of view, looks like a very fast, multi-port bridge. The bus is actually a virtual PCI bus, which can support multiple chains of devices in a tree topology. Within a switch, there must be at least one Primary port and several secondary ports. Each port appears from the CPU side as a two-tiered set of PCI-to-PCI bridges with a virtual, high-throughput internal PCI bus. From the HT technology point of view, each Secondary port looks like the Master HT technology Host port. In short, a switch can be thought of as a host port multiplier/replicator.

At present, HT switch defined in the HT specification has been developed by some corporations such as API NetWorks Inc.'s AP4041 [9] and Newisys, Inc.'s HORUS [10]. API NetWorks Inc. announced the industry's first HT switch, the AP4041 on November 5, 2001. The AP4041 is a 4-way switch specifically optimized for HT designs. The AP4041 has, as part of its compliance with the HT specification, the ability to be daisy chained with up to 32 other devices.

Newisys, Inc., a sanmina-SCI company, achieved HORUS chip in September, 2004. HORUS extends every glue-less SMP feature of Opteron processors to multiple quads. HORUS lets server vendors design up to 32-way Opteron systems. HORUS is the only chip that targets Opteron processors in an SMP implementation. The HORUS chip has four cHT links and three remote links. The remote links provide interconnection between the quads. The HORUS CC protocol is limited up to eight quads (32 sockets total).

In summary, AP4041 and HORUS have respective different architectures and usages. The AP4041, as part of its compliance with the HT specification, is mainly used to extending I/O device. Since data stream can not be forwarded between primary ports, the HT switch model defined in HT specification such as AP4041 can not be used to build a cloud server. HORUS merges multiple 4-way Opteron systems into a larger, low latency cache coherence system. HORUS is a cHT switch in the 4-way Opteron system. HORUS does not meet the demands of our original motivation, to build a cloud server based on processors with noncoherent HT links integrated, as illuminated in Section 2.

3.2   Basic Architecture

HT has the two key characteristics important to a processor interconnect: high bandwidth and low latency. That is well beyond what is possible with previous bus-based microprocessor interfaces, such SysAD for MIPS processors and MPX for Motorola processors. And because HT is a point-to-point link, rather than a shared bus topology, overall latency is significantly reduced. As for momentum, HT has the advantage of being available on processors here and now. HT has become the processor interconnection point for AMD, many MIPS-based processors, as well as some graphics and security processors, and there are plans to extend it further. Figure 3 shows an original architecture of cloud server based on a novel HT switch topology to be exploited in Section 4.

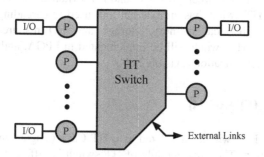

Fig. 3. HT switch-based cloud computing systems

The main features of the cloud server based on HT switch are shown as follows.

- The system is a cluster. Each processor with its peripheral devices in the system is an independent node, which has itself memory and I/O resources, and run an independent OS.
- The HT links, interconnects between processor and HT switch, are noncoherent HT links.
- Not maintain cache coherency among cluster nodes.
- As an optional item, HT switch has an external link to direct connect cascade switches.

Now Godson-3A processors are ideal to build a cloud server based on HT switch, but not limited to them, any high-performance general-purpose processor having the following features can be used in the cloud server, such as on-die memory controller, noncoherent HT links, multi-core processor technology, and low power.

The address space management of the cloud server is that each node, besides its local address space, has another global address window in the global address space.

In order to efficiently exploit the high performance of the cloud server based on HT switch, it is essential to develop user-level protocols, which can achieve high bandwidth and low latency. Generally, System Area Network (SAN) used in cluster systems has the embedded processors in their NICs, which makes it powerful for the NIC to offload the processing of communication protocol from the host processor [11][12]. As a cloud server, it is essential to develop user-level protocols for the cloud server based on HT switch. In view of the development of chip multiprocessor technology, the better solution is that choosing the multi-core processors as the building blocks of system, and using one core of multi-core processor to offload the processing of communication protocol from the other cores.

3.3   Object Systems

Based on the above-mentioned architecture of cloud server based on HT switch (reference to Section 3), our goal is to build a multiple processors cloud server based on HT switch. The system architecture is shown in Figure 3.

The system includes some building blocks such as Godson-3A processors and a HT switch. The HT links between processor and HT switch are noncoherent HT links. Besides HT links, HT switch has an external link used to cascading switches. Each processor has its self local memory, storage and I/O resources, and run an independent OS. The HT switch will be implemented in FPGA, and its HT links are compliant with HT specification revision 2.00b.

4   Design of HT Switch

A logic module of HT switch, virtualized as a HT Cave (single link end) device, is defined in this section. The logic module of HT switch is different from that of HT protocols [6]. This section describes the functionality and features of HT switch used in cloud server. The external link interface is introduced briefly and is not labeled on relational figures.

4.1   Logic Model

According the Godson-3A processor features, not supporting double-host chains function, a novel logic module of HT switch has been presented for this case [13]. The logic module of HT switch is called virtual HT Cave device. The virtual internal bus is an abstract bus that interconnects all HT Cave interfaces within the switch. The logic model parses the data and determines whether packet coming from source node should be claimed or passed to the destination node.

HT switch contains a register set to control mapping of transactions between processors. According to discussion in Section 3, each node has its exclusive address window in the global physical space. To any node, the global address windows of all nodes in the cloud server are mapped with the memory-mapped I/O space of HT switch.

These address windows are defined in each node's extended configuration space. Read and Write requests are routed based upon these address windows by HT switch crossbar. Response routing is identical for both Read response and TargetDone response. HT switch must maintain a table of outstanding Non-Posted requests that pass through it. Typically, each Non-Posted request that arrives will create an entry in the table storing the original SrcTag, SeqID, UnitID, and ingress port. This allows the switch to reassign these fields to available values on the egress port. When the response to the request arrives, the table is used to match up the new SrcTag with the original request and the response can be forwarded to the original ingress port.

In order to guarantee support for full producer/consumer ordering, the topology and HT switch configuration must guarantee that there must be a single unique path between each pair of ports. HT switch must ensure that merged streams of ordered access are transmitted in consistent ordered sequences.

4.2   HT Switch Architecture

HT switch is a typical, complex network-on-chip system. Figure 4 shows the high-level diagram of 4-way HT switch architecture in part, which is used to construct the cloud server based on HT switch (reference to Section 3).

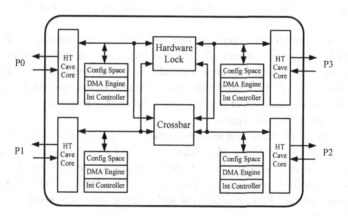

Fig. 4. 4-way HT switch architecture

HT switch is composed of HT Cave Cores and some auxiliary components such as DMA engines, Configuration Space, Interrupt Controllers, Hardware Locks, and so on. They are independent and have uniform internal interface to direct connect crossbar. DMA Engine integrated in HT switch makes it powerful for the cloud server to offload moving large data between nodes from processors. Configuration Space contains all configuration space registers of HT Cave, and handles write requests, read requests and response accesses to it. As a virtual Cave device, HT switch only uses the type 0 configuration header format. Interrupt Controller contains an IOAPIC used to configure interrupt vectors and to generate interrupt packets for processors. Furthermore, Interrupt Controller is responsible for system interrupt events. Hardware

Lock is a key component for the coordinating communication between processors. All the auxiliary components are designed to well support the message passing and data transfer between nodes in the cloud server. HT Cave Core implements HT protocol forwarding the traffic between HT link and internal interface. It can be seen as a tunnel that data passing in and out. HT Cave Core is comparatively independent and integrated IP core in HT interconnects fabric. There are many researches on it, so HT Cave Core is not discussed in this paper [14]. We place our focuses on discussing HT switch, including the following aspects.

- *Packet structure*

Obviously, HT switch packet format is compliant with HT specification. Packets are transmitted over internal interface signals. Except for Nop and Sync/Error, transfer packet types include all surplus HT packet types.

- *Virtual channel set*

Virtual channel set of internal interconnection depends on virtual channel set of HT Cave Core. HT defines a set of three required virtual channels that dictate transaction management and ordering: Posted Requests, Non-Posted Requests and Responses. HT Cave Core is responsible for managing the virtual channels of internal interconnection. Each HT Cave Core implements separate command/data buffers for each of the three required virtual channels. Doing so ensures that transactions moving in one virtual channel do not block transactions moving in another virtual channel.

- *Internal interface protocol*

HT switch uses a modified Altera Atlantic interface as its internal interface. The modification includes show-ahead synchronous mode and simplifying control/status signals. The internal interface is implemented on two unidirectional sets of signals. Each set consists of 128-bit data signals, one Request signal, one ACK signal, one Start of Packet signal, one End of packet signal, and one CLK signal.

- *Crossbar Interconnection system*

The internal interconnection implements high-speed packet transfers between HT Cave interfaces. HT switch has independent crossbar for each virtual channel. When packets are sent over a virtual channel, they are sent in one of the crossbar. The crossbar interconnection system is composed of crossbar links and crossbar interface logic. Crossbar interface logic is compliant with internal interface protocol.

- *Ordering rules*

Ordering rules coverts interactions between the three virtual channels of the same port. Transactions in different ports have no ordering rules. Enforcing ordering rules between transactions in the same port prevents deadlocks from occurring and guarantees data is transferred correctly. HT Cave Core is responsible for enforcing ordering rules of internal interconnection.

- *HT switch arbitration*

Two types of transaction arbitration provide the method for managing isochronous transactions and differentiated services: Virtual Channel Arbitration and Port Arbitration. HT Cave Core is responsible for Virtual Channel Arbitration based on ordering rules. Port Arbitration determines the priority of transactions with the same virtual channel assignment at the egress port, based on the priority of the port at which the transactions arrived. Port Arbitration mechanism is non-configurable hardware-fixed Round Robin arbitration (Equal or Weighted) scheme.

5   Implementation and Evaluation of an Cloud Server Based on HT Switch

In this section, we evaluate the architecture of the cloud server based on HT switch, which is described in Section 3 and 4. A prototyping system followed by results of performance testing is implemented.

5.1   Prototyping Systems

Serving as the primary reference for the cloud server based on HT switch, a HT switch prototyping system is implemented. The prototyping system is composed of three server boards, a 3-way HT switch board and a cascade switch board as Figure 5(a) shown. The server board is a special device used in I/O solutions. As Figure 5 shown, it is composed of a Godson-3A processor and some chipsets such as AMD8131 and AMD8111. AMD8131 is a HT Tunnel. A HT slot, direct connecting AMD8131's side B, is integrated on the motherboard. HT slot features are 8-bit links and transfer rates of 1600, 800, and 400 mega-transfers per second. The functions and architecture of the HT switch chipset are compliant with HT switch definitions in Section 4. The HT switch chipset is implemented in Altera Stratix FPGA. At the moment, each port of HT switch can run at a frequency of up to 400Mhz with a link width of 8 bits supported. The HT switch board integrates the same three HT slots as that of server board. The HT switch board and three server boards are connected together through three HT adapters as Figure 5(a) shown.

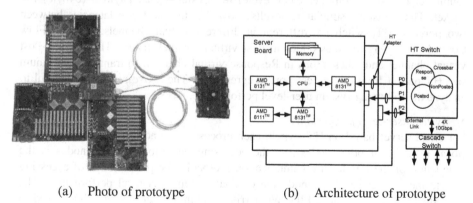

(a)   Photo of prototype   (b)   Architecture of prototype

Fig. 5. Prototyping system

According to the fact that AMD8131 is a HT Tunnel, the prototyping system (as Figure 5 (b) shown) is compliant with the object system (as Figure 3 shown) in functions and architectures. Embedding AMD8131 between processor and HT switch does not change the features of cloud server, excepting for the latency performance reduced a little.

Furthermore, the prototyping system based on multi-board makes use of devices in existence efficiently, avoids the risks of implementation of motherboard, quickens the schedule, and meets the demands of functionality verification and performance evaluation. Based on above analysis, the prototyping system is absolutely competent for the research on the cloud server based on HT switch.

The logic model of HT switch (reference to Section 4) is implemented in FPGA, so HT switch becomes the bottleneck of the cloud server in performances. The HT switch board has three, 8-bit, 400Mhz ports that can give 800Mbyte/s bandwidth in each direction, yielding an aggregate bandwidth of 1.6Gbyte/s per port and 4.8Gbyte/s for the entire device. The links of HT switch are compliant with HT specification revision 1.03.

5.2   Performance Testing and System Evaluating

The performance test of the prototyping system includes two parts: HT switch hardware level performance testing and system user-level performance testing. In view of the bottleneck effect of HT switch in the cloud server, we must obtain the HT switch hardware-level performance before testing system user-level performance so that the latter can be evaluated correctly.

• *HT switch hardware-level performance*
Each HT switch port supports a peak bandwidth of 800Mbyte/s in each direction, but the maximum effective bandwidth of a HT switch port is 533.33Mbyte/s. The maximum effective bandwidth is decided by internal interface protocol and packet routing process. Generally, it takes 6 clock cycles (5 transfer clock cycles and 1 routing clock cycle, 20ns per clock cycle) to transfer a max payload (64byte) HT packet. The statistical simulating results show that the hardware latencies between two ports of HT switch are different in different virtual channels. Without Flow Control generating, it takes 600ns in Post virtual channel, takes 431ns in Non-Post virtual channel and takes 436ns in Response virtual channel, to transfer a minimum size HT packet from the ingress port to egress port. The above results are helpful to analyze the following system user-level performance.

• *System user-level performance*
For cloud server based on HT switch, each processor can access its remote memory (local memory of other nodes), so the accessing operation between nodes is the foundation of the low-level communication protocol. The performance of accessing remote memory can truly embody the optimal system user-level performance. The accessing operation includes PIO, WC (write-combining), and DMA. PIO is used to draw out the system latency information. WC is used to draw out the system bandwidth information under processor controlling. DMA is used to draw out the system bandwidth information under HT switch controlling. The test of the prototyping system is detailed in the followings.

Firstly, when payload is 4bytes, PIO read latency is 1,436ns, and PIO write latency is 1,032ns. According to the above HT switch hardware-level latency testing results, HT switch shares 60 percent of the system user-level latency. Obviously, it is important to reduce the HT switch hardware-level latency. Furthermore, corresponding to PIO read request of any data length, the response data is divided into many response packets, and the payload of each response packet is limited to an unchangeable length (4bytes). PIO write request is as same as PIO read response. The interval between PIO write request packets is shorter than that of PIO read response packet, so increasing of PIO write latency is much slower than that of PIO read latency as Figure 6 (a) shown.

Secondly, the bandwidth testing results as Figure 6 (b) shown. PIO read and PIO write obtain the reasonable user-level bandwidth. As a result of full payload (64byte per packet) and burst transfer (no gap between Write request packets), WC achieves a bandwidth of 533Mbyte/s.

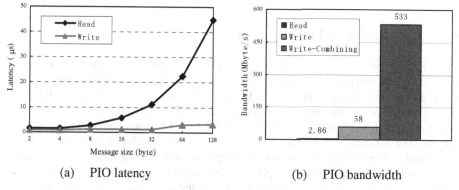

(a)   PIO latency   (b)   PIO bandwidth

Fig. 6. PIO performance

In order to offload data transfer from processors, HT switch integrates an essential auxiliary component called DMA Engine. As two high-speed data transfer modes, DMA and WC bandwidth performance are all limited by the HT switch hardware-level performance. Furthermore, DMA Engine needs a given time to configure and enable, so its bandwidth performance is a little lower than that of WC, as Figure 6(b) and Figure 7 shown.

In summary, the above fundamental testing results are help for the researches on the cloud server based on HT switch. Obviously, HT switch hardware-level performance plays an important role in the cloud server based on HT switch. Improving link frequency of HT switch ports to achieve the port bandwidth matching with that of processors is important to build a high-performance cloud server. If the link frequency is mismatched, the throughput may be noticeable impacted.

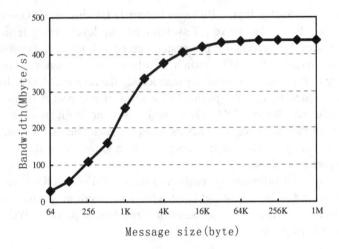

Fig. 7. DMA bandwidth performance

6   Conclusion and Future Work

Processors architecture and key interconnects technologies are crucial foundations to construct cloud computing systems. A logic module of HT switch, virtualized as a HT Cave device, is defined in this paper. Based on the logic module of HT switch, we have explored an architecture that constructs a cloud server. The building blocks of the cloud server based on HT switch include Godson-3A processors and a HT switch chipset. For efficiency, the cloud server based on HT switch has hardware support optimized to handle data moving and interrupt message passing between processors. To evaluate the system, a prototyping system followed by results of performance testing is implemented. This prototyping system serves as the primary reference for the cloud server based on HT switch. The testing results show that the prototyping system obtains reasonable user-level communication performance, and prove that the cloud server architecture, which based on HT switch, is feasible and effective to achieve the cloud server.

We will devote ourselves to the researches on the cloud server based on Godson-3A processors and HT switch, and continue the above-mentioned goal including a 32-CPU server and the communication protocol. On the other hand, Southbridge will be integrated into HT switch to strengthen I/O capabilities, Furthermore, we will keep on looking for the best approaches to improve the performance of HT switch, such as selecting high-performance FPGA or ASIC as the next generation HT switch platforms.

Acknowledgment. The authors thank everyone in the collaboration for their contributions. The work is supported in part by the National High-Tech Research and Development Plan of China under grant numbered 2013AA01A209, and by Beijing City Committee of science and technology plan project numbered D141100003414001.

References

1. Sassone, P.: Commercial trends in off-chip communication, Technical Report, Georgia Institute of Technology (May 2003)
2. Hu, W., Wang, J., Gao, X., Chen, Y., Liu, Q., Li, G.: Godson-3: A Scalable Multicore RISC Processor with x86 Emulation. IEEE Micro 29(2), 17–29 (2009)
3. Gao, X., Chen, Y., Wang, H., Tang, D., Hu, W.: System Architecture of Godson-3 Multi-Core Processors. Journal of Computer Science and Technology 25(2), 181–191 (2010)
4. Hu, W., Gao, Y., Chen, T., Xiao, J.: The Godson Procssors: Its Research, Development, and Contributions. Journal of Computer Science and Technology 26(3), 363–372 (2011)
5. Trodden, J., Anderson, D.: HyperTransport System Architecture, 1st edn. Addison-Wesley Professional (2003)
6. HyperTransport Technology Consortium, HyperTransport I/O Link Specification Revision 3.00, Document #HTC20051212-0046-0008 (2006)
7. Dawning Information Industry Co., Ltd., http://www.sugon.com
8. HyperTransport Technology Consortium, HyperTransport I/O Link Specification Revision 1.05c, Document #HTC2002104-0005-0005 (2003)
9. APINetWorks Inc., Starfish AP4041: 4-Port HyperTransport Switch, datasheet, http://www.mic-roway.com/download/AP4041/AP4041datasheel.pdf
10. Kota, R.: HORUS: Large Scale SMP using AMD Opteron processor, Newisys Inc., A Sanmina-SCI Company, Technical Report (May 2005)
11. Yang, X., Wu, D., Sun, N.: Design of NIC Based on I/O Processor for Cluster Interconnect Network. In: International Conference on Networking, Architecture, and Storage, NAS 2007, Guilin, China, July 29-31, pp. 3–8 (2007)
12. Yang, X., Guo, L.-l., Zhang, P., Sun, N.: Design of system area network interface card based on intel IOP310. In: Wu, Z., Chen, C., Guo, M., Bu, J. (eds.) ICESS 2004. LNCS, vol. 3605, pp. 165–171. Springer, Heidelberg (2005)
13. Yang, X., Chen, F., Cheng, H., Sun, N.: A HyperTransport-Based Personal Parrallel Computer. In: The 2008 IEEE International Conference on Cluster Computing, Tsukuba, Japan, September 29-October 1, pp. 126–132 (2008)
14. Chen, F., Cheng, H., Yang, X., Liu, R.: Design and Implementation of an Effective HyperTransport Core in FPGA. In: The Second International Workshop on High Performance I/O Systems and Data Intensive Computing (HiperIO 2008), Tsukuba, Japan, September 29-October 1, pp. 437–443 (2008)

A New Storage System for Exabytes Storage

Haitao Chen, Jinwen Li, and Wei Zhang

School of Computer, National University of Defense Technology,
Changsha 410073, China
{htchen,jwli,wzhang,ydong}@nudt.edu.cn

Abstract. A novel storage system - NebulaStorage is proposed to solve the storage challenge wall for high performance computer. NebulaStorage designs a new storage architecture in which computing and storage subsystems are loosely coupled. It uses embedded thin storage nodes to build massive storage, and uses software-based erasure code to replace the popular RAID disk array. Simulation tests show that its scalability and fault tolerance ability are better than mainstream luster parallel file system.

Keywords: exabytes storage, high performance computing, storage architecture, erasure code.

1 Introduction

Big data usually comes from the simulation and observation of science, engineering, society and network areas, especially in seismic processing, petroleum exploration, bioinformatics, visual fields. With the more and more emergence of big data, data-intensive application is becoming one of the most important trends of current large-scale parallel applications. Traditional high performance computers were mainly designed for computing-intensive application, so its storage capacity lags far behind the computing and communication capabilities. For example, the average storage bandwidth for each CPU kernel of Tianhe2 supercomputer which is the fastest computer in the world is less than 1MB/S while the storage bandwidth of a home PC with a single disk and four CPU kernels is higher than 80MB/S. Data-intensive parallel applications have much higher requirements for I/O storage bandwidth and storage capacity than computing-intensive parallel applications, so I/O storage wall is becoming a more critical challenge in high performance computing research field. Especially the scalability and reliability of exabytes storage system are big challenges. Large scale storage systems in the future must be able to provide continuous storage service under frequent failures of hardware and software.

Based on the in-depth analysis of related researches, we find that distribution is the key to solve the scalability problem. So we design a new distributed storage architecture which can maximize the localization of I/O requests. The architecture abandons the use of RAID disk array, instead uses software-based distributed erasure codes to tolerate disk failure and dynamically monitor the data health.

W. Xu et al. (Eds.): NCCET 2014, CCIS 491, pp. 140–147, 2015.

2   Related Works

The architecture with independent computing and storage subsystem occupy the current dominance of high performance computing parallel storage areas, in which computing nodes use storage client to access remote shared storage subsystem [1]. The biggest advantage of this architecture is that centralized data storage simplifies storage management, especially for computing-intensive applications.

The architecture with I/O forwarding and buffering layer introduces a middle layer between computing subsystem and storage subsystem. The forwarding capacity is used to merge the I/O requests of computing nodes, reduce the number of directly-connected clients for storage nodes, and decrease the disorderly competition between multi clients. The IBM BlueGene super computer added dedicated I/O forwarding nodes in hardware [2]. The buffering capacity is used to reduce I/O access latency and improve the I/O bandwidth by deploying dedicated nodes with big memory or SSD devices [3]. The Tianhe 2 super computer greatly improved application I/O bandwidth by using SSD as intermediate storage devices.

The architecture with integrated computing and storage dominates cloud computing area[4][5]. It realized localized I/O operations by integrating storage device on the computing nodes. The user tasks can be scheduled on computing nodes with wanted data. This architecture can provide highly concurrent storage services for loosely coupled cloud applications, but it cannot meet the high continuous reading and writing performance requirement for large files, so it isn't approved in the field of high performance computing.

The above three kinds of storage architectures which can cope well with the petabytes storage system, will face great challenges of scalability and fault tolerance if extending to exabytes storage system. Novel parallel storage architecture needs to put more attention on the combination relation of computing node and storage node, and maximize data locality while preserving I/O interfaces.

3   Storage Architecture of NebulaStorage

Designed for storage requirements of extra-scale high performance computer, Nebula storage system is different from the current mainstream storage system in the storage architecture and fault tolerance technology.

3.1   Storage Architecture with Loosely Coupled Computing Nodes and Storage Nodes

Related researches show that high degree of concurrency and access localization are the most important techniques to achieve scalability. High degree of concurrency depends on the storage architecture and advanced scheduling algorithm to eliminate the bottleneck resources, allowing millions of disks to provide data service at the same time. The access localization needs to reduce data access path and data movement overhead.

The architecture with independent computing and storage subsystem is easy to manage. But because all I/O operations are global, it will face severe competition and lock contention under exabytes storage scale. Global metadata server is easy to become a bottleneck resource and data path is too long. The architecture with forwarding and buffering layer eases the pressure of too many clients, but cannot fundamentally solve the problem. This paper proposes a kind of new storage architecture with loosely coupled computing and storage nodes, which can shorten the data access path, reduce the number of concurrent serving clients, make computing nodes get nearby storage service with low latency, as detailed in Figure 1.

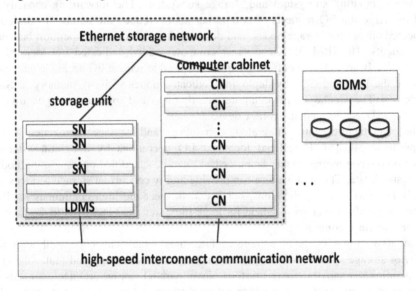

Fig. 1. Hardware components of NebulaStorage. CN is the abbreviation of computing nodes. GDMS is the abbreviation of global data management server. LDMS is the abbreviation of local data management server. SN is the abbreviation of thin storage node.

The storage architecture consists of global data management server, local data management server, thin storage node, storage unit, low speed Ethernet storage network and high-speed interconnect communication network.

A local data management server and a number of thin storage nodes constitute a storage unit. Each storage unit deploys directly in the computer cabinet or nearby several computer cabinet, which provide adjacent storage service for one or several computer cabinet. A combination of all storage units can work as a single image file system and provide global storage service for all nodes.

Computer cabinets and storage units connect via two networks. Low-speed Ethernet storage network is mainly used for computing nodes to access adjacent storage services, while high-speed interconnect communication network is mainly used for connecting computing nodes and accessing global storage service. Storage node is only connected with Ethernet storage network. Local data management server, global data management server and computing nodes are simultaneously connected with two networks.

In this storage architecture, computing nodes will firstly try to access local storage service. It will access global storage service only when the local storage service cannot meet the requirements of I/O requests. Local storage service is provided by adjacent storage unit, so the I/O operation is localized. Global storage service is provided by global data management server, computing nodes can access any remote storage unit by the high-speed interconnect communication network.

3.2   Fault Tolerance Based on Erasure Code

Data from Google shows that disk failure rate is between 1.7% to 8.6% in one year, meaning that average failure interval of EB storage system will less than several hours. A robust massive storage system must work under continuous failure situations. Reliability is the most crucial factor for selection of storage system. Replication-based mechanism has been used to achieve data reliability for Hadoop Distributed File System, but cannot be applied to the EB storage systems due to its huge storage space overhead. RAID redundancy is the most popular technique to deal with disk failure in high performance computing field, but it has several unavoidable disadvantages. One is that failure of a single storage node may lead to global failure. Another is that data recovery time of a single disk failure is linear growth with the disk storage space. For example one disk with 2TB capacity needs several hours to rebuild all data. During the recovery process, storage service may face performance degradation. It is a terrible situation for a massive storage system with too many hard disks.

Mass storage system using RAID technology usually builds with fat storage node which has powerful capacity and can tolerant disk failure. NebulaStorage uses a new design ideas, massive storage capacity is based on aggregate thin storage nodes, which simplifies the design of the storage nodes and reduces the power consumption. The so-called thin storage node refers to the storage nodes using low-power processors and giving up RAID technology. Single thin storage node is small in size and weak in storage performance, but software scheduling based on file and hard disk scale can help reducing disorderly competition between multi I/O requests. Simple logic of thin storage node is easy to manage and facilitates aggregation of multi nodes to meet the high-performance I/O bandwidth requirements of data-intensive parallel application. Nebula storage uses software-based erasure code to distribute one file to several storage nodes. Erasure code is a forward error correction (FEC) code for the binary erasure channel, which transforms a message of k symbols into a longer message (code word) with n symbols such that the original message can be recovered from a subset of the n symbols[6,7,8,9,10]. So NebulaStorage can tolerant concurrent disk and storage node failures, greatly improving storage reliability in similar storage space overhead compared with RAID-based storage system.

One of the most important concerns on the application of erasure code algorithm is about the excessive computational overhead of encoding and decoding. According to our tests, along with the development of multi-core technology, computational overhead of encoding and decoding may not a key problem. The machine for experimentation is a server with two intel XEON E5-4650 CPU which has 8 cores.

We test open source erasure coding library named Jerasure on the server. Jerasure is a C library released in 2007 that supports a wide variety of erasure codes, including RS coding, CRS coding and so on. Only CRS coding is used in test. As can be seen from figure 2 and figure 3, encoding speed is linear growth, a single CPU core can reach a encoding speed not less than 450MB/s, the total encoding speed can exceed 7500 MB/s, decoding speed is linear growth, a single CPU core can reach a decoding speed not less than 1680MB/s, the total decoding speed can exceed 26891 MB/s. It is very clear that the encoding and decoding speed of erasure code is much higher than the reading and writing speed of a single disk. So the computational overhead will not become the bottleneck resource of storage system.

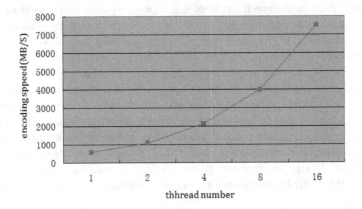

Fig. 2. Encoding performance test of CRS algorithm in Jerasure library. The parameters of CRS alogrithm is k=5, m=3, w=3, packetsize=81920Byte, blocksize=960KByte.

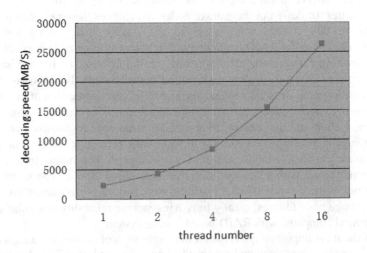

Fig. 3. Deconding performance test of CRS algorithm of Jerasure library. The parameters of CRS alogrithm is k=5, m=3, w=3, packetsize=81920Byte, blocksize=960KByte.

4   Designing and Optimization of NebulaStorage Software Stack

High performance storage software stack is the basic framework of the whole data management system, plays a very important role in the system scalability and aggregation performance. Based on user mode file system interface, this software stack supports function module with plug-ins style, is designed for data-intensive application. The function modules are distributed on computing nodes, global data management server, local data management server and storage node, as detailed in Figure 4.

- I/O request forwarding and client-side cache modules are deployed on computing nodes. I/O request forwarding module is responsible for receiving and forwarding application I/O requests and results, at the same time, high level logic optimization of some I/O requests. Client-side cache module is responsible for accelerating hit I/O requests by maintaining a cache using local memory.
- Global metadata management and load balance modules are deployed on global data management server. Global metadata management is responsible for the management and maintenance of file metadata, providing a global view of storage space for computing nodes. The load balancing module is responsible for monitoring all adjacent storage unit work load, ensuring that all I/O requests are fairly distributed to the adjacent storage units.
- I/O request receiving, I/O request aggregation, local metadata management, data coding and decoding, fault-tolerance management and local data cache modules are deployed on local data management servers. I/O receiving module is responsible for receiving I/O requests from clients and processing according to affinity scheduling algorithm. I/O request aggregation module is responsible for aggregating and compressing multiple I/O requests to reduce the number of I/O operations. Local metadata management is responsible for storing and maintaining metadata of storage unit. Data encoding and decoding module is responsible for the data encoding and decoding operations. Fault-tolerance management module is responsible for periodically checking state of data health and recovering sick data. Local data cache module uses memory and local SSD device to accelerate I/O requests.
- Local storage service module is deployed on storage node. It is responsible for mapping local disk as a storage service. Logic design is simple in order to guarantee the performance and robustness.

Nebula storage software stack use several design optimization to improve performance.

- Lazy single file system image: Normal single file system image means that all storage clients have the same global data view at any time. Nebula storage proposes a kind of lazy single file system image by relaxing consistency time requirements without affecting the application correctness. So global data view and local data view may have inconsistence for a short time. For example, when writing a newly created file, only local computing nodes can see the file. Only when the file is closed, its metadata will be synchronized to the global data management server. After that this file can be seen in global data view. The lazy single file system image can localize and parallel many I/O operations to increase the scalability of the system.

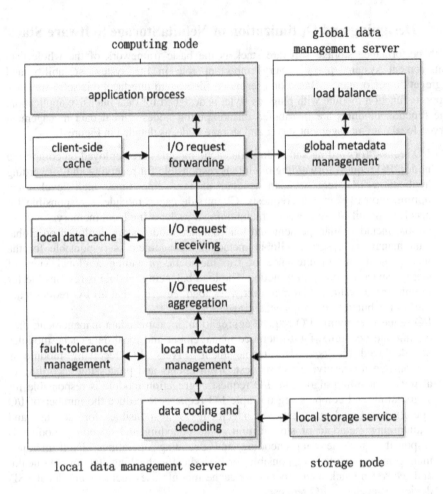

Fig. 4. Nebula storage software stack

- Affinity storage scheduling policy: Due to different distance between computing node and different storage units, the affinity storage scheduling policy try its best to schedule I/O requests to adjacent storage unit and prevent centralized data management server become bottleneck resource. Distributed and localized I/O requests weak the competition from different application process and improve concurrency.
- Adaptive fault management: Original file is erasure coded and distributed to K+M storage nodes, tolerating the failure of any M storage nodes. Each storage node regularly checks the integrity of local data and reports to local data manager server. The local data manger server will manage the health of local files. Only when the degree of data loss is greater than a certain threshold value or a reading request for the data, restore operation will be started.

5   Conclusions

To deal with scalability and fault tolerance challenges of EB storage system, this paper proposes a new architecture with loosely coupled computing and storage nodes. It improves system scalability by maximizing localized I/O operations and parallelizing a large number of I/O operations, reduces the performance degradation caused by the disorderly competition of massive I/O requests. NebulaStorage also uses erasure code instead of RAID to improve reliability without improving storage space overhead. Hardware prototype is under development. Some software test have show a promising future.

References

1. High-performance Storage Architecture and Scalable Cluster File System. Lustre File System White Paper (December 2007)
2. Isaila, F., Garcia Blas, J., Carretero, J., Latham, R., Lang, S., Ross, R.: Latency hiding file I / O for Blue Gene systems. In: 9th IEEE / ACM International Symposium on Cluster Computing and the Grid, CCGrid 2009 (May 2009)
3. Nisar, A., Liao, W., Choudhary, A.: Scaling parallel I / O performance through I / O delegate and caching system. In: Proceedings of the 2008 ACM / IEEE Conference on Super Computing (SC 2008) (November 2008)
4. Ghemawat, S., Gobioff, H., Leung, S.: The Google file system. In: Proceedings of the Nineteenth ACM Symposium on Operating Systems Principles (SOSP 2003) (October 2003)
5. Borthakur, D.: The Hadoop Distributed File System: Architecture and Design. The Apache Software Foundation (2007)
6. Huang, Z., Wang, C., Yuan, Y., Liu, L., Peng, Y.: Improve readability with Exact Hierarchical Codes in Distributed Storage Systems. Information-An International Interdisciplinary Journal 15(11a), 4411–4416 (2012)
7. Gulati, A., Merchant, A., Uysal, M., Varman, P.J.: Efficient and Adaptive Proportional Share I / O Scheduling. In: Proc of Conf. on File and Storage Technologies (FAST 2009) (2009)
8. Xing, J., Xiong, J., Sun, N., Ma, J.: Adaptive and Scalable Metadata Management to Support Trillion Files. In: International Conference for High Performance Computing, Networking, Storage and Analysis, SC 2009 (November 2009)
9. Xianghong, L., Jiwu, S.: Summary of Research for Erasure Code in Storage System. Journal of Computer Research and Development 49(1), 1–11 (2012)
10. Dimakis, A.G., Ramchandran, K., Wu, Y., et al.: A Survey on Network Codes for Distributed Storage. In: Proceedings of the IEEE (March 2011)

A High-Accuracy Clock Synchronization Method in Distributed Real-Time System

Hongliang Li, Xuan Feng, Song Shi, Fang Zheng, and Xianghui Xie

State Key Laboratory of Mathematical Engineering and Advanced Computing, China
hongliangli@263.net

Abstract. Clock synchronization is mostly needed in the distributed real-time system. Currently, the most popular Network Time Protocol (NTP) algorithm cannot meet the needs well due to its low accuracy (about 10 milliseconds) and high cost. Thus, an improved high-accuracy clock synchronization method is proposed in this paper to overcome errors and offsets. With this method, the error of clocks among computer nodes in distributed real-time system can be less than 2 milliseconds and high availability can be achieved. The method has been applied in national key engineering project.

Keywords: Clock Synchronization, Distributed Real-Time System, High-Accuracy, High Availability.

1   Introduction

In distributed real-time system, precise time synchronization between participating host computers and the standard clock is required, usually with error in several milliseconds, to guarantee the processing of real-time transactions in distributed system. Since there are usually errors in initial setting of the clock, and the clock will drift itself, clocks in distributed system must be corrected periodically to keep consistent with the standard clock.

Generally, there are two main clock synchronization protocols for distributed networks, which are client-server-based Network Time Protocol (NTP) and master-slave-based Precision Time Protocol (PTP).

NTP is built on software protocols and readily adaptable [1] Since NTP costs large system resources and the error is measured in milliseconds, it is suitable for wide area networks (WAN) and other distributed systems where requirements for accuracy of time synchronization are less demanding, incapable of networks that require real-time and high accuracy.

On the other hand, specified in IEEE 1588 standard, PTP allows hardware support and simplified the protocol itself [2] With customized hardware, the error of PTP can be assured in a few microseconds which outperform NTP. Simulations with OPNET have presented noticeable ability of IEEE 1588 [3] Integration into Substation Automation System (SAS) even implemented an accuracy of 80 nanoseconds [4] However, high accuracy of PTP can only be achieved on the condition of high cost and special designed hardware. Thus, NTP-based synchronization method is adopted in the following study.

W. Xu et al. (Eds.): NCCET 2014, CCIS 491, pp. 148–157, 2015.
© Springer-Verlag Berlin Heidelberg 2015

For NTP, a new approach termed Classless Time Protocol (CTP) is developed, in which convex optimization theory is applied to evaluate the clock offset and better performance is achieved [5] Based on Kalman filter, a clock skew and offset tracking method is also developed in modeling of clock drift [6]

Recently, researches in clock synchronization have paid much attention in Wireless Sensor Networks (WSN) [7] Representative traditional algorithms include Reference Broadcast Synchronization (RBS) [8], Timing-sync Protocol for Sensor Networks (TPSN) [9], Time Diffusion Synchronization Protocol (TDP) [10], Delay Measurement Time Synchronization (DTMS) [11], Flooding Time Protocol for Sensor Networks (FTSP) [12], Lightweight Tree-based Synchronization (LTS) [13] etc. These methods provide efficient solutions in terms of key path bandwidth, delay uncertainty, fault-tolerance, robustness and network monitoring.

A study has been done to improve security and stabilization of the clock synchronization in WSN [14]. Some enhanced algorithms are also proposed to solve problems like network delay and clock drift, such as Black Burst Synchronization (BBC) [15] and PulseSync [16].

Considering the requirements for high-accuracy in clock synchronization and high availability in large-scale network put forward by the study, the following method is proposed to synchronize clocks in distributed real-time system in addition to NTP.

2   Synchronization Mechanism Structure

In the clock synchronization mechanism proposed by this paper, clock server connected with the standard clock will receive standard time information and adjust the time of local processor to synchronize with the standard clock. Clock clients connected to the clock server via LAN will use TCP/IP protocol for communication to make every clock in system synchronized with the standard clock.

In case that the clock server crashes, a primary clock sever and a secondary clock server are both used, respectively receiving time information from different standard clock. Under normal circumstances, clock clients are synchronized with time of the primary clock server. Otherwise, when the primary clock server crashes, clock clients will be automatically synchronized with the secondary clock server, which will be converted into the primary one in the meantime to achieve fault tolerance.

From the perspective of clock synchronization, the structure of clock synchronization mechanism can be represented in Figure1, in which the standard clock is consistent with the clock of National Time Service Center (NTSC) with 10^{-12} clock offset.

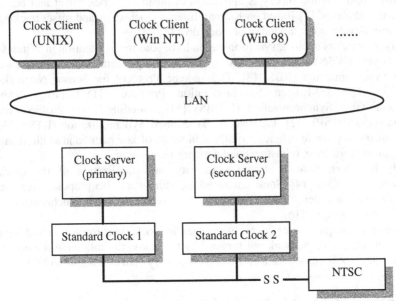

Fig. 1. The structure of clock synchronization mechanism

3   Clock Synchronization Method

In the system, the clock synchronization mechanism in each computer node is divided into two parts, one is the synchronization between clock server and the standard clock, and the other is the synchronization between clock clients and clock server.

3.1   Synchronization between Clock Server and the Standard Clock

By connecting with the standard clock, clock server can get periodical input of standard time code and adjust the server's time to synchronize with the standard clock. The delay time of information transmission from the standard clock to clock server is equal to system error, which could be obtained by measuring and used to correct the delay when setting the clock of the server.

3.2   Synchronization between Clock Clients and Clock Server

Clock clients are synchronized periodically with the time on clock server through network. As the message transmission delay in the network differs when network load is different, the correction of system time on clock server cannot be based on a static network delay time which is considered as a constant value, but the current delay time value at the time of correction.

The time correction method by which clock client periodically obtains time from clock server through network is represented in Figure2.

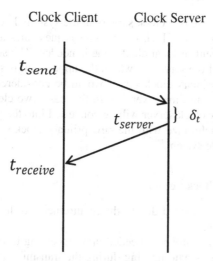

Fig. 2. Synchronization between clock client and clock server

As can be seen from Figure2, the detailed steps of synchronization process between clock client and clock server are as follows:

Clock client take note of the timestamp t_{send} before sending a message to clock server

When the message from clock client is received, clock server write the local time t_{server} into the response message immediately and send it back to clock client

Clock client take note of the time $t_{receive}$ when response message from clock server is received and abstract the time of clock server from the message

Actually, the delay time δ_t in clock server between receiving the request from clock client and sending local time can essentially be treated as a constant since it requires a paragraph of fixed instructions. And considering the transmission time in LAN is very short, the study assumed that the network load stays unchanged from the time message is send to the time message is received. Thus, the time to be set in clock client should be:

$$t = t_{server} + \frac{(t_{receive} - t_{send}) - \delta_t}{2} \qquad (1)$$

4   High Availability

In this chapter, some major problems and corresponding methods to achieve high availability in the system will be discussed.

4.1   Switch of Clock Servers

As mentioned earlier, there are two clock servers in the system, known as the primary and the secondary clock server. Clock client send request message to the primary clock server when adjustment of local clock time is needed. The study used time-out strategy to infer the state of the server, in which the upper limit is set to 5 seconds for now. That is, the current primary clock server would be considered as crashed when there is no response for a long time (over 5s). In this case, two clock servers will be switched and the secondary clock server will be converted into the primary one. Then, clock client will try to synchronize with the new primary clock server again to keep time coherence in the whole system.

4.2   Error Control of Clock Server

Fault tolerance is extremely needed due to the requirements of high availability in a distributed real-time system.

Firstly, processing of byte stream is needed upon receiving time information from the standard clock. If there is byte missing during the transmission, the error will be passed backwards and result in decoding errors of all the time ever after. Secondly, due to the time-sharing characteristic of UNIX, ongoing clock process may be switched off the processor in some cases [17]. Thus, system time cannot be set in a timely manner and large time errors will be caused.

To solve these two problems, the study worked out the following fault-tolerant processing procedure:

Clock server reads the data in byte stream and decodes it to standard time $t_{standard}$. When there is obvious error such as a year greater than 2100, indicating the input clock information in byte stream is incorrect, turn to step 5 to handle the error.

The difference between $t_{standard}$ and t_{system} (the current system time of clock server) will be compared with τ, which is the maximum possible value of the difference between the standard clock and the system clock under normal circumstances. That means τ should satisfy the relation:

$$\tau > (E_{machine} + E_{standard}) * t_{interval} + \Delta t \tag{2}$$

in which:

$E_{machine}$、$E_{standard}$ stand for the clock excursion rate in computer node and standard clock respectively

$t_{interval}$ stands for the timed interval to set the clock

Δt stands for the system error of clock setting

If $\left| t_{standard} - t_{system} \right| > \tau$, indicating that the time information transmitted in byte stream might be incorrect, turn to step 5 to handle the error.

Else if $\left| t_{standard} - t_{system} \right| \leq \tau$, adjust the system time according to the received standard time information and turn back to step 1.

Determine the number of consecutive errors. If it is greater than n, the received time data is considered correct while the system time is incorrect. In that case, system time will be adjusted to synchronize with the standard clock. Otherwise, input buffer will be emptied, request for new time information will be send to the standard clock immediately, the number of consecutive errors will be pulsed one, and the whole procedure will turn back to step 1.

What's worth being mentioned is that the threshold number n cannot be set arbitrarily. If n is too large, the clock server transition may result in a long time inconsistence between clock server and the standard clock. Considering the reliability of reading byte stream time information in system, take 2 as the number of n could fulfill the requirements.

By this method, transmission errors of time information can be effectively controlled. The large time delay caused by ongoing process switched off CPU can also be prevented as well. Practice has showed that this approach works totally well enough to meet design requirements.

4.3   Clock Error Processing between Clock Client and Clock Server

Since network transmission rate is very high in LAN, the transmission delay $(t_{receive} - t_{send})$ is usually less than the minimum resolution of system clock, which results in unavailability of actual network delay time and errors in clock adjustment. Therefore, the study adopted the error-sharing strategy to solve this problem through n times of continuously transmission. Considering that network transmission delay in LAN is relatively very small compared to that in WAN, the study assumed that change in network load during several successive transmissions is minor. In such conditions, the time to be set in clock server should be:

$$t = t_{server} + \frac{(t_{receive} - t_{send}) - \delta_t}{2n} \tag{3}$$

When receiving time data from the primary clock server, the receiving program in clock client should be suspended in the absence of incoming data to reduce occupancy for system resource. However, if the primary clock crashes while clock client is waiting for data, program in clock client will die. Therefore, prior to data receiving, whether the current primary clock server is working properly need to be determined, based on which to decide which clock server is the primary one.

In addition, as it is with standard time information receiving program, client program may also be switched off the processor in UNIX systems, which means the process of successive time data sending and receiving with clock server cannot be completed within single time slice, resulting in inability to set system time in time and large errors. Therefore, the same fault-tolerant and error-sharing strategy is adopted here, which is also one of the strategies to ensure system time error reach to reserved standard.

4.4　Priorities of Processes

In UNIX systems, one process may be switched off CPU by higher priority process. That clock client or clock server is witched off during processing may affect the accuracy of system time setting and result in a large error. The previous fault-tolerant processing cannot completely guarantee the requirements for errors, because there will still be large time errors if the switching of process happened before the system call of system time setting was executed. Therefore, it is really necessary to raise priorities of some processes to ensure the atomicity of executions in clock server and clock client.

5　Test and Evaluation

The rsadj synchronization measurement technique is used to observe the behavior of the clock synchronization mechanism presented previously [18].

5.1　Determination of Synchronization Interval

The length of synchronization interval is related to how often the system will be disturbed by clock program and the synchronization accuracy of system clock. If the interval is too long, too much interruption will be caused to system. Otherwise, the synchronization accuracy between clock server and the standard clock, clock client and clock server will be affected. Let $t_{excursion}$ stands for the time excursion of computer. Then the minimum synchronization interval $t_{interval}$ to be set should meet the relation $t_{interval} < t_{error}/2t_{excursion}$. Taking into account that time in clock client and clock server cannot be completely synchronized during correction, the range from 30 minutes to 60 minutes for interval value would be appropriate.

5.2　Time Error between Clock Server and the Standard Clock

The delay time of time communication interfaces between processing nodes is taken as the reference value of error between server and the standard clock.

5.3　Time Error between Clock Client and Clock Server

When using only network time protocol (NTP) software to synchronize clocks, the measured clock errors (absolute value) between clock client and clock server are shown in Figure3 (where the total number of samples is 425):

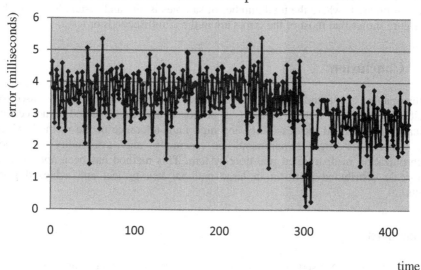

Fig. 3. Statistics of the 425 NTP experimental results

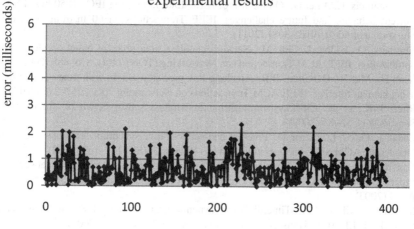

Fig. 4. Statistics of the 398 NTP & clock synchronization experimental results

As can be seen from Figure3 above, clock error between computer nodes is relatively large without extra synchronization mechanism.

When the clock synchronization method discussed previously is applied, the measured clock errors (absolute value) between clock client and clock server are shown in Figure4 (where the total number of samples is 398 and system load is high). The figure shows that most of the errors are in the 2 milliseconds or less.

6   Conclusion

In this paper, a method to keep clock time accurately synchronized based on distributed real-time system in LAN is proposed and implemented. Practice and evaluation has proved the feasibility and high fault tolerance of the method, which fully meets the high requirements in accuracy and availability of clock synchronization in distributed real-time system. This method has been applied to a large-scale distributed platform in large national key project and achieved good results.

References

1. Mills, D., et al.: Network time protocol version 4: Protocol and algorithms specification. IETF RFC5905 (June 2010)
2. Lee, K., et al.: IEEE 1588-Standard for a Precision Clock Synchronization Protocol for Networked Measurement and Control Systems. In: Conference on IEEE, vol. 1588 (2005)
3. Depari, A., et al.: Evaluation of timing characteristics of industrial ethernet networks synchronized by means of IEEE 1588. In: Instrumentation and Measurement Technology Conference Proceedings, IMTC 2007. IEEE (2007)
4. De Dominicis, C.M., et al.: On the use of IEEE 1588 in existing IEC 61850-based SASs: Current behavior and future challenges. IEEE Transactions on 60 Instrumentation and Measurement 60(9), 3070–3081 (2011)
5. Gurewitz, O., Cidon, I., Sidi, M.: Network classless time protocol based on clock offset optimization. IEEE/ACM Transactions on Networking (TON) 14(4), 876–888 (2006)
6. Kim, H., Ma, X., Hamilton, B.R.: Tracking low-precision clocks with time-varying drifts using kalman filtering. IEEE/ACM Transactions on Networking 20(1), 257–270 (2012)
7. Rhee, I.-K., et al.: Clock synchronization in wireless sensor networks: An overview. Sensors 9(1), 56–85 (2009)
8. Elson, J., Girod, L., Estrin, D.: Fine-grained network time synchronization using reference broadcasts. ACM SIGOPS Operating Systems Review 36(SI), 147–163 (2002)
9. Ganeriwal, S., Kumar, R., Srivastava, M.B.: Timing-sync protocol for sensor networks. In: Proceedings of the 1st International Conference on Embedded Networked Sensor Systems. ACM (2003)
10. Su, W., Akyildiz, I.F.: Time-diffusion synchronization protocol for wireless sensor networks. IEEE/ACM Transactions on Networking 13(2), 384–397 (2005)
11. Ping, S.: Delay measurement time synchronization for wireless sensor networks. IRB-TR-03-013, Intel Research Berkeley Lab (2003)
12. Maróti, M., et al.: The flooding time synchronization protocol. In: Proceedings of the 2nd International Conference on Embedded Networked Sensor Systems. ACM (2004)
13. van Greunen, J., Rabaey, J.: Lightweight time synchronization for sensor networks. In: Proceedings of the 2nd ACM International Conference on Wireless Sensor Networks and Applications, ACM (2003)

14. Hoepman, J.-H., et al.: Secure and self-stabilizing clock synchronization in sensor networks. Theoretical Computer Science 412(40), 5631–5647 (2011)
15. Gotzhein, R., Kuhn, T.: Black Burst Synchronization (BBS)–A protocol for deterministic tick and time synchronization in wireless networks. Computer Networks 55(13), 3015–3031 (2011)
16. Lenzen, C., Sommer, P., Wattenhofer, R.: Optimal clock synchronization in networks. In: Proceedings of the 7th ACM Conference on Embedded Networked Sensor Systems. ACM (2009)
17. Stevens, W.R.: Unix Network Programming: Networking APIs: Sockets and XTI, vol. 1 (1998)
18. Troxel, G.D.: Time surveying: Clock synchronization over packet networks. Massachusetts Institute of Technology (1994)

Soft-Input Soft-Output Parallel Stack Algorithm for MIMO Detection

Fan Luo, Zhiting Yan, Guanghui He, Jun Ma, and Zhigang Mao

School of Electronic Information and Electrical Engineering,
Shanghai Jiao Tong University, Shanghai, China
{luofan,guanghui.he}@sjtu.edu.cn

Abstract. This paper presents a reduced-complexity soft-input soft-output parallel stack algorithm (SISO-PSA) for multiple-input multiple-output (MIMO) wireless communication systems employing Turbo iterative processing at the receiver. The proposed algorithm incorporates hybrid enumeration and a modified tree pruning criterion to support soft-inputs, which results in significant computational complexity saving. Moreover, a leaf enumeration scheme is proposed to reduce the number of expanded leaf nodes. In addition, the parallelism at algorithm level provides high throughput while reduces area compared to hardware level parallelism, which is very suitable for VLSI implementation. The simulation results show that the proposed algorithm can achieve better performance than SISO K-Best algorithm (K=50) and SISO-FSD with 60% memory saving and significantly reduced computational complexity in terms of the number of visited nodes in a 4×4 64QAM MIMO system.

Keywords: Multiple-input multiple-output (MIMO), soft-input soft-output (SISO), parallel detection, stack algorithm.

1 Introduction

Multiple-input multiple-output (MIMO) systems have great potential to increase spectral efficiency by transmitting independent data streams concurrently on multiple antennas. MIMO technology constitutes the basis for many new wireless communication standards, such as IEEE 802.11n, IEEE 802.11ac and 3GPP LTE-Advanced. There is an increasing demand for Gbps throughput wireless systems in recent years. Communication standards such as IEEE 802.11ac and 3GPP LTE-Advanced target for Gbps throughput with MIMO technology. However, it poses significant challenges for the design of MIMO detection algorithm with high throughput and low complexity for VLSI implementation.

Many detection algorithms for MIMO systems based on tree search are proposed to reduce computational complexity. Tree-search algorithm can be categorized as breadth-first search algorithm, depth-first search algorithm and best-first search algorithm. Breadth-first search algorithms such as K-Best[1] and FSD[2] attains a

W. Xu et al. (Eds.): NCCET 2014, CCIS 491, pp. 158–169, 2015.
© Springer-Verlag Berlin Heidelberg 2015

fixed-complexity without backtracking, which is hardware-friendly. However, they suffer from high computational complexity to achieve near maximum a posteriori (MAP) detection performance. A typical depth-first search algorithm STS-SD[3] can achieve optimal performance and each node is visited at most once, but backtracking in the tree search procedure hinders high throughput. Best-first search algorithm[4] stores expanded nodes to a stack and expands best node in the stack to its best child and best sibling and then replaces the best node with its best child and best sibling. Advanced stack algorithm[5] is one of the best-first search algorithms. It's proved to be optimally efficient because it visits the least number of nodes among all optimal tree-search-based MIMO detectors on condition that the stack is large enough, but the throughput is significantly limited when the SNR (signal noise ratio) is low and the memory consumption is huge for VLSI implementation.

To achieve the demand for Gbps throughput of MIMO detector, hardware level parallelism is popular among literatures. VLSI implementations in [6-7] duplicate the detection core to achieve Gbps throughput at the cost of significant increase of area. In contrast to hardware level parallelism, algorithm level parallelism is more efficient and less area consuming. Parallel stack algorithm[8] provides parallelism at algorithm level, which multiplies the throughput without increasing the area. However, parallel stack algorithm doesn't support soft-inputs. In the case of soft-input soft-output MIMO detection, the presence of a priori information in the partial metric function prevents the applicability of zigzag search since the desirable geometrical properties are annihilated. Finding the exact Schnorr-Euchner (SE) order for SISO MIMO detection requires exhaustive calculation and sorting of partial metrics of all constellation points, which is inefficient for hardware implementation.

In order to solve the problems of parallel stack algorithm, we propose a soft-input soft-output parallel stack algorithm (SISO-PSA). Hybrid enumeration[9] is adopted in the proposed SISO-PSA to avoid the costly full enumeration and sorting (FES) procedure without performance degradation. Since a priori information in each layer are independent, the a priori-based metrics can be computed and sorted at the beginning of a tree search procedure, which leads to negligible complexity increase. Moreover, the tree pruning criterion is modified to adapt to hybrid enumeration. To further reduce the computational complexity, we proposed a simplified leaf enumeration to avoid inefficient full expanding and sorting of leaf nodes in SISO detection . With the parallelism at both algorithm and hardware level, the proposed algorithm can achieve high throughput and small area at the same time.

The rest of this paper is organized as follows. Section 2 reviews the MIMO system model and iterative MIMO detection, and gives a brief introduction to parallel stack algorithm. Section 3 present our proposed soft-input soft-output parallel stack algorithm. Section 4 shows the simulation results of the proposed algorithm compared to other MIMO detection algorithms. Finally, Section 5 concludes the paper.

2   Fundamentals

2.1   System Model

Consider a MIMO system with N_t transmit antennas and N_r ($N_r > N_t$) receive antennas. The coded bits are mapped to N_t dimensional symbol vectors $s \in O^{N_t}$, where O is the complex scalar constellation set with $|O| = 2^q$, and q is the modulation order. Each symbol s is associated with a label vector x that contains $N_t q$ binary values chosen from the set $\{+1, -1\}$. And $x_{i,b}$ denotes bth bit of the ith entry of the symbol vector $s = [s_1 \ldots s_{N_t}]^T$. The associated complex baseband input-output relation is given by

$$y = Hs + n, \tag{1}$$

where H is the $N_r \times N_t$ complex channel matrix and n is $N_r \times 1$ vector of zero mean independent and identically distributed Gaussian entries with variance N_0. The receiver is assumed to have perfect channel state information, i.e., the H and N_0 are perfectly known to the receiver.

The channel matrix H can be QR decomposed as $H = QR$, with Q a unitary $N_r \times N_t$ matrix and R an $N_t \times N_t$ upper triangular matrix with elements R_{ij}. Then the system model can be rewritten as

$$\tilde{y} = Rs + Q^H n, \tag{2}$$

where $\tilde{y} \triangleq Q^H y$ and $Q^H n$ is a noise vector with the same statistics as n because Q is a unitary.

2.2   Soft-Input Soft-Output MIMO Detection

The receiver for soft-input soft-output (SISO) MIMO systems consists of a SISO MIMO detector and a SISO channel decoder. The detector and the decoder exchange reliability information for each coded bit iteratively.

Using Bayes' theorem and max-log approximation, intrinsic max-log LLRs can be computed according to [10]

$$L_{i,b}^D \approx \min_{s \in \chi_{i,b}^{(-1)}} \{d(s)\} - \min_{s \in \chi_{i,b}^{(+1)}} \{d(s)\} \tag{3}$$

$$d(s) = \frac{1}{N_0} \|\tilde{y} - Rs\|^2 - \log P[s], \tag{4}$$

where $\chi_{i,b}^{(+1)}$ and $\chi_{i,b}^{(-1)}$ are the sets of symbol vectors whose bth bit of the ith entry equal to +1 and -1 respectively. d(s) is the path metric of s. For each bit, one of the two minima in (3) corresponds to

$$\lambda^{ML} = \frac{1}{N_0} \|\tilde{y} - Rs^{ML}\|^2 - \log P[s^{ML}]. \tag{5}$$

λ^{ML} is associated with the ML solution

$$s^{ML} = \underset{s \in O^{N_t}}{\arg\min} \left\{ \frac{1}{N_0} \|\tilde{y} - Rs\|^2 - \log P[s] \right\}. \tag{6}$$

The other minimum in (3) can be written as

$$\lambda_{i,b}^{\overline{ML}} = \min_{s \in \chi_{i,b}^{\overline{ML}}} \{ \frac{1}{N_0} \|\tilde{y} - Rs^{ML}\|^2 - \log P[s^{ML}] \}, \tag{7}$$

where $\chi_{i,b}^{\overline{ML}} \triangleq \chi_{i,b}^{(x_{i,b}^{\overline{ML}})}$ and $x_{i,b}^{\overline{ML}}$ denotes the counter-hypothesis to the ML hypothesis. With the definitions (5) and (7), (3) can be written in a compact form as

$$L_{i,b}^D = \begin{cases} \lambda_{i,b}^{\overline{ML}} - \lambda^{ML}, & x_{i,b}^{ML} = +1 \\ \lambda^{ML} - \lambda_{i,b}^{\overline{ML}}, & x_{i,b}^{ML} = -1. \end{cases} \tag{8}$$

Extrinsic LLRs can be computed as[3]

$$L_{i,b}^E = L_{i,b}^D - L_{i,b}^A, \tag{9}$$

where $L_{i,b}^A$ is the a priori LLR.

2.3   Parallel Stack Algorithm

Stack algorithm[11] uses a stack to store all the expanded nodes, and expands the node in the stack with the minimum metric, and then replace it with all its children. The number of nodes in the stack grows exponentially with the tree search procedure, and the memory consumption is too large for VLSI implementation. Advanced stack algorithm only expands the best node to its best child and best sibling, which dramatically reduces the stack size.

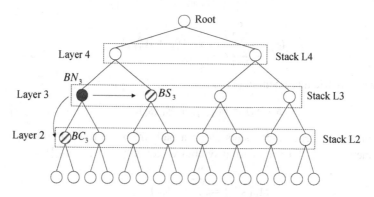

Fig. 1. Parallel stack algorithm

Parallel stack algorithm[8] further divided the stack into small stacks (Stack L4 to Stack L2), as shown in Fig. 1, each of which stores the expanded nodes in each layer. There is no stack for Layer 1 because leaf nodes are not stored. Best node in each layer expands to its best child and best sibling and then it is removed from the stack.

For example, BN_3 in Stack L3 expands to its best child BS_3 and best sibling BC_3. BS_3 stores to Stack L3 and BC_3 stores to Stack L2, and then BN_3 is deleted from Stack L3. Nodes in each stack expand concurrently, which multiplies the throughput of MIMO detector. And this parallelism at algorithm level can save area significantly compared to hardware level parallelism. However, parallel stack algorithm does not support soft-inputs. The a priori information in the partial metric in soft-input case prevents the applicability of the efficient zigzag enumeration, and requires full enumeration and sorting. The great computational complexity is not suitable for VLSI implementation.

3   Proposed Soft-Input Soft-Output Parallel Stack Algorithm

3.1   Hybrid Enumeration

In soft-output-only MIMO detection algorithm, the two-dimensional constellation diagram is divided into subsets consisting of rows or columns. Within a subset the next constellation point can be chosen by zigzag enumeration. For the ordering of points across subsets, the distance of closest constellation point in each subset is computed, and the node with smallest partial metric is chosen as the next node. However, according to (4), the additional a priori information in the metric function prevents the usage of the geometrical properties of constellation diagram and traditional zigzag enumeration is no longer applicable. We define the two terms in (4) as channel-based partial metrics (CMs) and the a-priori-based partial metrics (AMs) respectively as follow[12]

$$M_C(s_i) = \frac{1}{N_0} \left| \tilde{y}_i - \sum_{j=i+1}^{N_t} R_{ij}s_i - R_{ii}s_i \right|^2 \tag{10}$$

$$M_A(s_i) = \sum_{b=1}^{q} \frac{1}{2} \left(-x_{i,b}L_{i,b}^A + |L_{i,b}^A| \right), \tag{11}$$

and rewrite metric increment in (4) as

$$M_P(s_i) = M_A(s_i) + M_C(s_i). \tag{12}$$

The sum of the metric increments along a path from the root to node s_i yields the partial metric $M_P(s^{(i)})$ for a partial symbol vector $s^{(i)} = [s_i, \ldots, s_{N_t}]^T$

$$M_P(s^{(i)}) = \sum_{j=i}^{N_t} M_P(s_j). \tag{13}$$

In order to avoid full enumeration and sorting, CMs and AMs are enumerated independently. AMs can be computed and sorted at the beginning of the tree search procedure with small effort. CM enumeration is similar to the partial metrics in soft-output-only situation, which can also make use of geometrical properties of constellation point by using zigzag search. Hybrid enumeration works by comparing corresponding partial metrics of enumerated CM and AM, and choosing the one with smaller partial metric. For example, $O_1 \sim O_4$ are constellation points in the hybrid enumeration procedure as shown in Fig. 2. CMs and AMs of $O_1 \sim O_4$ are marked in the horizontal and vertical ordinate respectively.

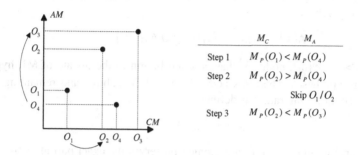

Fig. 2. Hybrid enumeration example

At first, O_4 and O_1 are chosen in AM and CM enumeration respectively, and then their partial metrics are computed and compared. O_1 has the smaller partial metric, so it is chosen as the next candidate. Then the PM of the next one in CM axis (O_2) is computed and compared with the PM of O_4, and O_4 is chosen. The next two in AM axis (O_1 and O_2) were enumerated, so they are skipped and the next one (O_3) is enumerated. Then PMs of O_2 and O_3 are compared. The above process is repeated until all nodes that are not qualified to be pruned are enumerated, as shown in the table in Fig. 2.

From the enumeration procedure described above, we know that CM enumeration may skip an arbitrary number of enumerated nodes, so the original zigzag enumeration scheme needs to be optimized. Before zigzag search, the enumerated nodes are masked first, and then the zigzag search will skip them.

Hybrid enumeration only needs to compute two partial metrics at a time, which only adds small computational complexity to traditional zigzag enumeration, and dramatically reduces the computational complexity compared to full enumeration and sorting.

3.2   Pruning Criterion

In order to reduce the number of visited nodes, a node will be visited only when its partial metric may lead to the update of ML hypothesis or counter-hypotheses. Consider the nodes $s^{(i)}$ on layer i corresponding to the label bits $x_{j,b}$ ($j = i, \dots, N_t, b = 1, \dots, q$), and the subtree originating from this node corresponding to the label bits $x_{j,b}$ ($j = 1, \dots, i - 1, b = 1, \dots, q$) has not been expanded yet. The node $s^{(i)}$ described above may affect the update of ML hypothesis or counter-hypotheses in following two sets

$$A_1(s^{(i)}) = \{f^{-1}(\Lambda_{j,b}^{\overline{ML}}, L_{j,b}^A, x_{j,b}^{ML}) | (j > i, \forall b) \cap (x_{j,b} = \overline{x_{j,b}^{ML}})\} \tag{14}$$

$$A_2(s^{(i)}) = \{f^{-1}(\Lambda_{j,b}^{\overline{ML}}, L_{j,b}^A, x_{j,b}^{ML}) | j \le i, \forall b\}. \tag{15}$$

The set of hypotheses which may be affected during the search in the subtree from node $s^{(i)}$ is given by

$$A(s^{(i)}) = \{a_l\} = A_1(s^{(i)}) \cup A_2(s^{(i)}). \tag{16}$$

If $d(s^{(i)}) > max\{a_l\}$, node $s^{(i)}$ has no contribution to the update of ML hypothesis or counter-hypotheses. Then this node along with its subtree and remaining siblings can be pruned. Pruning radius is defined as

$$r = max\{a_l\}. \tag{17}$$

However, hybrid enumeration no longer preserves the exact partial metric order of constellation points, so the next sibling's partial metric may be smaller than that of current node. Pruning all the remaining siblings may result in pruning the nodes whose partial metrics are smaller than the pruning radius, which will cause a performance loss. In order to avoid pruning useful nodes without much increase in the number of visited nodes, two pruning metrics are defined as follow[12]

$$M_i^{sibl} = M_C(s_{C,i}^{(k)}) + M_A(s_{A,i}^{(k)}) + M_P(s^{(i+1)}) \tag{18}$$

$$M_i^{sub} = M_C(s_i^{(k)}) + M_A(s_i^{(k)}) + M_P(s^{(i+1)}). \tag{19}$$

where $s_{C,i}^{(k)}$ and $s_{A,i}^{(k)}$ are selected by channel- and a priori-based enumerations respectively at step k, and $s_i^{(k)}$ is the one with smaller partial metric. If $M_i^{sibl} < r$, current node along with its subtree and remaining siblings are pruned. And if $M_i^{sub} < r$, only current node and its subtree are pruned.

3.3   Leaf Enumeration

ML hypothesis and counter-hypotheses are updated once a leaf node is reached. However, not all leaf nodes lead to the update of the hypotheses. At the layer just above leaf nodes, only the best child and the useful siblings are expanded, we define useful siblings as follow

$$US_b = \underset{s \in \chi_{1,b}^{\overline{BC1}}}{\arg\min}\{d(s)\}, \quad b = 1, ..., q, \tag{20}$$

where BC_1 is the best child at leaf layer, and $\chi_{1,b}^{\overline{BC1}}$ is the set of symbol vectors whose bth bit in the first entry is complement to BC_1. When $d(BC_1)$ updates the ML hypothesis, US_b may update counter-hypotheses, and other leaf nodes will not affect hypotheses. Similarly, when $d(BC_1)$ updates a counter-hypothesis, only US_b will affect counter-hypotheses.

Computing a US_b needs to compute and sort the partial metrics of the nodes whose bth bit in the first entry is complement to BC_1, which will introduce much additional computational complexity. However, by taking advantage of Grey mapping for the constellation symbols, each US_b can be considered as the best node in $\sqrt{2^q}/2$ subsets of the constellation points whose bits vectors flip the bth bit in the first entry of BC_1. According to the above property, BC_1 and US_b can be obtained through simple quantization in the real and imaginary dimensions of the constellation diagram before computing their partial metrics.

In SISO parallel stack algorithm, however, BC_1 cannot be obtained by simply quantization because of the presence of M_A. The following nodes need to be found first:

$$SN_b^c = \underset{s \in \chi_{1,b}^c}{\arg\min}\{d(s)\}, \quad b = 1, \dots, q, c \in \{+1, -1\}, \tag{21}$$

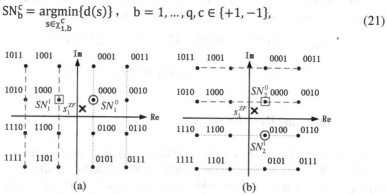

(a)   (b)

Fig. 3. Leaf enumeration example

where $\chi_{1,b}^c$ is the set of symbol vectors whose bth bit in the first entry is c. An example is shown in Fig. 3 (a), where s_1^{ZF} is zero-forcing solution of leaf node, and the subsets of constellation points whose first bit is 0 or 1 are arranged in columns. So SN_1^0 and SN_1^1 can be obtained by simply quantizing the image component of s_1^{ZF}. Similarly, the subsets in Fig. 3 (b) are arranged in rows, and SN_2^0 and SN_2^1 are obtained by quantizing the real component of s_1^{ZF}.

Except for SN_b^cs described above, the influence of M_As is also taken into consideration. The partial metrics of SN_b^cs and the n smallest M_As are computed, and the node with smallest partial metric is selected as BC_1. With this leaf enumeration scheme, at most $2q + n$ partial metrics have to be computed, which brings down the computational complexity compared to full enumeration.

3.4   Hypotheses Update

ML hypothesis and counter-hypotheses are updated by the partial metric of leaf nodes. The algorithm is initialized with $\lambda^{ML} = \Lambda_{i,b}^{\overline{ML}} = \infty$ ($\forall i, b$). When a leaf node with corresponding label x has been reached, ML hypothesis and counter-hypotheses are updated according to the following rules.

1) if $d(BC_1) < \lambda^{ML}$, then $d(BC_1)$ will become the new ML hypothesis. The former ML hypothesis and $d(SN_b^c)$ will update the counter-hypotheses according to

$$\Lambda_{i,b}^{\overline{ML}} \leftarrow f(\lambda^{ML}, L_{i,b}^A, \overline{x_{1,b}^{ML}}), \quad x_{i,b}^{BC1} = \overline{x_{1,b}^{ML}} \tag{22}$$

$$\Lambda_{1,b}^{\overline{ML}} \leftarrow \min\{f(\lambda^{ML}, L_{1,b}^A, \overline{x_{1,b}^{ML}}), f(d(SN_b^c), L_{1,b}^A, \overline{x_{1,b}^{ML}})\}, \quad x_{1,b}^{BC1} = \overline{x_{1,b}^{ML}} = \overline{c}, \tag{23}$$

followed by the updates $\lambda^{ML} \leftarrow d(BC_1)$ and $x^{ML} \leftarrow x_{BC1}$. In other words, for each bit in the ML hypothesis that is changed during the update process, the metric of the former ML hypothesis becomes that of the new counter-hypothesis.

2) if $d(BC_1) > \lambda^{ML}$, then the ML hypothesis stays the same. $d(BC_1)$ and $d(SN_b^c)$ will update the counter-hypotheses according to

$$\Lambda_{i,b}^{\overline{ML}} \leftarrow \min\{\Lambda_{i,b}^{\overline{ML}}, f(d(BC_1), L_{i,b}^A, \overline{x_{1,b}^{ML}})\}, \quad x_{i,b}^{BC1} = \overline{x_{1,b}^{ML}} \tag{24}$$

$$\Lambda_{1,b}^{\overline{ML}} \leftarrow \min\{\Lambda_{1,b}^{\overline{ML}}, f(d(SN_b^c), L_{1,b}^A, \overline{x_{1,b}^{ML}})\}, \quad c = \overline{x_{1,b}^{ML}}. \tag{25}$$

4   Simulation Results

In this section, the proposed SISO-PSA is verified and compared with other algorithms. We considered a 4×4 64-QAM MIMO system over spatially uncorrelated Rayleigh channel with additive white Gaussian noise. According to the 3GPP-LTE standard, the system uses the Turbo code with block size = 1024bits, code rate =1/2 and 8 internal iterations. The stack size of each layer in proposed SISO-PSA is set to (1,10,10) from Layer 4 to Layer 2 respectively, and the total stack size is 21.

4.1   Detection Performance Simulation

Fig. 4 shows the performance of the proposed SISO-PSA with the iteration number from 1 to 4. When iteration number is 1, there are no soft-inputs, so the SISO-PSA is the same as the soft-output-only parallel stack algorithm. It can be observed that iterative MIMO detection obtains significant performance gains compared to soft-output-only MIMO detection. With performing 4 iterations, the proposed SISO-PSA shows a performance improvement (compared to the first iteration) of more than 3 dB at BER=10^{-4}. Additionally, it can be found that the performance gain shrinks while iteration number increases. Further increase of the iteration number will not yield significant performance improvement.

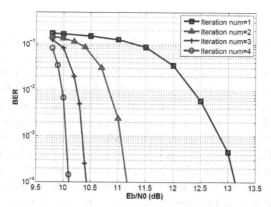

Fig. 4. BER performance of SISO-PSA for 4×4 64QAM iterative MIMO system with Turbo code rate 1/2

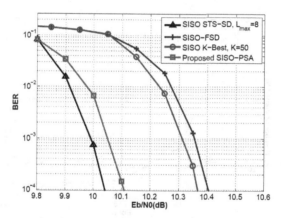

Fig. 5. BER performance of various algorithms for 4×4 64QAM iterative MIMO system with Turbo code rate 1/2 and 4 iterations

The performance of the proposed SISO-PSA is compared with other typical soft-input soft-output tree search algorithms in literatures. Fig. 5 compares the performance of the proposed SISO-PSA with SISO STS-SD with $L_{max} = 8$, SISO K-Best with K=50, and SISO-FSD with $L_{2N_t-1}^m = [7,7,5,5,3,3,1,1]$[2]. Each of them performs 4 iterations. The performance of STS-SD is given as the reference since it can achieve the max-log MAP detection if the clipping value L_{max} is sufficiently large. As shown in Fig. 5, our proposed SISO-PSA improves the performance by 0.26dB and 0.29dB compared to SISO K-Best and SISO-FSD respectively at BER=10^{-4}. Meanwhile, the proposed SISO-PSA shows only 0.07 dB degradation compared with SISO STS-SD at BER=10^{-4}. Furthermore, SISO K-Best and SISO-FSD both have a list size of 50, while the stack size of the proposed SISO-PSA is 21, which saves nearly 60% of memory compared with SISO K-Best and SISO-FSD. The proposed SISO-PSA achieve better performance and lower memory consumption at the same time.

4.2   Complexity Analysis

Usually, the computational complexity of tree search algorithm is measured by the total number of nodes visited by the detector[3]. Fig. 6 compares the number of visited nodes (4 iterations) of the proposed SISO-PSA with SISO STS-SD, SISO K-Best and SISO-FSD mentioned above. SISO K-Best and SISO-FSD have fixed complexity, so their number of visited nodes does not change over Eb/N0. SISO STS-SD and SISO-PSA, however, visit more nodes with the decrease of Eb/N0. The proposed SISO-PSA visits fewer nodes than SISO STS-SD especially when Eb/N0 is lower than 12 dB, because the stack size of SISO-PSA can be used as a tradeoff between performance and complexity to slow down the increase of complexity. It can be observed that SISO-PSA visits the least number of nodes among all the algorithm above, except when Eb/N0 is lower than 11.8 dB, this number will slightly more than SISO-FSD. The low computational complexity indicates that the proposed SISO-PSA is suitable for VLSI implementation.

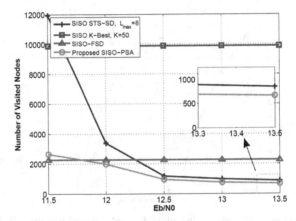

Fig. 6. Average number of visited nodes of various algorithms with 4 iterations

5   Conclusions

This paper has proposed a novel soft-input soft-output parallel stack algorithm for iterative MIMO detection. The proposed SISO-PSA adapts parallel stack algorithm to support soft-inputs. Hybrid enumeration is employed in the proposed algorithm to avoid inefficient full enumeration and sorting. Moreover, a modified tree pruning criterion is employed for the hybrid enumeration. In addition, a leaf enumeration scheme is proposed to further reduce the computational complexity. Furthermore, because of the parallel feature at algorithm level, SISO-PSA can achieve high throughput without increasing area. Simulation results indicate that our proposed algorithm can achieve a near MAP optimal performance. Compared to the SISO-FSD and SISO K-Best algorithm, the proposed algorithm provides better performance with reduced computational complexity and memory consumption. Due to the properties of algorithm level parallelism and low memory consumption, SISO-PSA appears to be an promising solution for VLSI implementation of high throughput MIMO detector.

Acknowledgement. This work is supported by National Natural Science Foundation of China under Grant No.61306026 and Important National Science & Technology Specific Projects under Grant No.2014ZX03001003.

References

1. Chen, S., Zhang, T., Xin, Y.: Relaxed K-Best MIMO Signal Detector Design and VLSI Implementation. IEEE Trans. VLSI Systems 15, 328–337 (2007)
2. Chen, X., He, G., Ma, J.: VLSI Implementation of a High-Throughput Iterative Fixed-Complexity Sphere Decoder. IEEE Transactions on Circuits and Systems II: Express Briefs 60(5), 272–276 (2013)
3. Studer, C., Bolcskei, H.: Soft-input soft-output single tree-search sphere decoding. IEEE Trans. Inf. Theory 56(10), 4827–4842 (2010)
4. Shen, C.A., Eltawil, A.M., Mondal, S., Salama, K.N.: A best-first Soft/Hard Decision Tree Searching MIMO Decoder for a 4x4 64-QAM System. IEEE Trans. VLSI Systems 20, 1537–1541 (2012)
5. Prasad, N., Kalbat, K.Y., Wang, X.: Optimally Efficient Max-log APP Demodulation in MIMO systems. In: Proc. IEEE Global Commun. Conf., USA, pp. 1–5 (December 2010)
6. Borlenghi, F., Witte, E.M., Ascheid, G., Meyr, H., Burg, A.: A 2.78mm2 65nm CMOS Gigabit MIMO Iterative Detection and Decoding Receiver. In: Proc. IEEE European Solid-State Circuits Conference (ESSCIRC 2012), pp. 65–68 (2012)
7. Sun, Y., Cavallaro, J.R.: Trellis-Search Based Soft-Input Soft-Output MIMO Detector: Algorithm and VLSI Architecture. IEEE Transactions on Signal Processing 60(5), 2617–2627 (2012)
8. Yue, Z., He, G., Li, J., Ma, J., Mao, Z.: A soft-output parallel stack algorithm for MIMO detection. In: 2013 IEEE Workshop on Signal Processing Systems (SiPS), pp. 30–35 (2013)
9. Liao, C.H., Lai, I.W., Nikitopoulos, K., Borlenghi, F., et al.: Combining orthogonalized partial metrics: Efficient enumeration for soft-input sphere decoder. In: Proc. IEEE 20th Int. Symp. Pers., Indoor Mobile Radio Commun., pp. 1287–1291 (2009)
10. Hochwald, B.M., Ten Brink, S.: Achieving near-capacity on a multiple-antenna channel. IEEE Trans. Commun. 51(3), 389–399 (2003)
11. Baro, S., Hagenauer, J., Witzke, M.: Iterative detection of MIMO transmission using a list-sequential (LISS) detector. In: Proc. IEEE Int. Conf. Commun., pp. 2653–2657 (2003)
12. Witte, E.M., Borlenghi, F., Ascheid, G., Leupers, R., Meyr, H.: A scalable VLSI architecture for soft-input soft-output single tree-search sphere decoding. IEEE Trans. Circuits, Syst. II 57(9), 706–710 (2010)

Current Reduction Phenomenon in Graphene-Based Device

Honghui Sun and Liang Fang

State Key Laboratory of High Performance Computing,
National University of Defense Technology,
Changsha, Hunan, P.R. China, 410073
School of Computer, National University of Defense Technology,
Changsha, Hunan, P.R. China, 410073
{hh_sun,lfang}@nudt.edu.cn

Abstract. A current reduction phenomenon was observed in back gate graphene-based field effect transistor. The drain current I_D became smaller in next measurement even though the sweep range of the back gate bias V_{BG} increased. We consider the reason for this phenomenon is that the contaminations produced during the device fabrication inevitably may serve as trap centers at the electrode-graphene interface, which would weaken the extent of p-type doping by trapping electrons when V_{BG} is positive.

Keywords: Graphene based field effect transistor (G-FET), current reduction, trap center, doping.

1 Introduction

Since its discovery in 2004 [1], graphene has attracted lots of interest in exploring its novel intrinsic properties and attempting to apply this ultrathin 2-dimensional material to modern semiconductor industry. High intrinsic carrier mobility [2] and thermal conductivity [3], unique ambipolar conduction property [4], and extremely thin 2-dimensional monatomic material [4], etc., all of these properties make it become one of the most promising alternatives for Si, to step into the new generation of technologies beyond the limitations of conventional semiconductor materials. Back-gate graphene based devices were broadly employed to investigate the intrinsic properties of graphene and device performance for its simple structure [1, 3, 5]. In recently years, several researches were focused on the effect of back gate on the contact resistance [6, 7] and channel conduction [8]. In this paper, we present a current reduction phenomenon with increasing the sweep range of back gate bias V_{BG} in ambient condition.

2 Experimental Setup

Graphene flakes were prepared by mechanical exfoliation using adhesive tape from natural graphite and transferred on a heavily p-doped silicon which was covered by a

W. Xu et al. (Eds.): NCCET 2014, CCIS 491, pp. 170–175, 2015.

300 nm thermal SiO_2 in order to distinguish the graphene thickness under optical microscope [1]. To remove residual glue, process of rising in warm acetone/isopropyl alcohol was carried out before device fabrication. The ratio of I_{2D} to I_G and the full width of half maximum (FWHM) of the 2D peak in Raman spectrum indicates that the graphene used in this back gate G-FET is bilayer graphene [9, 10], as is shown in Fig. 2. Then, photolithography and electron beam evaporation (EBE) were implemented one after the other to form the source-drain metal electrodes. Scanning electron microscope (SEM) image of typical device is

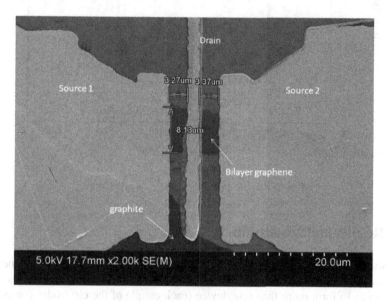

Fig. 1. SEM image of back-gate G-FET

Shown in Fig. 1. Unlike the normal electron beam lithography (EBL), here, we used the MicroWriter™ to define the source/drain patterns. It can precisely locate the pre-defined pattern on the destined position with the maximum error of 0.1 um. Another advantage is that there is no need to form markers on the substrate before sample preparation, and this benefit could make a further contribution to increase the possibility of obtaining single layer or bilayer graphene without metal markers on the substrate. The source and drain electrodes were made of 2 nm Ti as the adhesion layer and 30 nm thick Au. A 350℃ annealing procedure in H_2 and Ar was employed to remove the residual photoresist during the lithography process and optimize the metal-graphene interface. Electrical measurements were implemented in ambient condition by Semiconductor Parameter Analyzer Agilent B1500A.

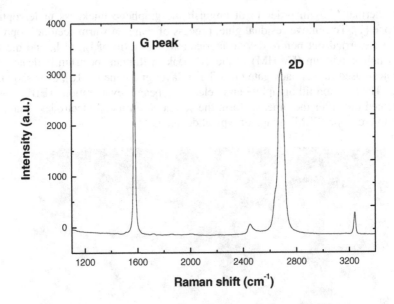

Fig. 2. Raman spectrum of the graphene flake

3   Results and Discussion

Fig. 1 shows a SEM image of the back-gate G-FET in which a bilayer graphene flake serves as the conducting channel. Three metal electrodes were defined on the same sample so as to form more than one device (each couple of the electrodes composes a back gate device). However, the Drain and Source 1 electrodes were shorted by a thick graphite flake. The only device which consists of source (Source 2) and drain (Drain) electrodes was practicable in electrical measurement.

Fig. 3 shows the output characteristic of the back gate G-FET for gate bias V_{BG} =0 V. The non-linearity of output curve indicates non-Ohmic contact nature between the electrodes and graphene. Several factors, such as the mismatch of work function between metal and graphene, contaminations at the metal-graphene interface, may result in forming the potential barrier between metal and graphene and deteriorating the transport property of the device.

This contamination which consists of glue from the adhesive tape, residual photoresist, desorbed H_2O and other molecules would breakdown easily by high gate voltage in ambient condition. Large amount of heat from the breakdown may further burn out the graphene under the contact area. To avoid this destructive breakdown, V_{BG} was enhanced step by step. As is shown in Fig. 4 (d), V_{Dirac} (the gate voltage at the minimum of the transfer characteristic curves) locates at about +16 V, indicating that graphene was p-type doping. A current reduction phenomenon was observed for each measurement when increased the sweep range of V_{BG}. In both Fig. 4 and 5, it clearly illustrates that the maximal drain current at negative gate bias in latter sweep is less than the minimum at positive gate bias in former sweep, though the sweep range increased.

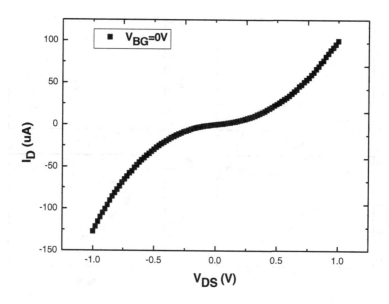

Fig. 3. Output characteristic of the device for back gate bias $V_{BG}=0$.

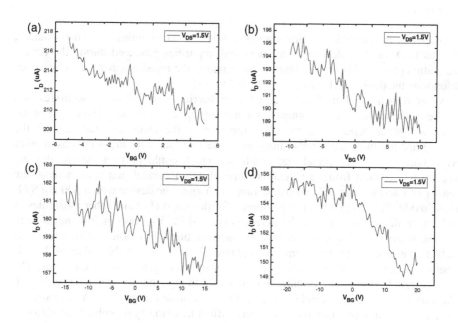

Fig. 4. Transfer characteristics (I_D–V_{BG}) of G-FET at the drain source bias of 1.5 V during the sweep of back-gate bias V_{BG} from (a)–5 to 5 V, (b) -10 to 10 V, (c) -15 to 15 V, (d) -20 to 20 V, respectively.

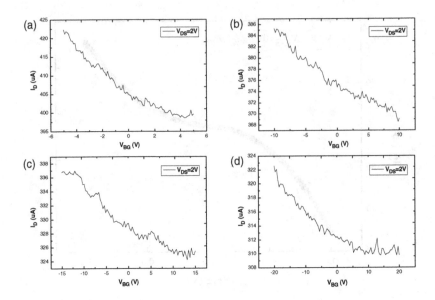

Fig. 5. Transfer characteristics (I_D–V_{BG}) of G-FET at the drain source bias of 2 V during the sweep of back-gate bias V_{BG} from (a)–5 to 5 V, (b) -10 to 10 V, (c) -15 to 15 V, (d) -20 to 20 V, respectively

Graphene is sensitive to some contamination due to its ultimate thinness nature, such as H_2O, other molecules in ambient and impurities produced during the device fabrication process. The contamination, particular at the metal-graphene interface, may deteriorate the device performance seriously [11-13].

As aforementioned in Fig. 3, a potential barrier exits between electrodes and graphene due to the contaminations at the metal-graphene interface. The height of the potential barrier depends on the work function of the metal and the state of the metal-graphene interface. Contaminations at the interface not only serves as another layer material between metal and graphene, which could prevent current flowing directly into (or out from) graphene as through Ohm contact, but also increase the density of interface-trapped and oxide trapped charge. The device with a 300 nm SiO_2 as the oxide dielectric shows p-type doping for desorbed H_2O and other molecules in ambient, which is consistent with references [14-16]. As V_{BG} sweeps from negative to positive values, the charge carrier type in graphene turns from hole to electron. These surface states serve as trap center to capture electrons when the value of V_{BG} is positive. So the degree of p-doping is weaken by these gate-induced electrons. The drain current I_D decreases evidently in next sweep though the sweep range is enlarged. The variation of I_D is relatively bigger in Fig. 4 because the gate bias V_{DS} is smaller and the contaminations aforementioned may affect I_D seriously in ambient condition.

We repeatedly changed the sweep range of V_{BG} and the current reduction phenomenon was clearly observed. The reduction depends on the sweep range of V_{BG} in last sweep, which indicates that charge trap-induced doping of graphene is the origin of current reduction.

4   Conclusion

In summary, we report a current reduction phenomenon in back gate G-FET. Charge trap-induced doping of graphene, particularly at metal-graphene interface, may be the main reason for this peculiar behavior. Contaminations during the device fabrication process should be further reduced and current annealing method could be applied before electrical measurements in subsequent researches.

Acknowledgment. This work is supported by the National Natural Science Foundation of China under Grant No. 61332003.

References

1. Novoselov, K.S., et al.: Electric Field Effect in Atomically Thin Carbon Films. Science 306(5696), 666–669 (2004)
2. Castro, E.V., et al.: Limits on electron quality in suspended graphene due to flexural phonons. arXiv preprint arXiv:1008.2522 (2010)
3. Balandin, A.A., et al.: Superior thermal conductivity of single-layer graphene. Nano Letters 8(3), 902–907 (2008)
4. Schwierz, F.: Graphene transistors. Nature Nanotechnology 5(7), 487–496 (2010)
5. Wang, X., et al.: Room-temperature all-semiconducting sub-10-nm graphene nanoribbon field-effect transistors. Physical Review Letters 100(20), 206803 (2008)
6. Khatami, Y., et al.: Metal-to-multilayer-graphene contact—Part I: Contact resistance modeling. IEEE Transactions on Electron Devices 59(9), 2444–2452 (2012)
7. Khatami, Y., et al.: Metal-to-multilayer-graphene contact—Part II: Analysis of contact resistance. IEEE Transactions on Electron Devices 59(9), 2453–2460 (2012)
8. Di Bartolomeo, A., et al.: Effect of back-gate on contact resistance and on channel conductance in graphene-based field-effect transistors. Diamond and Related Materials 38, 19–23 (2013)
9. Ferrari, A.C.: Raman spectroscopy of graphene and graphite: disorder, electron–phonon coupling, doping and nonadiabatic effects. Solid State Communications 143(1), 47–57 (2007)
10. Ferrari, A., et al.: Raman spectrum of graphene and graphene layers. Physical Review Letters 97(18), 187401 (2006)
11. Shih, C.-J., et al.: Understanding Surfactant/Graphene Interactions Using a Graphene Field Effect Transistor: Relating Molecular Structure to Hysteresis and Carrier Mobility. Langmuir 28(22), 8579–8586 (2012)
12. Jia, K., et al.: Stability analysis of a back-gate graphene transistor in air environment. Journal of Semiconductors 34(8), 084004 (2013)
13. Jang, C.W., et al.: Rapid-thermal-annealing surface treatment for restoring the intrinsic properties of graphene field-effect transistors. Nanotechnology 24(40), 405301 (2013)
14. Nouchi, R., Saito, T., Tanigaki, K.: Observation of negative contact resistances in graphene field-effect transistors. Journal of Applied Physics 111(8) (2012)
15. Tian, J., et al.: Ambipolar graphene field effect transistors by local metal side gates. Applied Physics Letters 96(26), 263110 (2010)
16. Luo, X., et al.: Current-carrying Capacity of Long & Short Channel 2D Graphene Transistors. In: Device Research Conference. IEEE (2008)

Dynamic Mapping Optimization for LSQ Soft Error Rate Reduction under 3D Integration Technology

Chao Song and Min-xuan Zhang

School of Computer Science, National University of Defense Technology,
Changsha 410073, China

Abstract. With the progress of integrated circuit technology, the soft error problem is getting worse, which has become a challenge that researchers have to face. 3D integration technology can stack several circuit layers in a vertical direction, and 3D chips have an effect of shielding, which is capable of reducing the soft error rate of the inner circuit. In this paper, we propose a dynamic mapping optimization method to reduce the soft error rate of LSQ based on the observation of the characteristics of the LSQ access behavior using 3D integration technology. The experimental result shows that, the proposed method can significantly reduce the soft error rate by 86.6% and 85.7%, on average, for the load queue and store queue respectively.

Keywords: soft error rate, LSQ, 3D technology.

1 Introduction

Higher performance is always the main goal of microprocessor designers, and the feature sizes, operating voltage and the parasitic capacitance are simultaneously reduced, highlighting the reliability problem of integrated circuit[1]. Researches show that soft errors have become a major aspect of integrated circuit reliability problems[2][3]. Different from traditional hard errors, the duration of soft errors is not permanent, and the state of the circuit is temporary wrong and will again return to normal within a short time. Typically, the errors caused by energetic particles striking are called soft errors and the energetic particles are mainly from the atmosphere and chip packaging material[4].

Under advanced process, there will be more particles that can lead to soft errors, as the decreases of feature size, operating voltage and parasitic capacitance will result relatively low energy particles having the ability to raise soft errors. Therefore, soft errors have become an issue that designers must face. Conventional methods, e.g. hardware redundancy approach taken to reduce the probability of occurrence of soft errors will bring a decrease in performance and increase in cost, including power consumption and area overhead.

3D integration technology has changed the traditional structure of the chip[5]. In the chip using 3D integrated technology, several circuit layers are stacked in the

W. Xu et al. (Eds.): NCCET 2014, CCIS 491, pp. 176–183, 2015.

vertical direction, and the interlayer interconnection technologies, such as TSV (Through Silicon Vias), are used to connect the adjacent circuit layers. Besides the improvement in the overall length of the chip connections, latency and power consumption[6], 3D integration technology can reduce the likelihood of soft errors[7]. The energetic particles that are mainly from packaging materials have different effects to different circuit layers, as the circuit layer adjacent to packaging material can shield particles for the circuit layers away from packaging materials. Researchers have used the shielding effect brought by 3D integration technology to improve the reliability of microprocessor cores or the on-chip memory.

In this paper, we use the features of 3D integration technology and the architectural improvements to achieve reliability enhancement compared to traditional two-dimensional chips. We focus on the load and store queue in the microprocessors. The access behavior of each entry in the queue is observed at fine-grained level. Based on the observation, we propose a new dynamic mapping optimization method to improve the reliability.

2   Background

2.1   Soft Error

Soft error problem has a long history and more attention is paid along with the progress in technology.

Soft error rate depends on two aspects, one is the raw soft error rate of the circuit in chip, which is the probability that soft error occurs in circuit, and the another is the shielding effect to soft errors brought by architecture, which means that the final output is not affected in the case of soft error occurring in the circuit. For example, the soft error is shielded if the memory cell is written new data, instead of reading incorrect data. 3D integrated technology can reduce the negative impact of the above two aspects, enhancing the reliability of the chip. Architectural Vulnerability Factors(AVF) is proposed to quantify the shielding effect, and can be calculated through ACE (Architecturally Correct Execution) analysis[8].

2.2   3D Integration Technology

In 3D integrated circuits, each layer of the circuit is manufactured in accordance with the traditional process technology, and the vertical connections between layers can be achieved by TSV (Through Silicon Via). Figure 1 is a schematic of 3D integrated circuits, and in this 3D integrated circuits, two layers are stacked, using F2F (face to face) binding, i.e. two metal layers are adjacent(fig. a), or F2B (face to back) binding, i.e. the metal layer and the substrate are adjacent(fig. b).

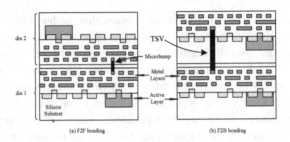

(a) F2F bonding   (b) F2B bonding

Fig. 1. 3D integration technology

When high-energy particles strike into the semiconductor material, the particles collide with the silicon lattices. In this process, the kinetic energy of the particles is decreased, and the speed is gradually reduced. If the energy is not sufficient to penetrate the semiconductor material, the particles will eventually stop in the material. The kinetic energy of the particles determines the maximum distance that the particles can pass through. Thus, the circuit layer adjacent to the packaging materials can stop the high energy particles for the inner circuit layer, which is known as shielding effect.

Raw soft error rate of the circuit is co-decided by the circuit characteristics and the outside particle environment. For the same circuit, more high-energy particle striking means more soft errors. Shielding effect can reduce the energy and number of the particles that reach the internal circuit layers, and the final chip soft error rate is therefore reduced.

3   Access Behavior Analysis and Architectural Optimization

In this section, we analyze the access behavior of the LSQ at fine-grained level. Based on the analysis and combined with 3D integration technology, architectural optimization method, dynamic mapping optimization is proposed to reduce the soft error rate.

3.1   Access Behavior Analysis

LSQ is designed as a FIFO queue that the entry occupied first logically will be released first unless the entire queue is flushed. In each cycle, some entries are occupied and some entries are released. If in a period of time, release is blocked but occupancy is still allowed, the queue will be full eventually, and such an extreme situation will disappear when the first occupied entry is released.

Another extreme case is that the entire queue is empty, and this situation will not last forever, as memory access operations are essential. We constructed a multiple issue, out-of-order microprocessor in the simulator, and the access behavior of LSQ was observed. LSQ is set to 32 entries (specific settings, see 4.1).

Figure 2 shows the ratio that LSQ is empty or non-empty across all cycles. It can be seen from (a) that, in the load queue, the proportion of empty is from 3.4% to

47.2%, with an average of 22.9%; and the proportion of non-empty is from 52.8% to 96.6%, with an average of 77.1%. The (b) shows that, in the store queue, the proportion of empty is from 24.7% to 90.6%, with an average of 57.1%; and the proportion of non-empty is from 9.4% to 75.3%, with an average of 42.9%.

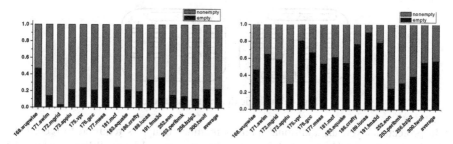

Fig. 2. (a). The nonempty cycles of load queue   **(b).** The nonempty cycles of store queue

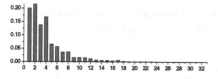

Fig. 3. (a). The utility of load queue   **(b).** The utility of store queue

Figure 3 shows the ratio of the number of occupied entries across all non-empty cycles. It can be seen from (a) that, in the load queue, the number of cycles that two entries was occupied has the highest proportion of non-empty cycles, 21.5%. In most non-empty cycles, the number of occupied entries is less than one third of the capacity of the queue, that is to say the efficiency of load queue is low. It can be seen from (b) that, in the store queue, the cycle that only one entry is occupied has the highest proportion, 41.6%. In most non-empty cycles, the number of occupied entries is less than a quarter of the capacity of the queue, and this means that the utility ratio of store queue is less than the load queue.

3.2   Architectural Optimization

The LSQ is layout to the inner and outer, using 3D integration technology. For the shielding effect, the inner layer is protected and the outer layer is unprotected, and the logical structure is shown in Figure 4. LSQ is in default mode or maximum spatial mode. In the default mode, the logic space of the LSQ is mapped to only the protected inner layer; and in the maximum spatial mode, the logical space is mapped to all circuits. The mode shift depends on the utilization of queue. When the protected inner layer is not fully occupied, the queue is in default mode. When the required physical space is larger than the protected inner layer, the queue is shifted to the maximum spatial mode.

H in figure 4 represents the oldest occupied entry, and if the entry is released, H moves to the right, the next occupied entry. T represents the entry that can be occupied in current cycle, and moves to the right if this entry is occupied or stays unchanged if this entry is not occupied.

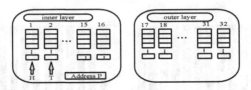

Fig. 4. The logic diagram of structure

In protected layer, an additional address memory unit P is required to record the entry in the protected layer when T enters the unprotected layer. When reaches that entry, H leaves the protected layer and enters the unprotected layer to maintain the correct logical order and the P is unset.

When T is back from unprotected layer, if P is unset, the first entry in protected layer is occupied by T. If P is set, the entry after P is occupied by T. The control flow of T and H is shown in Figure 5.

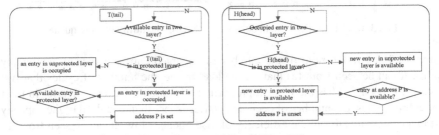

Fig. 5. The control flow of T and H

4   Experimental Methodology

We use the architectural reliability analysis tool Sim-SODA to calculate AVF[9], selecting 16 SPEC 2000 benchmarks as the application loads. The basic configuration of the processor is shown in Table 1. We use Sim-Point analysis techniques to select a representative segment[10], and 100M instructions are executed for each benchmark.

Table 1. Processor Configuration

Pipeline Stages	7
Fetch, issue, commit width	4/4/4
Instruction Queue	20
ROB	80
Register File	80
Load/store Queue	32/32
Instruction/Data TLB	128/128

We consider the following three different scenarios: base, 3D and 3D_ optimized. The soft error rate of basic circuit is shown in Equation 1:

$$SER_{base} = \sum_{i=1}^{32}(SER\_RAW \cdot AVF_i) = SER\_RAW * \sum_{i=1}^{32}AVF_i \qquad (1)$$

SER_RAW is the raw soft error rate of circuits, and $AVFi$ is AVF of entry i.

The soft error rate of circuits that are layout to different layers using 3D technology, i.e. the policy of 3D, is shown in Equation 2:

$$SER_{3D} = \sum_{i=1}^{16}(0.1*SER\_RAW \cdot AVF_i) + \sum_{i=17}^{32}(SER\_RAW \cdot AVF_i) \qquad (2)$$

$$= SER\_RAW * (0.1*\sum_{i=1}^{16}AVF_i + \sum_{i=17}^{32}AVF_i)$$

The raw soft error rate is proportional to the radiation intensity of energetic particles[11]. Through the analytic model simulation, for the particles from packaging materials, the radiation intensity of the protected circuit is 10% of the original intensity.

The soft error rate of circuits that are layout to different layers using 3D technology and are optimized by the dynamic mapping, i.e. the policy of 3D_optimized, is shown in Equation 3. In this policy, the AVF of each entry is different from Eq.1 and Eq.2.

$$SER_{3D\_optimized} = \sum_{i=1}^{16}(0.1*SER\_RAW \cdot AVF'_i) + \sum_{i=17}^{32}(SER\_RAW \cdot AVF'_i) \qquad (3)$$

$$= SER\_RAW *(0.1*\sum_{i=1}^{16}AVF'_i + \sum_{i=17}^{32}AVF'_i)$$

5   Results

In this section, we list the results obtained by simulation.

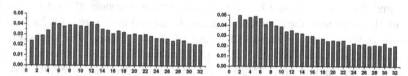

Fig. 6. (a). The AVF of each entry in load queue   **(b).** The AVF of each entry in store queue

Figure 6 shows the percentage of the AVF of each entry that are not optimized by dynamic mapping. Figure 6(a) shows that, in the load queue, the entries that have higher proportion of AVF appear in the first half of the load queue, and the sum of the first half AVF proportions is 60%. Figure 6(b) shows that, for the store queue, data, the sum of the first half AVF proportions is 63.7%.

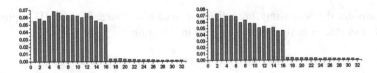

Fig. 7. (a). The optimized AVF of each entry in load queue **(b).** The optimized AVF of each entry in store queue

Figure 7 shows the percentage of the AVF of each entry that are optimized by dynamic mapping. Figure 7(a) represents the results of the load queue, and the figure 7(b) represents the results of the store queue. As can be seen, the proportion of AVF of the entries located in the first half of queue is much higher than the remains. The sum of AVF percentage of entries in the first half are respectively 96.2% and 95.2% for load and store queue, indicating the good effect of dynamic mapping optimization.

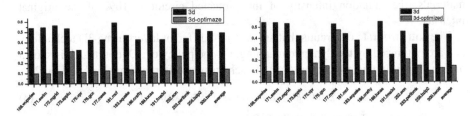

Fig. 8. (a). The normalized SER of 3D and 3D_optimized of load queue **(b).** The normalized SER of 3D and 3D_optimized of store queue

Figure 8 represents the normalized soft error rate respect to the policy of basic circuit for the policy of 3D and 3D_optimized. Figure 8(a) shows the result for the load queue. For the policy of 3D, the minimum decrease in the soft error rate is 41.3%, and the maximum is 67.5%, with an average decrease of 51.3%. For the policy of 3D_optimized, the minimum decrease in the soft error rate is 68.7%, and the maximum is 90%, with an average decrease of 86.6%. Figure 8(b) represents the result of store queue. For the policy of 3D, the minimum decrease in the soft error rate is 45.2%, and the maximum is 75.2%, with an average decrease of 57.3%. For the policy of 3D_optimized, the minimum decrease in the soft error rate is 52.6%, and the maximum is 90%, with an average decrease of 85.7%.

6   Conclusions

In response to increasingly serious soft error problem, researchers have presented various methods to reduce the probability of soft error occurring. 3D integration technology can not only improve the performance of the chip, also can reduce the radiation intensity of high-energy particle in chip. This paper proposed a dynamic mapping optimization method based on 3D integration technology, which can effectively reduce the soft error rate of load and store queue. Experiments show that the soft error rate of load queue and store queue that using 3D integration technology has an reduction of 51.3% and 57.3% on average, with respect to the basic circuit, and has an reduction of 86.6% and 85.7% on average, with respect to the basic circuit when taking 3D integration technology and dynamic mapping optimization method.

Acknowledgments. The research is supported by National Natural Science Foundation of China with Grant No. 61076025, and by Specialized Research Fund for the Doctor Program of Higher Education of China with Grant No. 20124307110016.

References

1. Shivakumar, P., Kistler, M., Keckler, S.W., et al.: Modeling the Effect of Technology Trends on the Soft Error Rate of Combinational Logic. In: Proc. of the 2002 International Conference on Dependable Systems and Networks (DSN 2002), Bethesda, MD, USA, pp. 389–398. IEEE CS (2002)
2. Mitra, S., Seifert, N., Zhang, M., Shi, Q., Kim, K.S.: Robust System Design with Built-in Soft-Error Resilience. IEEE Transactions on Computer 38(2), 43–52 (2005)
3. Baumann, R.C.: Radiation-Induced Soft Errors in Advanced Semiconductor Technologies. IEEE Transactions on Device and Materials Reliability 5(3) (September 2005)
4. Baumann, R.C.: Soft errors in advanced semiconductor Devices Part I: the three radiation sources. IEEE Transactions on Device and Materials Reliability 1 (2001)
5. Banerjee, K., Souri, S.J., Kapur, P., Saraswat, K.C.: 3-D ICs: a novel chip design for improving deep-submicrometer interconnect performance and systems-on-chip integration. Proceedings of the IEEE 89(5), 602–633
6. Xie, Y.: Processor Architecture Design Using 3D Integration Technology. In: VLSID 2010, pp. 446–451 (2010)
7. Zhang, W., Li, T.: Microarchitecture soft error vulnerability characterization and mitigation under 3D integration technology. In: MICRO 2008, pp. 453–446 (2008)
8. Mukherjee, S.S., Weaver, C.T., Emer, J., Reinhardt, S.K., Austin, T.: A Systematic Methodology to Compute the Architectural Vulnerability Factors for a High-Performance Microprocessor. In: MICRO 2003 (2003)
9. Fu, X., Li, T., Fortes, J.: Sim-SODA: A Unified Framework for Architectural Level Software Reliability Analysis. In: Proceedings of Workshop on Modeling, Benchmarking and Simulation (2006)
10. Sherwood, T., Perelman, E., Hamerly, G., Calder, B.: Automatically Characterizing Large Scale Program Behavior. In: ASPLOS 2002 (2002)
11. Heijmen, T.: Analytical Semi-empirical Model for SER Sensitivity Estimation of Deep-submicron CMOS Circuits. In: IOLTS (2005)

Author Index

Printed in the United States
By Bookmasters